With Wellington's Light Cavalry

With Wellington's Light Cavalry

Campaigning with the 16th Light Dragoons in the Peninsular and Waterloo Campaigns of the Napoleonic Wars

William Tomkinson

With Wellington's Light Cavalry: Campaigning with the 16th Light Dragoons in the Peninsular and Waterloo Campaigns of the Napoleonic Wars

Originally published in 1894 under the
title *Diary of a Cavalry Officer*

Published by Leonaur Ltd

Material original to this edition and its origination in
this form copyright © 2006 Leonaur Ltd

ISBN (10 digit): 1-84677-099-8 (hardcover)
ISBN (13 digit): 978-1-84677-099-9 (hardcover)

ISBN (10 digit): 1-84677-088-2 (softcover)
ISBN (13 digit): 978-1-84677-088-3 (softcover)

http://www.leonaur.com

Publishers Notes

In the interests of authenticity, the spellings, grammar and place names used in this book have been retained from the original edition.

The opinions of the author represent a view of events in which he was a participant related from his own perspective;
as such the text is relevant as an historical document.

The views expressed in this book are not necessarily those of the publisher.

Contents

Editor's Preface	7
Sailing to Portugal	9
Winter of 1811 and Spring of 1812.	134
The Waterloo Campaign	275

Editor's Preface

Although it may appear late in the day to publish for the first time a record of military life in the Peninsular and Waterloo campaigns, at a date now separated from us by the greater part of a century, I am encouraged by the opinion of many friends to hope that the contents of this book may prove not without interest to the general public, and possibly of some value to the student of military history.

A recent perusal of the "Memoirs of General Marbot" make me fully sensible of the fact that, in comparison with the thrilling scenes and incidents with which that book of contemporary history abounds this volume may appear tame, if not dull. The good horse "Bob" at Grijo cannot claim to emulate the deeds of "Lisette" at Eylau, although, like her, he saved his helpless rider from death or captivity; nor had his master the opportunities, even if he had the will, to perform such deeds of desperate daring as the French General describes. Something, possibly, should be allowed for the difference of nationality and temperament of the two writers; and, in any case, the writing of the English Cavalry Officer carries with it, I venture to think, by its directness and simplicity, a conviction of accuracy and absence of exaggeration.

The original volume was written near the scene of the events described in it, and bears at its commencement the superscription "Copied from some memoranda made at the time." Both ink and writing have stood the test of age well, and are still for the most part clear and legible; though, fortunately for the Editor, a fair copy was also made some thirty-five years later. It has been thought best to publish it almost exactly as it was written, suppressing no names, and to let it tell its own story. Consequently, little is needed by way of introduction or explanation.

The Author, Lieutenant-Colonel William Tomkinson, was

the youngest son of Henry Tomkinson, Esq., of Dorfold Hall, Nantwich, Cheshire.

Born in 1790, he was gazetted to a cornetcy in the 16th Light Dragoons in December, 1807; joined his regiment in April, 1808; and in 1809 entered on that period of military adventure described in this volume. He was thanked in the general orders of the day of January 22nd, 1811, and recommended for promotion in the Duke of Wellington's despatch to the Horse Guards of May 14th of the same year. In 1812 he was gazetted a Captain in the 60th Regiment, from which he exchanged back into his old regiment without leaving it. It is somewhat remarkable that, while severely wounded in four places in almost his first skirmish, he passed practically unscathed through four years' service in the Peninsula and the Waterloo campaigns, although under fire, to the best of his recollection, on nearly one hundred occasions. He received the Peninsular and Waterloo medals, with clasps for the actions of Busaco, Fuentes, Salamanca, and Vittoria.

Of his character it may be said that, simple in tastes and habits, quiet and unassuming in demeanour, yet prompt and decisive in action, of iron constitution, and an excellent rider, he was in all respects a worthy follower of the great leader under whom he served. He retired on half pay in 1821, and settling at Willington in his native county, engaged actively in the duties and pursuits of a country gentleman, as a magistrate, landlord, and sportsman. In the hunting field he became as distinguished as in the field of battle, and with his two brothers formed one of the trio sung by the Cheshire poet as "The brothers three from Dorfold sprung whom none of us could beat."

He married, in 1836, Susan, daughter of Thomas Tarleton, Esq., of Bolesworth Castle, Cheshire (by Frances, daughter of Philip Egerton, Esq., of Oulton Park), and sister of the late Admiral Sir Walter Tarleton, K.C.B., and died in 1872, in his 83rd year, leaving surviving issue four sons and two daughters. One of the former is Lieutenant-Colonel Henry Tomkinson, now in command of the 1st Royal Dragoons, and upon me, as his heir and successor, devolves the duty of editing his diary.

JAMES TOMKINSON. Willington Hall, Tarporley.

Chapter One
Sailing to Portugal

April 1st, 1809. One squadron of the 16th Light Dragoons arrived at Falmouth and embarked yesterday, and the one to which I belonged this day marched in from Truro and immediately embarked. My bay horse (Bob), as he was in the slings, twice kicked himself out, and was near being lost. He stood on the deck of the vessel for some time, whilst they were putting a fresh pair of slings on him, and nearly killed the second mate of the vessel by knocking him overboard. The man fell the whole height of the vessel, there being no water near the quay at which we embarked, from the tide being out. He was left behind sick at Falmouth.

We sailed on the 7th, and arrived, after an excellent passage, on the 15th at Lisbon. Being a junior officer, I was left to take a vessel no one chose to select. Mine was, however, overlooked by those above me, being one of the best in the fleet.

We kept the head of the convoy the whole voyage, and made the passage with half the sail some others were obliged to carry. We made the Tagus on the evening of the 15th, running in the first; on the frigate, the *Magicienne* (our convoy), making a signal for the fleet to put into the river. Some vessels anchored off the bar, and one with Lieutenant Buchanan* on board ran ashore on the bar, and kept firing guns of distress. They got off without injury on the return of the tide. We disembarked the following morning. Some of the vessels landed their horses by means of large boats on the river, and others ran in close to the shore, which was the best plan, as the horses then had water to stand in on coming down, and ran no chance of being injured. There was not, I think, a single accident; and the only horse I heard of as lost was one shot and thrown overboard in the harbour at

---
* *Of Hales, Market Drayton*

Falmouth, being suspected of farcy. The regiment consisted of eight troops of eighty horses each; total, 640 horses.

We were put up in the cavalry stables at Belem, belonging to the Royal Palace. The officers were billeted on the inhabitants. There was not a single individual who could speak a word of the language. I quite dreaded going home at night to my quarter, from the numberless questions I was asked by the inhabitants of the house. Their curiosity in looking at my appointments was very great, and they conceived the round buttons on our jackets to be real silver, being plated in a manner they did not conceive was possible. I was not very well satisfied with this idea, having some apprehension I might lose some of them.

We remained a week at Lisbon, and then commenced our march by a squadron each day up the country. I belonged to Captain Swetenham's troop, which formed a squadron with Captain Ashworth's,* commanded by the latter. A subaltern officer was sent on to procure billets, and I was ordered on that duty for our squadron. Our first day's march was to Povoa; second, Villa Franca; third, Santarem. From Santarem I proceeded, on the night before the squadron, to Torres Novas to procure billets, missed my way, was out until midnight nearly, wandering about without knowing more of the language than the name of the place I was going to, in a wild country covered with rock and heath, and by roads almost impracticable, with a sergeant and a dragoon equally at a loss with myself. On arrival at Torres Novas, I found an order to return to Santarem, and marched back the following day with the squadron which had preceded ours on the march. We remained about a week at Santarem. Our march up to join the rest of the army was retarded by want of supplies ; so deficient was our commissariat at this period of the war that they could not supply one cavalry regiment on its march through a country abounding in supplies—at least, ample for so much as was required for us. Whilst we remained at Santarem, Sir Arthur Wellesley landed from England to assume the command of the army, and Sir John Craddock returned home. On his road up he sent an order for the 16th to march, and in consequence

* *Of Somerford Booths, Congleton.*

we moved up to Coimbra by the following route:—May 2nd, Rio Mayor; May 3rd, Battalia; May 4th, Leiria; May 5th, Pombal; May 6th, Coimbra.

At Coimbra we found Sir Arthur and all the army. Both infantry and cavalry were reviewed on the 7th, the whole amounting to about 17,000 men. The 14th and 16th Light Dragoons, with one squadron of the 20th Light Dragoons, form a brigade under Major-General Cotton.* There are two heavy cavalry regiments expected out from England, and General Payne has come out and joined the army as commander of the cavalry. We hear that Soult is at Oporto, with his advance on the Vouga. Our entrance into Coimbra was hailed by the inhabitants as a happy event, in the hopes we might protect them from the French, and showers of flowers were poured down from the windows as we entered the town. We marched on the 8th to Avelans, and on the 9th to the bank of the Vouga, where, for the first time, we turned into a field to bivouac for the night. This was an event much thought of, and every officer was employed in bringing into use the various inventions recommended in England for such occasions, many of which were found useless; and, again, many essentials had been left behind, from a determination to face the campaign with the fewest number of comforts, whereby many requisites were omitted which were now found indispensable. But we were young soldiers, had listened to every suggestion, and can only learn by experience.

Our surprise at hearing the noise made by the frogs was very great, but quite common in Portugal. They were to be heard for miles.

The river is not fordable, and our passage over it is by a bridge close to our bivouac. The French piquets are said to be a league from the bridge, and the Portuguese have a cavalry piquet on the other side the river, about a mile in advance.

After a great deal of preparation to pass the night, being the first we had ever an idea of spending in the open air, and just as we had laid ourselves down for that purpose, Captain Cocks**

---

* *Sir Stapleton Cotton, Bart., afterwards Viscount Combermere, Field Marshal.*
** *The Hon. Charles Somers Cocks, eldest son of the first Lord Somers.*

of the 16th came round to our tents, saying the cavalry was to advance immediately, for the purpose of surprising the enemy's piquets at daylight. Captain Cocks had come out before the regiment, and had been attached to General Cotton's staff. He was still on the same service. We moved about eleven at night, and immediately on passing the Vouga the road ascends through a narrow pass, only admitting one horse at a time. The men, from the constant halts and delay, fell asleep; and what is but too common, lost the man before them, and so the road. On thinking the halt rather long, I got up to the dragoon asleep, and finding we had missed our way, I rode on, attempting to make it out; and on perceiving a Portuguese vidette standing near the road with a peasant boy near him, I made the boy, by threats, show me the road, and was by him conducted to the top of the hill, where I found the regiment formed on a heath waiting for the rear, which had been delayed by the circumstance above mentioned. We then moved forward, marching through the night. The boy was excessively frightened, and could only be made to proceed by my drawing my sword and threatening to kill him if he did not show the road. Every yard he advanced he fancied he was going close up to the French piquet, and on my perceiving the rest of the regiment and releasing him, he set off back again in the greatest haste.

"Go on, 16th! for shame, 16th." This was said by Cocks, being much annoyed any delay should take place, and at this time too young a soldier, and too anxious, to make the usual allowance for blunders on a night march. We afterwards often laughed at this.

May 10th. At daylight in the morning, the advance came up with the French piquet in front of Albergueria Nova. The piquet retired in great haste through the village, and the brigade formed on the plain, having the village on its right; there we halted in line, and saw the French cavalry turning out of their camp in a fir grove in the greatest confusion. They, in a short time, sent out some skirmishers, and in about half an hour they commenced firing some shots, which were the first we encountered. The halt was said to in consequence of the enemy having a couple of companies of infantry in the wood, and that it was necessary we should wait the arrival of some of our own infantry before we advanced. In about an hour a regiment of Portugese infantry and two guns came up, on seeing which the enemy began to move off in great haste. We then moved to our left, and by going round the wood, advanced with it on our right. Here we found four squadrons of French light cavalry formed, for the purpose of covering the retreat of their main body, consisting of two regiments. There were two squadrons in advance (of the enemy's), with the other two in support. The 16th passed a small ravine, and on forming moved to the brow of a small hill, from the top of which, about two hundred yards distant, on an easy declivity, the two squadrons were formed. The squadron I belonged to, and another of the 16th, were the two in advance. These were the two which charged. The instant we saw the enemy from the top of the hill, the word was given. The men set up an huzzah, advanced to the charge. The enemy fired a volley at us when about fifty yards from them, and then went about, setting off as hard as they could ride, we pursuing, cutting at them, and making all the prisoners in our power. Their other two squadrons in support went about, and the whole retired in no small confusion. The affair was more like a skirmish at a field day than an affair with an enemy.

From the enemy being in such haste with their fire, all the shots went over our heads, and no accident appeared to us to happen to any one. The enemy retired with their four squadrons over a ravine, the banks of which were very steep, and a couple of guns were brought up to fire a few shots, but without any execution, as they ascended the opposite bank by a winding steep road in single file. Thus ended our day's affair. We had Major Stanhope* (the Hon. Lincoln) very slightly wounded by a sabre in the shoulder, and two men also, but slightly, and one man and horse missing. We were in great spirits at our success, and, for the first affair, nothing could be more encouraging.

We marched and halted for the night near the village of Oliviera, bivouacking in a fir grove. The infantry occupied

---

* *Second son of Charles, third Earl of Harrington; he died in 1840.*

the village. Lieutenant-General Arthur Paget commanded the advance of the infantry in Olivia.

Sir Arthur Wellesley in his despatch states the enemy as having four regiments of cavalry, one of infantry and artillery. This could not be so; for had they that force, they certainly would have shown more than they did. We never saw a gun, scarcely any infantry; and if there were four regiments of cavalry, they must be very weak.

Sir Arthur's statement was probably founded on information from the peasants, who made the enemy's numbers probably greater than in reality they were, that he might send a large force to ensure success, and thereby get them away from that neighbourhood.

"The infantry of the army was formed into three divisions for this expedition, of which two, the advanced guard, consisted of the Hanoverian Legion, and Brigadier-General R. Stewart's brigade, with a brigade of six-pounders and a brigade of three-pounders under Lieutenant-General Payne, and the brigade of Guards; Brigadier-General Campbell's brigades of infantry, and a brigade of six-pounders under Lieutenant-General Sherbrooke, moved by the high road from Coimbra to Oporto; and one composed of Major-General Hill's and Brigadier-General Cameron's brigades of infantry, and a brigade of six-pounders under the command of Major-General Hill, by the road from Coimbra to Aviero."

Sir Arthur Wellesley's despatch.

Dated Oporto, May 12th, 1809.

May 11th. Two squadrons cavalry were ordered to march with the brigade under General Paget in advance of the army—the one I belonged to, of the 16th, and one of the 20th Light Dragoons, both under the command of Major Blake of the 20th. Major-General Hill, with his brigade, had embarked on the 9th at Aviero, and landed yesterday near Ovar, and was moving from thence to Oporto on the enemy's right flank. We marched for about a couple of hours from Olivia. The infantry were in front, the country being enclosed and not adapted for cavalry.* On passing Santo Redondo, we came up with the enemy's rear guard, which was immediately attacked and driven from their camp and position through a fir grove on the road to Oporto. The enemy's force consisted of 4,000 infantry and some squadrons of cavalry, though from the ground we occupied neither were to be seen, being stationed in rear of a fir grove, ready to act if required. The fire was very sharp, though on our side always advancing. We lost some men in this attack (infantry). After remaining stationary for some time, we were ordered to advance and follow up the rear of the army. We advanced over the ground they had occupied as a camp and the rising ascent they had held and been driven from by our infantry.**The two squadrons then descended the hill and entered a fir wood along a deep, narrow, sandy lane, leading to Oporto and close to the village of Grijo. The wood terminated half a mile before the road entered the village, having vineyards and enclosures to the right, with the same on the left. The ground on the left was very steep and rocky, and afforded a strong position for infantry. The enemy's rear guard was here posted. The main body to our left of the road, with a couple of battalions in the fields and vineyards to our right. They consisted of about 3,000 infantry. The two squadrons, on entering the wood, were obliged to proceed in file; and we had not gone half the distance through it, before we were met and turned back by Dashwood of the Adjutant-General's department, saying the enemy were so posted as to render it impossible for cavalry to act. We were retiring, when someone in our rear ordered us to go about and proceed in advance. Dashwood again ordered us to retire, repeating what he before said. We, however, advanced to the edge of the wood, where the road became so narrow that the troops got into single file.

---

* *On the road from Olivia we passed three priests the French had murdered for some cause or another. They were hanging on a tree, close to the roadside, and must have been a full month in that situation from their appearance.*

**An infantry soldier killed here was the first dead man I had ever seen.*

The 16th were in front, and Captain Cocks'** troop being on the right of the squadron, was the one in advance.*** The road was very deep, and as we stood in it the enemy kept firing in the direction of where we stood, causing the leaves from an oak tree to fall on us in great numbers. The person who had given the orders from the rear was Captain Mellish, who had come from the rear with orders from the Hon. General Stewart (adjutant-general) for us to advance. Captain Mellish, without seeing the position of the enemy, called out that it was the positive order of General Stewart for us to advance, and Dashwood stood at the head of the lane saying it was impossible. Here we stood in the lane, and I rode from my own troop in the rear of our squadron to see what was going on, Dashwood still standing at the head of the lane forbidding our advance.

In this position we remained; and Captain Mellish, on coming past the dragoons in getting to the front, was heard to say, without seeing the position of the enemy (I heard him myself), that if no one would head us that he would himself (Dashwood was not in the attack). Dashwood and myself were the only two officers in front at the head of the lane. On hearing this, we could not avoid advancing; and in single file, along a narrow, bad lane, did we proceed to attack these 3,000 infantry so posted. Captain Mellish did not head us, nor did he leave the wood with the advance. We galloped about one hundred yards down the road, and then turned into the enclosures to the right, through a gateway in a stone wall, sufficiently wide for one horse. I was nearly off, my horse turned so suddenly.

On getting into the enclosure, we rode at a gallop up to the enemy, who, strange to state, ran away. They were scattered all over the field, and I was in the act of firing my pistol at the head of a French infantry man when my arm dropped, without any power on my part to raise it. The next thing I recollect was my horse galloping in an ungovernable manner amongst this

** *He (Captain Cocks) was not with his troop, being on General Cotton's staff.*
*** *I belonged to Captain Swetenham's troop in the rear, and being anxious to see what was going on, I left my own men and got to the head of the column.*

body of infantry, with both my hands hanging down, though I do not recollect being shot in the left arm. In this state one of their bayonets was stuck into him, and he fortunately turned short round; and I had, in addition, the good luck to keep my seat on him. He went full gallop to the rear, and on coming to a fence of an enclosure he selected a low place in it under a vine tree, knocked my head into it, when I fell off him. This again made me insensible, and my next recollection was being supported by a French infantry soldier across the field to the rear and to the shade of a wall, where he laid me on my back. In a short time some of the German infantry came up (belonging to our advance under General Paget), and began to plunder me, taking out of my pocket a knife containing many useful things for campaigning. They were prevented proceeding any further by the arrival of a private of the name of Green, of Captain Cocks' troop, who took me for Captain Swetenham, telling me I was certainly killed, and that it was a sad thing to order men on such a duty. There were only eight men who went into the field to the right with me. Green was the only one who escaped, and one man was shot in nine places. Green was made a sergeant.

I remained about half an hour where the Frenchman had laid me, when a surgeon of the artillery came up, cut off my clothes, and dressed my wounds. I fancied myself to be hit in the body, from the difficulty I had at first in breathing; yet on that subsiding, I did not conceive it could be so.

On taking off my clothes, I was found to be wounded by a musket-shot in the neck. It had entered above the left shoulder and come out in the front. A second through the right arm above the elbow, and a third musket-shot through the left, below the elbow, with a bayonet-wound close by the latter. The wounds were dressed in the common and best manner, being bound up in their own blood, and I was taken by my servant Robinson to a small hovel close by, where I was placed for the night. From the loss of blood and shock I had received, delirium came on at intervals, with a considerable degree of fever. My servant was ordered not to let me move, and from lying on my back in one position I was so uncomfortable and irritable that considerable disputes occurred between us, my wishing him to move me and he knowing it would be injurious. I, however, said so much at one time that he was induced to relieve me in some degree from the position I so much complained of.

The remainder of the two squadrons went down the road; and the enemy, conceiving cavalry would never make such an attack unsupported by infantry, retired towards Oporto, and were followed by the squadrons through Grijo towards Oporto, in which retreat they lost nearly five hundred, taken prisoners. When we turned into the field to the right of the road, we were exposed to the whole fire of the enemy stationed on the other side of the road; and had they stood their ground, it would have been impossible for us to get at them, and even if it had been in our power, from the enclosed state of the country and difficulty of our advance, they might have defied us.

Captain Mellish behaved very ill in insisting on our advance, at all events in using the language he did. Dashwood was quite right in his instructions, on seeing the position of the enemy. General Stewart was more to be condemned than any for sending the orders he did; but for this there was perhaps some reason, and not perhaps the most liberal. Major Blake too, of the 20th, who commanded the two squadrons, ought to have come to the head of the lane; and having for some time been on service, it was his duty as an old officer to have taken upon himself the responsibility, and not have attacked. The infantry were not half an hour's march behind, on seeing which the enemy would have retired, when we might have pursued and availed ourselves of some open ground beyond Grijo.

Had this affair occurred later in the war, no cavalry officer would have made the attack without representing the enemy's position.*

May 12th. I was this day put on a door and carried to a house in the village of Grijo, where I was left with the remainder of

---

* *Notes.*
Green remained with me all night. I was returned "severely wounded."
Loss in the affair of the 11th May: infantry and cavalry, 19 killed, 63 wounded, 14 missing.

the wounded in yesterday's affair. I was quite delirious nearly the whole day, and through the night could scarcely be kept in bed. I lost my horse (Bob), and was fortunate in seeing him this day pass through Grijo, having been taken by a commissary from some peasants into whose hands he had fallen. I had a spare jacket in my valise, and the peasants had cut off the buttons, fancying they were silver. The house I occupied belonged to a priest, who had left it to reside in some other village during the time the enemy were in the neighbourhood. He occasionally came to visit me, pestering me with inquiries in a language I could not understand, with his head close to my ear, talking very loud to make me understand, and not unfrequently for twenty minutes at a time.

My dragoon (Robinson) showed him my jacket with the buttons cut off, and I rather conceive he was the means of my having them nearly all returned, as each day some peasant brought a few; my dragoon told me some people had been sent to prison, and that the buttons were returned in hopes of obtaining their release; however, I got nearly all of them.

One of the dragoons, in Captain Cocks' troop, who went into the field with me, was shot in nine places, and lived for some days. In about a week, they began to remove the wounded from Grijo to Oporto, over a very bad, rugged, rocky road. The distance is about six miles, and this they wanted me to travel on a common bullock-car of the country, drawn by two oxen at the rate of about two miles an hour, or not so much; the wheels made of solid pieces of wood, very low, fixed to the axle-tree, which turns round, and from the friction and noise may be heard to a great distance from the creaking. Not infrequently the wheels are not round, and consequently give a jerk in every circle they make. I, however, refused to go in them, and they were obliged to procure me a sedan-chair which was sent out.

In putting me on the door to carry me to Grijo, they had either let my head slip or it had happened from the wound sloughing, but the wound in my neck was at first only two holes, and from either one cause or the other, the two holes had broken across, and the space from where the ball went in to where it came out was one opening. The wound in my left arm was most painful, and I was constantly asking the surgeon who attended me if it was not broken. This wound was merely like a prick with a bayonet, and the cause assigned for the pain was that some of the cloth was taken in with it.

May 22nd. I this day moved into Oporto in the sedan chair, and was about two hours and a half on the passage. I was dreadfully tired, and frequently begged them to stop and allow me to rest a little. I never got out of the chair, and having only one hand to use, and not much power in that, I was frequently in great pain from not being able to relieve myself from any position in which I was uncomfortable. I was dreadfully irritable, and wished the dragoon to shoot the Portuguese who held up the curtains of the sedan windows to look at me, which they repeatedly did on my entering the town.

I, however, arrived safe at the house I was to occupy, and had a tolerably good night, which was the first I had passed without delirium since I was wounded. I had not been a day in Oporto before my servant Robinson was taken so ill that he could not stir from his chair. He was, however, very attentive in sitting by my bedside, keeping off the mosquitos; and the only person I had to attend to my horses, and procure any little thing I wanted, was a dragoon (Fisher), who generally, when he went out, did not return for hours, and neglected everything as much as he dared without allowing Robinson, my horses, and self to starve.

The Hon. Captain Neville,* of the 14th Light Dragoons, called to see me, and made me a present of a mosquito-net: the most acceptable thing I could possibly have received.

The 16th had followed the enemy up to Motalegre, when Soult having abandoned Portugal, they returned with the remainder of the army to Oporto. It was then determined I should proceed, when sufficiently recovered, to England; and on the army leaving Oporto (on its march for Coimbra) I

---

* *Henry, second son of the second Lord Braybrooke. He died in Spain in the same year, after the battle of Talavera.*

was moved (through Captain Cocks) to the house of Viscount Balsamam, which had been occupied by General Cotton. The house was very large; I had the best room in it, and was supplied with every comfort. The Viscount spoke English, and came frequently to see me.

I still continued to complain much of the pain occasioned from the wound in my left arm. It was so painful, I could not move it, nor allow the blood on the hand, which had clotted on it (from never being washed), to be removed. The dressings began to be very scarce, no ship having arrived with medical supplies, and what few the army could spare, with those found in the town, were nearly expended. I had once or twice been dressed with something like tallow or hog's-lard, and my wounds kept bound up for want of dressings, so that they began to smell before they dared again to open them, fearing they should soon be quite without any dressing.

From lying constantly on my back in one posture, the skin came off the shoulder-blades, which was painful when I was raised and put down again. In about ten days after I had removed to the Viscount's house, the surgeon who attended me discovered I had something in my left arm and fancied it was a bullet; one shot had gone quite through, and the one which gave me so much pain, and in which he fancied there was something, did not appear above a quarter of an inch long, but was torn a little, as if with the point of a bayonet. I had now poultices put to it, and kept the inside part of my arm undermost as much as possible, the substance being in the sinews. A vessel arrived in the Douro, and I had an ample supply of lint and proper salve: a greater comfort could not be conceived.

June 17th. The skin on the left arm, over what was supposed to be a bullet, began to change colour, and whatever was in the arm began to show itself near the surface. The surgeon said he should bring his instruments and take it out the next morning.

June 18th. He arrived at his usual hour, about 12 a.m., with another surgeon to assist him, and what with instruments and preparation I thought they were going to undertake some operation. He placed my arm as he wished it, and at the first cut came against the substance, and took it out with his fingers with the greatest ease. It proved to be a button* off the front row of my jacket, which were very large! The ball had struck against my breast, and driven the button off into my left arm, leaving the shank on the jacket.** The relief was instantaneous. I moved all my fingers immediately, and was employed the whole day in putting my hand in hot water and getting off the clotted blood from my hand; it was a very busy day. My arm was much wasted from lying so long in one position, and I had no power of moving it.

However, from getting the button out I could lie on my side a little, and vary my position from the one I had been accustomed to. My wounds healed by degrees, but being so much reduced by the great discharge from the one in the neck, I had not strength to show any amendment in more than one at a time. The neck healed in some degree the first; and when it showed decided symptoms of amendment, the surgeon told me he had apprehended that the sloughing, which was very great, would have laid bare the artery, in which case I should have died. He might, however, in this have shown as much ignorance as in allowing the button to remain such a length of time in my arm. I, however, began to gain strength, and could walk about for a few minutes in the room.

Among the incidents of this time was the circumstance of shooting at the cats on the opposite side of the street, going along the roof of a low house. Of one that sat in the window, which was open, and an old woman being in the room when the dragoon fired. We shot with a pistol.***

---

* *The button—originally round—is now in my possession; one-half is driven completely into the other, forming a concave side with jagged edges; its weight is nearly half an ounce. Also the jacket worn on the occasion; the arms are cut open from top to bottom, and the neck down to the shoulder. All the buttons are in their place, except one besides that discovered in the arm—which possibly saved his life.-ED*

** *I recollect, when I came to my senses (after falling off my horse), fancying I was shot through the body, from the difficulty I had in breathing, which was probably occasioned by the blow from the ball striking against my breast.*

*** *My father used to tell this story to me when a child; the reason was the dreadful noise made by the cats, which prevented sleep.*

Excellent attendance of Jones, a dragoon of the 16th, in Swetenham's troop, who was left sick at Oporto and came to wait upon me. My servant Robinson still very unwell from rheumatism, and scarcely able to walk. Robinson and I playing at all-fours. Jones holding my cards, and we two playing Robinson. The friend I made of Jones, he telling me all the tricks dragoons practised. Jones' attempts to amuse me through the day. The songs he sung to me, and my learning one or two from hearing them so often. We all three lived the same. The Viscount went to Lisbon, but left three cooks in the house. Each meal was sent up with ample wine for dinner. One large bottle nearly holding two quart bottles. I drank what little I wanted (which was very little), and they finished the remainder in the room next to mine, eating the dinner, which was excellent and enough for three. They scarcely ever left me, and the time Jones employed to fetch things from the hospital, etc., was very short. No two men could behave better.

1821. Jones came to see me when quartered at Manchester, near where he now resides, having been discharged. I was playing at ball with some officers in the barrack yard. He was very glad to see me, and the more so as I had the use of my arms.

June 27th. The French prisoners taken at Oporto, and the sick left in their hospitals capable of being moved, were ordered to England (they amounted to about 700). A fleet of transports was ordered to leave the Douro with from 400 to 500 of the above, in one of which I was ordered to embark, and was placed under the care of Assistant-Surgeon Williams, 52nd Regiment. There were forty-five French infantry soldiers in the same transport. We sailed on the 28th, and for some days I suffered considerably from the rolling of the vessel and pain in my wounds, having only one side on which I could lie, being frequently turned on the other by the motion. I was sea-sick for the first two or three days. When I recovered a little, I found great benefit from the sea air, and got on deck for several hours at a time. The wind was quite against us, and for the first fortnight we, each day, got farther off our destination. The vessel was a very miserable one, and nearly the worst sailer in the fleet.

We parted convoy about the 23rd, and were alone through the whole of the 26th.

The master from his reckoning was off the French coast, as he supposed; but we could not see it, and by his manner he evidently betrayed considerable anxiety from the fear of the prisoners rising and carrying the vessel into a French port. They had certainly some idea of it, approaching to the quarter deck—which they had never done before we separated from the convoy—and coming frequently to look at the compass. As night fell, it was our opinion they would have made some attempt. We were only fifteen in all, against forty-five, and without any means of defence. Fortunately about 4 p.m. we spied a sail, and before dark were hailed by a British seventy-four, having a large convoy from America. We joined the fleet, and kept in the middle of them the whole night. The next morning we spied the land, being the coast of Cornwall, and sailed close past the Eddystone, with a fine sharp breeze from the west. We here joined our own fleet, with another from the West Indies, and proceeded up Channel in company with 300 sail. We made Spithead on the 28th, when we immediately landed, and in a couple of days proceeded to London.

Note.

The master of the vessel, when we saw land, was certain it was the Isle of Wight, and persisted in pointing out to us a fancied opening in the land which he called the Needles. Had it been night, he would possibly have persisted in it, and attempted to run in. He was so much out in his reckoning, that nothing but the Eddystone direct ahead would convince him. It is through such ignorance that many a vessel is lost.

Letter from Sir Stapleton Cotton.

May, 1809.

Dear Sir,—

I hope my letter will be in time to give you a true account of your son before Mrs. Tomkinson and yourself have been alarmed by any exaggerated one which may appear in the papers, and which is but too much the case upon these occasions.

Your son, I am sorry to say, was wounded in an attack made by the 16th upon the enemy's infantry on the 11th inst. One ball passed through his neck, and he received a wound in each arm; but none of these wounds are dangerous, and the surgeon assures me that your son is doing well. I found him yesterday in very good spirits, and not in the least alarmed about himself. After the disagreeable task of informing a parent of a misfortune having befallen his son, I have the pleasing one of saying that nothing could exceed the gallant and soldier-like conduct of Lieutenant Tomkinson upon this and every other occasion.

You may depend upon hearing regularly from me until your son is perfectly recovered.

I beg my best compliments to Mrs. Tomkinson and all your family.

I am, dear sir,
Yours faithfully and obediently,
S. COTTON.

From Captain Swetenham.

May, 1809.

Dear Sir,—

From the circumstance of your son having been wounded in a charge with the squadron which I had the honour to command on the 11th inst. and fearing that you might feel alarmed from the public accounts, I think it a duty incumbent upon me to state that he is not in the least danger, but doing well, although he received no less than three wounds. It was on an occasion when the squadron suffered much. My own horse was shot, and my bridle reins in two places. We entered Oporto with little resistance yesterday. You need be under no alarm respecting your son, and if you direct to him at Oporto he will receive your letters, provided you pay the postage to Falmouth. Excuse this hurry. I have only a few minutes, and wish to send a line to my own friends.

I am, dear sir,
Yours faithfully and obediently,
C. SWETENHAM.

From Major the Hon. Lincoln Stanhope.

Porto, May 31st, 1809.

Dear Sir,—

Feeling that you must be anxious to hear news of your son, I take advantage of an opportunity that offers of sending to Lisbon to let you know that he is going on as well as possible. I write this in his room, and have not the smallest doubt of his doing well. I understand General Cotton wrote to you soon after your son was wounded. But perhaps in the hurry he might not have been so explicit as the anxiety of a father might have wished. My poor friend Tomkinson received a ball through each arm, and one through the neck; however, most fortunately they are all flesh wounds. I conceive it the best plan for him, as soon as he is well enough, to go to England; for though he is doing as well as possible, yet his wounds are likely to render him too weak to undertake active service for some time. I have therefore spoken to General Pain, who commands the cavalry, to allow him to go home the first opportunity that offers. Nothing could exceed his gallantry on the day he got his wounds, which is only what you will hear from every one who witnessed the engagement. Trusting that you will soon see your son in a convalescent state,

I remain, dear sir,
Your most obedient humble servant,
LINCOLN STANHOPE.

Tomkinson begs me to give his best love to Mrs. Tomkinson and to his sisters and brothers,

OPORTO, June 2nd, 1809.

Dear Father,—

I suppose you have ere this received General Cotton's letter, which I requested him to write the day I met with my accident. Conceiving that it will be a satisfaction to my mother and yourself to hear from me by my own pen, I have taken the opportunity of General Paget's aid-de-camp going to England to send this scrawl to say that I am doing as well as possible. I received a ball through the flesh part of each arm and one in the left side of my neck. All the pain has now left my three wounds, my appetite and spirits are very good, and if the surgeon was here to loose the bandage on this right arm, I think I could have written a letter that would have given you more satisfaction. I intended, when first I was wounded, to have come to England; but I am now so much better, that I don't know whether or not it will be necessary. I shall be obliged in case the army advances into Spain, but of that circumstance we are at present ignorant. The 16th did their duty, and behaved famously. Major Stanhope wrote to you the other day for me. With kindest remembrances and best wishes to all friends,

                I remain, dear father,
                Your affectionate son,
                                    W<small>M</small> T<small>OMKINSON</small>

Chapter Two
The Campaign of 1810

March 20th, 1810. I embarked this day on board the *Norge*, a seventy-four, for Lisbon; and sailed the same day, our party consisting of Lieutenant-General Sir Stapleton Cotton; Lord Tweeddale, his quarter-master general; Lieutenant Dudley, 16th Light Dragoons, his aid-de-camp.

We arrived in Lisbon on the 29th, having made the Tagus late on the 28th. The vessel struck against a rock when off Fort San Julian, and was obliged to be sent round to Gibraltar to repair. From the gloomy state of affairs in England before we left, we expected to hear at Lisbon of the retreat of the army. Headquarters were at Vizeu, with our outposts on the Agueda, where the 95th Infantry had had an affair with the enemy at Barba del Puerco, they having attempted to surprise them at night, in which they failed, being driven back with considerable loss.

During our stay at Lisbon, Sir Stapleton occupied Quintella's house, one of the best in Lisbon. I bought an English mare and two Portuguese ponies: the two latter for baggage.

Quintella is very opulent; he has the monopoly of all the snuff sold in Portugal.

There are two passages into the Tagus: one close to Fort St. Julian, which is narrow and not very deep, and the other farther south, wider and most usually selected on entering the Tagus. The *Norge* is one of the largest seventy-fours in the navy; and the master, having been in her and off the Tagus with Sir John Duckworth, at the time of the Convention of Cintra, when it was in agitation to have entered the Tagus and bombard and get possession of Fort San Julian, for which purpose he had been employed in taking soundings, and particularly of the inner passage, thought himself capable of taking in the ship without a pilot, in which case half the pilotage goes to the master. The captain of the vessel had never been in the Tagus; it was his first voyage in the *Norge*, and, much against his inclination, a pilot was not taken. We were very close in shore, with every sail set, going twelve or fourteen knots an hour, a man heaving the lead, and the wind blowing very fresh off shore on our larboard quarter. The vessel struck twice on a rock, the masts quite bent; but fortunately going so quick she got off. It was at the dinner hour of the men, and all excepting 100 or 150 were below, and on feeling her hit, in an instant from 500 to 600 hands were on deck. The vessel made from three to four feet of water immediately and the pumps were set going before we came to an anchor. The master considered it very unreasonable in the captain to wish for a pilot, his own knowledge of the harbour being so correct, and the captain distinctly stated that the master took the whole responsibility on himself. The captain in my opinion ought to have insisted on one.

April 15th. We this day arrived at Coimbra, having moved by the usual stages, and here halted one day.

The 6th Portuguese Regiment of the line was here, under Colonel Ashworth, brother to Captain Ashworth of the 16th. The men were very fine and steady under arms, and from all appearances should make excellent troops.

We made two short days' marches from Coimbra to Santa Combadao, where we found the headquarters of the 16th, seven leagues from Coimbra. The following day Sir Stapleton moved on to Vizeu. The regiment was by no means recovered from the effects of the Talavera campaign; but from the quantity of green forage in the neighbourhood of every quarter, great changes were evident in a short time.

Headquarters with right squadron, Santa Combadao, with the remainder of the regiment in the adjacent village.

The day after I joined, I was ordered to Frieshada, a small village on the right of the main Vizeu road, to take care of the horses sent there for grazing.

The regiment was brigaded with the 1st Hussars, K.G.L., who were up in the front, doing the outpost duty, under Brigadier-General Crawford, on the Agueda.

April 27th. Headquarters of the army moved this day from Vizeu up to Celorico, eight leagues in advance, and two squadrons of the 16th marched to Vizeu.

April 28th. This day joined Captain Cocks' troop, and marched with the other two squadrons to Vizeu.

April 29th. Marched to Villa Cova; called by the peasants four leagues from Vizeu, though from the badness of the road it was near night before we got in, raining nearly the whole way.

April 30th. The regiment this morning occupied the following villages in the rear of Celorico:—

Mello, Right squadron and headquarters: Ashworth and Lyon, E. and G.

Left centre, Mesquitella: Hay and Swetenham, D.K.

Left, Gouvea: Murray and Pelly, F. and A.

Right centre, divided: Captain Belli's troop at Nabias; Captain Cocks at Villa Franca.

Headquarters of the army, Celorico:—

1st Division, Celorico: Lieutenant-General Sir Brent Spencer.

3rd Division, Pinhel: Major-General Picton.

4th Division, Guarda: Major-General Cole.

The 5th Division, as General Leith's corps was then called, was in the neighbourhood of Guarda.

The Light Division upon the Agueda.

Cavalry: Lieutenant-General Sir Stapleton Cotton.

Lieutenant-General Hill, with the 2nd Division, was at Castello Branco, having moved from the south at the same time headquarters advanced from Vizeu.

The houses here are far inferior to those in Estremadura, without chimneys, the people living in the midst of smoke and filth. This makes the inhabitants look twenty years older; and being naturally not the finest race in the world, I can't say much for their appearance.

The regiment was supplied in everything from the country; we got the corn in by cars, passing our receipts for it on the commissary at Celorico, which were paid when presented. Cocks rather did this in a summary manner, and a commissary was sent to Villa Franca to inquire into the complaints of the peasants. We asked him to dinner, and gave him as much wine as he wished, when he said the complaints were groundless.

We heard about the 12th of this month that Massena, the Prince of Essling, had arrived at Valladolid with a considerable reinforcement, and had assumed the command of the army of Portugal.

June 1st. An order arrived last night for the 16th to move to some villages in front of Celorico, and orders were at the same time given to the first division to hold itself in readiness. The regiment occupied the following villages:—

Headquarters, Right squadron: Marcal de Chao.

Right centre: Minuchal.

Left centre: Carnicais.

Left: Frasches.

Headquarters of the cavalry came to Minuchal.

This move was in consequence of the enemy having pushed a considerable force down to Ciudad de Rodrigo, and having thrown some bridges over the river, all preparatory to the siege of the place, and not with any idea of an attack on us before they take it. Deserters come in daily, and all report the enemy as short of supplies. They must say something, and this is perhaps the only good reason they can give for an act, under almost any circumstances, highly disgraceful to a soldier.

Every one, almost, thought Rodrigo would not hold out forty-eight hours after the enemy's guns opened.

On the 19th of June, Lord Wellington reviewed the 16th, which looked as well as at a review on Hounslow Heath.

General Anson arrived from England, and as it was necessary to relieve part of the Hussars with General Crawford, two squadrons of the 16th were ordered up. This I heard on dining at headquarters on the 20th, and that the whole brigade would have gone up, had General Anson been junior to Crawford.

June 23rd. The whole regiment moved up this day about two leagues to the front. Headquarters went to Povoa del Rey with the right squadron, and the remainder to adjacents. Captain Cocks' troop to Moimenteria.

June 24th. The two right squadrons of the 16th this day proceeded on their march to relieve the Hussars. We marched through Pinhel, halting at Valverde, in all four leagues. Major Stanhope had the command; Major Archer, with the headquarters of the regiment, remaining behind.

June 25th. We marched at daylight, passing the Coa at the bridge of Almeida. The banks are the most rugged and inaccessible I ever saw: a handful of men might defend the bridge against any force. Almeida is an irregular work, in tolerable repair. It is garrisoned by one regiment of the Portuguese line, the 24th, and two of Militia, with Colonel Cox, a British officer in the Portuguese service, for its governor.

Our route took us to La Alameida, the first village in Spain, two leagues from Almeida and three from Valverde. On our entering the village an order arrived to hasten on to Gallegos, the enemy having driven in our outposts from the other side the Azava, in front of Gallegos. On our arrival at Gallegos, as they had retired and all was quiet, we remained all day on the hill in front of Gallegos, and at night returned to La Alameida. The enemy established their piquets on one side the Azava and Agueda, with ours on the opposite bank. One of the enemy's powder waggons blew up through a shell from the town falling into it; the explosion was seen by us as far back on the march as between Almeida and La Alameida. The enemy's guns opened against the town.

June 26th. We marched from La Alameida so as to arrive at Gallegos by daybreak, and when the piquets were relieved, occupied the quarters which the two squadrons of Hussars had left in the village of Gallegos.

Brigadier-General Crawford had the command of this advanced corps, consisting as follows:—

43rd Regiment
52nd Regiment.

95th Regiment.
1st Portuguese Cacadores.
3rd Portuguese Cacadores.
Captain Ross' brigade of Horse Artillery.
2 squadrons 16th Light Dragoons.
2 squadrons 1st Hussars, K.G.L.

There were besides about 4,000 Spanish infantry in the village on the right, with Don Juliano de Sanchez's Guerrillas, about 200.

Piquets of infantry and cavalry occupied the line of the Azava from the right as far as Carpio, to its junction with the Agueda, and on that river at the ford of Molleno de Floris. General Crawford's headquarters with his infantry were in Gallegos; the Cacadores encamped on the hill on the right of Gallegos, opposite Carpio. Two squadrons of the 16th, with one of the Hussars, in Gallegos; the other detached to Villa de Puerca, a league to the left, watching the passes of Barba de Puerca, and the others up to our chain of posts.*

From the Azava to Gallegos is one short league, and two from that river to Ciudad Rodrigo. The enemy have about 8,000 men over the Agueda, which makes us particularly on the alert. We never unsaddle excepting in the evening, merely to clean the horses; and at night the men sleep in their appointments, with their bridle reins in their hands, ready to turn out in an instant. At two in the morning, the whole turn out and remain on their alarm ground until the piquets relieved, come in, and all is quiet.

The firing both from the town and enemy's batteries was very brisk. It begins before daylight, ceases in the heat of the day, and then again at night.

I was much struck with the difference between the Spaniards and Portuguese; and though from Val de la Meda to La Alameida (the two frontier villages of Spain and Portugal) is only one league, the difference in manners, customs, dress, and language

---

*The appearance of the 16th was good in comparison to what it had been; but looking in the condition of horses in England, this is perhaps saying too much—our appearance was good.

is as great as nations thousands of leagues distant. The Spaniards are particularly clean in their dress as to outward appearance and houses, each cottage affording one good room, with a small recess or two, large enough for a bed. Their floors are generally of a hard earth, with one small window, generally to the north or west, which in summer is particularly adapted for so warm a climate. The chairs, or rather stools, are as clean as hands can make them, and the walls kept constantly white-washed. In their persons they are not so clean, but in this respect far before the Portuguese.

June 27th. The 16th, this day, took their share of the duty. The three squadrons found four officers' piquets along the chain of posts. Right piquet at Carpio Ford, an officer, sergeant, and two corporals, and eighteen men supported by infantry at night.

The Mill Ford, an officer and eighteen, sergeant and corporal.

Marialva Bridge; the same, with infantry.

Molleno de Floris (on the Agueda), an officer and twelve of cavalry, with an officer and twenty of infantry.

There was a captain of the cavalry piquets who remained at night at the Mill Ford, with a field officer of the day, who visited the chain of posts without remaining out at night. Two guns were out night and day, ready to support the piquets.

June 28th. I, this morning, mounted my first piquet, relieving an officer of the Hussars, on the right at Carpio Ford.

The enemy had kept a large force of cavalry in and near the village of Carpio from the time they drove us over the Azava until yesterday, when it was removed. They wished, by this appearance, to make us abandon our line of posts; and on our not doing so, thought us stronger than we were.

June 29th. The fire at Rodrigo was very heavy this morning. I was relieved at daylight. All remained as usual. We had one alert in the course of this day, but soon turned in, as it was nothing more than one of the enemy's generals visiting their outposts, which may be a pleasant ride for them, though if they would not move their troops it would save us much unnecessary trouble.

June 30th. General Crawford, with the infantry and four

guns, retired to La Alameida, leaving Lieutenant-Colonel Arenchildt of the Hussars, with the three squadrons and two guns, in Gallegos.

The enemy, soon after daylight, brought two regiments of infantry and two guns to the village of Marialva, not a quarter of a mile from the bridge. This turned us out, and it was long before it was known they intended to leave them there. This, with the infantry having left us, makes our situation particularly nice, though perhaps we can get away the better alone; and as we must run whenever they come, we have less to risk.

Our baggage went with the infantry.

The besieging army consists of the 6th Corps d'Armee under Marshal Ney, Duc d'Elchinghen, of the 8th, under Marshal Junot, Duc d'Abrantes.

The whole amounting to 45,000 men. Massena superintends the whole operation.

The town has a garrison of from four to five thousand Spaniards.

July 1st. Mounted piquet at Molleno de Floris, relieving Lieutenant Alexander of the 16th. The piquet consisted of twelve men, finding at night three double videttes; so that when the relief was out, he had only the sergeant left with himself. The relief missed its way, and he, conceiving they were taken, came and reported himself that the enemy had passed the Agueda. This created much confusion, and on Captain Cocks' going up to the piquet (as the officer on duty), he found the corporal returned with his six men and all quiet. Alexander was put under arrest by General Crawford. In consequence of this I had six more men sent me. Considerable fire of small arms nearly the whole night at Rodrigo.

July 2nd. I was this morning relieved as usual, all quiet. On my arrival at Gallegos I found the troops formed in rear of the town in consequence of the enemy having pushed a force close to the Azava, apparently with a view to crossing. They remained there for two hours, and retired again when we turned in to our

---

★ *This was the best conducted, most regular chain of posts I saw during the whole war: 1814 this written.*

quarters. We were on duty almost every other night.

July 3rd. Mounted piquet this morning at the bridge of Marialva. The enemy approached close to the bridge, and by passing some light infantry down the opposite banks, attempted to remove the cars from off the bridge. At the same time their cavalry mounted for foraging, and their infantry got under arms; through this, I reported that the enemy had an intention of passing, and the troops in Gallegos turned out. At night all remained quiet. It was feared I had, at first, made a hasty report; but I was fully justified in sending word.

July 4th. The enemy this morning half an hour before daylight passed the ford close to Marialva with two hundred cavalry as an advance, driving in my piquet at a gallop; they were close at our heels for two miles, we firing as much as we could to give the other piquets notice, and cutting at them as they came up to us. I saw a light go down their line, as if they were counting men in their ranks on the opposite side the river. I mounted my men (which was fortunate), as they came on at a gallop, and I had some difficulty in getting all away. It was just grey in the morning when they came on. Sergeant Little was the sergeant of the piquet; and in order to keep himself and the men on the alert, he sang nearly the whole night, and behaved very well in retiring.

The troops at Gallegos were turned out on their alarm ground, which checked the enemy on the hill above, where they waited for their force to come up; by that means allowing time for our piquets on the right to come in. The enemy showed four regiments of cavalry on the heights, which caused us to retire in rear of Gallegos, placing our skirmishers on the brook and ravine lineable with the village. The enemy were kept in check some time by this, assisted by the two guns left with us, and allowed time for us to get everything clear away and retire gradually on the La Alameida road, forming behind the bridge and defile, a mile from Gallegos. Here the enemy, perceiving it our intention to withdraw over the brook, and that the greater part was already over, made a dash at our rear skirmishers, who were withdrawn in good order by Captain Krauchenburgh of the Hussars; and we, having allowed a certain number to pass the bridge, charged them back with great success. Two French officers, leading their men, behaved most gallantly, and were killed on the bridge. This success did not retard their advance one moment, for on our right they kept advancing with two regiments, and we remained rather too long. For the last half-mile we were obliged to gallop, with the French dragoons close at our heels, and formed in rear of the infantry, which was drawn up in line in front of the village La Alameida, and received the enemy with a volley which completely checked them, and through six guns opening, allowed the infantry to retire quietly over the Duos Casas on Port Concepcion, leaving the cavalry on the plain near La Alameida. Thus ended the day's business. The enemy lost at the affair at the bridge, and from the well-directed fire of our guns, nearly fifty; our loss, Hussars one man killed, three wounded—two horses wounded. The 16th lost one man, two horses wounded; had they brought guns, we should probably have suffered equally. This was the first time the Portuguese troops were engaged, and behaved well. Like all when first engaged, they were too quick with their fire.

The Light Division encamped near Val de la Mula, the 16th and Hussars on the plain between that and La Alameida, with our piquets extending from Fuentes de Onoro on the right to Aldea del Obispo on the left. The 14th Light Dragoons here joined General Crawford, taking the duty on the left.

The weather was extremely hot, and we were placed in the open plain without a tree to shade us.

The whole day's work took place in the midst of the most beautiful wheat ever seen, with which the plain about Gallegos is covered. We have now left that abundant country, and see nothing but rye. It reached nearly to our knees as we rode through it, and the grain flew out at every step.

The duty at Gallegos was very severe. Every morning before 3 a.m. on the alarm ground, and the subalterns were nearly every other night on piquet. When off duty in the daytime, we had so many alerts that little rest could be had. The evenings, from the heat of the weather, were the pleasantest part of the day, and at first we did not lie down so soon as we ought, considering the early hour we turned out. We soon learnt to sleep in the day, or at any time—never undressed—and at night all the horses were bridled up, the men sleeping at their heads, and the officers of each troop close to their horses altogether.

On the commissary of the Light Division complaining to Lord Wellington that General Crawford had told him he would have him hung if the supplies for the Division were not produced by a certain time, Lord Wellington replied, "Then I advise you to produce them, for he is quite certain to do it!"

July 5th. Retired this day over the Touron, the river which separates the two countries, encamping in a small wood to the right of Val de la Mula. Three squadrons of the 14th came into our camp; their fourth occupied Aldea del Obispo. We found three officers' piquets—one near Fuentes de Onoro, one at the bridge near La Alameida, and the third on the main road in the wood leading from that village to Fort Concepcion, of the same strength as on the Azava.

Very little firing for the two last days at Rodrigo; the enemy are said to be short of ammunition.

July 7th. Mounted on the Ford piquet, the one on the main road to La Alameida. In the evening General Crawford went with the cavalry to take some of the enemy's dragoons near Barquilla. They had been in the morning, but retired before he got there. The troops returned to their camp ground after dark. On the 9th the firing at Rodrigo was continued through the whole of the day, and so on the 10th until 4 p.m., when it entirely ceased.

At 10 on the night of the 10th, three squadrons of the 14th, two of the 16th, and one of the Hussars, marched from their camp to La Alameida, then turning to the left assembled in a hollow a mile from Villa de Puerca, about half an hour before daylight. We were concealed in a hollow, and were not perceived by the enemy on our march. At general went forward alone, and shortly returned, moving us at a trot in an open column of divisions, on the village; left in front. We were a little delayed and broken in crossing a defile close to the village, and the squadron of Hussars in front charged a square of the enemy's infantry of about 300. The infantry remained firm, and the Hussars having received their fire from the front side, opened out, passing right and left. The 16th were ordered to form line to the left, and pursue some cavalry near Barquilla. This we did, and secured them all, they laying down their arms on our approach. We made two officers and thirty dragoons prisoners. During this, General Crawford halted a squadron of the 14th, and ordered them to charge the infantry. They were led by Colonel Talbot in the most gallant manner; the dragoons rode up to the bayonets, and Talbot fell in the enemy's ranks, shot through the body. The charge, however, failed; and our general, in the room of carrying it at all risks, ordered the troops to retire. The detached squadron of Hussars that had been in Villa de Cerva made its appearance in the direction the enemy were expected; and the 14th, likewise coming from Villa de Puerca to Barquilla, were likewise mistaken for the enemy. In short, never was a business so badly managed. In the first place, had we shown our force, their infantry would have laid down their arms; but from the hurry and confusion in which we attacked, had they surrendered, we must have ridden over them. They beat us off once; and then, in the place of attacking each force with a squadron, we sent on one squadron by itself, which did all it could, but without success, and the enemy's infantry got clear away to Cismiero. We lost:—

14th Light Dragoons: 1 lieutenant-colonel, 1 quarter-master, 6 men, 13 horses, killed.

16th Light Dragoons: 1 man killed, 1 man wounded, 2 horses killed.

1st Hussars: 13 men wounded, 13 horses killed.

The charge was made in a scrambling manner. There were likewise two guns within a mile of the place, which ought to have been brought up. The French very justly made a flaming despatch. Their detachment should never have been allowed to go back to tell the story.

We followed the Hussars in their charge. I heard the fire from the enemy's infantry; but such was the haste with which the attack was conducted, that had it not been for the whizzing of the shot, I should not have known we were under fire, not seeing where the enemy stood.

To each of the cavalry piquets one of the infantry had been added, and the enemy patrolled down to the bridge of La Alameida, finding our posts, as usual, retired. We got to our encampment about 8 a.m., and the troops having been out all night, the piquets did not relieve before three in the afternoon, when I mounted on the right. It was with great difficulty I could keep awake.

Ciudad Rodrigo surrendered last night at 6 p.m., with the honours of war, after a most gallant defence of fifteen days from the enemy's batteries opening, and twenty-five from the opening of the trenches. The garrison were marched off prisoners of war to France. The enemy pushed their approaches to the crest of the glacis, when the governor was summoned, and the town surrendered.

July 13th, 1810. I was this morning relieved at the usual hour by a sergeant and twelve; this was a new arrangement. Through the Spanish cavalry having left Fuentes de Onoro, an officer was ordered there.

July 13th. The enemy showed a considerable force of cavalry on the right, between La Alameida and Fuentes. We assembled on our alarm ground in consequence, but soon returned again to our bivouac. We had been so long in this bivouac that we made huts for ourselves, many of the men doing the same.

July 14th. Mounted piquet this morning on the ford; all quiet. The enemy, as yet, have not shown the least disposition to advance. Since the town has surrendered, they have almost been quieter than before.

July 17th. The 16th and Hussars retired to San Padro, leaving the 14th at Val de la Mula, and our piquets keeping their former line. The enemy having pushed on toward Nava del Rey and close to our right piquet, it became necessary to protect the main road running to Almeida through San Padro.

July 18th. Mounted on the Ford piquet. The enemy during the day sent many patrols down in front of La Alameida, close

* *Of Dunse Castle, Berwick.*

to my videttes.

July 19th. At 4 this morning, I was relieved by Lieutenant Hay* of the 16th, for the purpose of going on a detached party with Captain Cocks. The right piquet was driven in from Fuentes to Villa Formosa, which delayed our march. The enemy retired about 9 a.m.; and at 10 we marched, our party consisting of thirty men from our own troop. We halted for the night in Villa Mayor, three leagues from San Padro, and one from the Coa. We here found Lieutenant Gwin of the 14th, who, in the morning, joined his regiment. Twelve men were detached to the right to Cornet Whych of the 1st Hussars, who had been out for some time, and now under Captain Cocks. The enemy have not made any movement of consequence, confining themselves to patrolling into Naver de Aver and the adjacent villages.

July 22nd. The distance was so great to communicate with General Crawford that the party moved to Mallihuda Sorda, one league to the left. The enemy's patrols came close to the village, and at night we bivouacked in its rear.

The enemy yesterday drove in our piquets from the line of the Dos Casas; and Fort Concepcion was blown up at three explosions. It was effectually done. Small parties like the one we are now on are of great service by way of gaining information. They should never attempt any operation by way of attacking the enemy's parties.

The enemy this day pushed our advance, under General Crawford, over the Coa. He had been a long time at this advanced duty, and was well aware that, on the army uniting, so great a command would fall from him. He was anxious to do something, and determined on a fight at the Coa. The enemy showed themselves in force early in the morning in front of San Padro, and on the plain near Fort Concepcion. There was time enough to have got the cavalry clear away; they waited till 10 a.m., when the enemy advanced in such force with their cavalry that ours were obliged to pass the bridge of Almeida in a hurry, their light troops, infantry, having come up, and being engaged with our light infantry.

Considerable confusion took place at the bridge, and half of the 43rd, under Major McLeod, charged the enemy's advance in the most gallant manner, and by that means secured the safe retreat of the remainder.

The infantry having got all clear over the bridge, took up a position on the left bank of the river, and the enemy attempted twice to force its passage. In each attempt they failed, the division keeping its ground. The enemy brought fresh troops down every half-hour, and from their numbers suffered a good deal from our artillery, etc. The affair was a very sharp one, the fire not ceasing till 4 p.m., when, on our ceasing, the enemy did the same. We lost Lieutenant-Colonel Hull of the 43rd, who had joined from England the day before, with fifteen other officers, killed and wounded. The infantry then retired nearly as far back as Celorico, the 3rd Division being withdrawn from Pinhel. Sir Stapleton with the cavalry took the outposts.

Lord W. was much displeased with Crawford for the last affair, though I consider him the best outpost officer in the army.

July 24th. The party moved back to Villa Mayor. The enemy having driven our advanced corps over the Coa, pushed troops over the river by the bridges at Almeida and Castello Bom. This rendered our situation not safe; and from reports of the advance of troops on our right, Captain Cocks, on the night of the 25th; crossed the Coa at the Ponte Sequeiros, a league from Villa Mayor, and occupied the village of Sardiera, a league on the other side. The enemy's patrols coming near, we did not remain long quiet, and occupied a high hill close to the village, on the top of which there is the convent of Nossa Senhora do Monte, where we were perfectly safe, having a view of the whole country. From the orderlies sent with reports to General Crawford, and patrols out, the party was reduced to four men, and a piquet from the 1st (Royal) Dragoons, belonging to General Slade's brigade, being sent to the point we occupied, it allowed us to go quietly into the village of Richoso, half a league in the rear.

Two patrols, of each two men, from our party were attacked by peasants—one in the village of Marmeliero, on the right, and the other in Richoso, close to our front. In Marmeliero they shot Williams with slugs in seven places, obliging his comrade to make away for his own safety. On Captain Cocks' going there he found the dragoon in the hands of the principal people of the village, who had taken care of him, and though wounded so severely, not in immediate danger; he was brought into the camp. At Richoso they shot Thompson through the body, and kept the dragoon of the Royals with them, tied the whole day to a tree, releasing him in the evening, when he returned to us, reporting what had happened. Captain Cocks, with the party, went out, found Thompson lying amongst the rocks dreadfully bruised with stones, and shot through the lungs. He was brought home, and will never again be fit for service.

Williams recovered; Thompson was invalided, and sent to England. The affairs were reported to General Cole in Guarda, and so on to Lord Wellington, who said he would burn the villages, though nothing was ever done.

The enemy have established their posts for the siege of Almeida, and have broken ground before the place. They subsist very much (the corps in advance) by the plunder they get in the villages between us and their posts, which are all nearly deserted by the inhabitants. The people, finding their parties do not consist of above one hundred men, have collected all their arms and assembled in bodies of 150 round about us. The country is particularly adapted for this, affording perfect shelter in the rocks, always a retreat from cavalry, and with people knowing the country it is impossible for troops to get at them. On the 14th, Captain Cocks called in his party under Whych, he being ordered to join his regiment.

August 16th. All the peasants collected this day for the purpose of destroying the mills on the Coa, which the enemy made use of to grind their bread. We took the party to prevent any small patrol of the enemy's annoying them, and went to Misquitella, on the banks of the river. The peasantry did not like going near the mills, where there were a few of the enemy. They commenced a fire from the rocks, when three French infantry ran out and got away; then the boldest ventured down, and said they had completely destroyed the mill. Five deserters this day came to us on the banks of the Coa. They say they are badly supplied, and that if the peasants would not hurt them, desertion would be more general. We hear a few shots daily from Almeida at the enemy in their trenches. From the nature of the ground the French do not make much progress, being obliged to carry on their whole work above ground, by means of fascines and gabions. Our communication by telegraphs is kept up from Freixedas.

August 23rd. Captain Cocks marched at night to surprise a French piquet near Misquitella. We were not able to find their lights, and returned at daybreak to our camp. Cocks is anxious to do something, though night expeditions seldom answer; and should we fall in with infantry, and lose two or three men, a whole piquet taken would not repay the loss. We had been the night before and saw their fires, and had they been lighted should have seen them, as I conceive we advanced in a right direction. We had only a couple of men with us the night before.

August 26th. The party again moved on the same ground after a plundering party of the enemy's, which had been in the habit of passing through the villages in front of their piquets; they had been earlier than usual, and had retired.

We patrolled up to their piquet, which left its post and all their bread, which we got; we caused them to light their beacon, and then returned to our camp. We saw the enemy's guns firing on the town, which was the first certain information we had of their batteries having opened, which they did yesterday.

August 27th. The party this day moved up from the old encampment to the hill of Nossa Senhora do Monte. The sergeant of Hussars coming off piquet reported having heard in the night an explosion towards Almeida.

August 28th. General Cole ordered us back to our former ground, as the explosion heard was the blowing up of the magazine in Almeida, and the town in consequence having capitulated with the honours of war. The two Militia regiments were sent back to their homes, having taken their oaths not to fight again against the French. The 24th of the line, with the governor, was marched to France. General Cole, with his light companies, remained in Guarda. The division moved back to

Prados, two leagues in the mountains, headquarters retired to Gouvea, and the whole of the infantry to the rear of Celorico. It rained hard the whole night; we put up in some houses close to the camp.

August 29th. General Cole ordered us to Joe Bugal to watch the main road from Almeida to Guarda. This day month we marched to the ground we now left. It was a most excellent camp, the trees affording capital shade; and from the length of time we had been there, each man had a good hut, and the encampment wore the appearance of a small village. We were much safer from any sudden attack; the men and horses both continued healthy from having plenty to eat and something to employ themselves with. The men got as much rye-bread, mutton, potatoes, and wheat-flour from the adjacent mills as they wanted, and the horses as much rye in the ear and thrashed as they could eat, and now and then some wheat nearly ripe. Cocks and myself had nothing with us but a change of linen, a pot to boil potatoes, and the same to make coffee in, with a frying pan, which were carried on his led horse. We never wanted for a single article excepting wheat-bread, which failed us occasionally, and with a person not accustomed to rye, it does not agree. We could always march in five minutes, never slept out of our clothes, and never enjoyed better health; half-past two in the morning was the hour we got up.

August 30th. We were ordered from Joe Bugal to the right on the Sabugal road, the enemy having pushed their troops to that place. The 2nd corps of the army of Portugal had moved from their cantonments on the Tagus up to Pena Macor, and it was not known whether the troops in Sabugal had come from thence or from either of the other two corps employed against Almeida. We rather thought from the second.

Sept. 2nd. At 2 this day, the beacon at Guarda was set on fire, and our party, with two squadrons of the Royals, all marched up the hill into the town. The light companies and Royals left Guarda under General Cole for Prados, leaving us in the town. We slept in the streets, not thinking it safe to put under cover. From lighting the beacon, several houses had taken fire; and there not being an inhabitant in the town, two or three were burnt down. I was too tired to get up and see the fire.

Sept. 3rd. We occupied the Bishop's Palace this morning, from which few things had been removed and many left to the mercy of the enemy; we saved a considerable quantity of wine, and a few other useful things to a soldier. The move from Guarda had been occasioned by the enemy's pushing back our piquets near Freixedas, which was only a reconnoissance. General Cole ordered us from Guarda to Prados, where we halted, and for the first time since we went up to Gallegos, slept without the fear of being turned out.

We left a sergeant of the Hussars with four men, who patrolled into Guarda every morning from the small village he was in, one league from the place.

Sept. 5th. General Cole went to the neighbourhood of Gouvea, and our party was under Sir Stapleton, whose headquarters were at Celorico. He ordered Cocks back to Guarda with fourteen men, leaving me at Prados with the remainder. On the 6th I sent ten men to reinforce Cocks, and Lieutenant Badcock of the 14th having joined him, I marched to my regiment at Misquitella and adjacents. Captain Cocks' troop was alone in Carvelera.

The enemy remain quiet, preparing for their advance; and the report is, we are to fight at the Ponte Murcella, five leagues on this side Coimbra. The Hussars and the 14th are doing the outpost duty in front of Celorico.

Since our first going up, five men of the 16th have gone over to the enemy; and though each has got into a scrape or lost his character before, yet, to people ignorant of the circumstances, it looks ill. Two of them had broken open a chapel, and feared a general court-martial. One was a man of the name of Jones, from Cocks' troop, and had formerly been of noted bad character.

Sept. 16th. We all assembled this morning at Villa Cortes. The enemy pushed back the advance a league on our side of Celorico, a little skirmishing took place, and in the evening the whole was withdrawn to Penhancos, six leagues from Celorico. Captain Persse of the 14th was taken this day.

Sept. 17th. The 16th marched a short league to the rear,

occupying St. Comba and San Miguel. Our squadron with the left went to San Miguel, the headquarters, with the remainder to Santa Comba. Headquarters of the army last night at Coa, and this day moved a short distance further to the rear.

The enemy's three corps all joined at Celorico, amounting to from 60,000 to 70,000. It was calculated at 65,000 infantry and 4,000 cavalry in three Corps d'Armee, the whole commanded by Massena, Marshal in the French service, and Prince desisting.

6th Corps d'Armee: Marshal Ney, Duc d'Elchinghen.
8th Corps d'Armee: Marshal Junot, Duc d'Abrantes.
2nd Corps d'Armee: General Regnier.

The enemy have broken the Vizeu road from Celorico, and merely sent patrols after us, as far as San Padro. Captain Cocks remains out with his party, in the neighbourhood of Mello, watching the enemy, and had they moved on the Gallicis road, he would have had a fine opportunity of counting their force; as it was, he ascertained to a certainty that they were moving on Vizeu, and sent Lord Wellington the only information he could receive to be relied on from his own outposts.

We here received our new helmets from England, and not before they were wanted. The old ones were completely worn out, and so warped by the sun that the men could scarcely wear them. They are bad things for a soldier, only looking well for a few months; the first rain puts them out of shape. All the silver to the edging comes off with both men and officers, and the sooner we adopt some other head-dress the better.

Sept. 18th. We marched this morning four leagues on the Ponte Murcella road, and encamped.

I here mounted my bay horse (Bob), which I left in charge of Owen of the 16th, and from his neglect I thought I should have lost him.

Sept. 19th and 20th. Each of these days we did not march above two leagues, and on the 20th encamped in rear of Gallicis, where a remount of fifty-four horses joined us from England. The Hussars remain in our rear near Coa. The whole force of the enemy has gone the Vizeu road.

Lord W. has assembled the army near the Ponte Murcella,

which is destroyed. The villages are all deserted by the inhabitants. We want no commissary, finding corn and meat in every village. It rained the whole night of the 20th, and the greatest part of the day.

Sept. 21st. By this time the whole of the enemy's force had passed the Mondego, and was assembled in the neighbourhood of Vizeu. Lord Wellington crossed with the whole excepting the 2nd Division, which, on Regnier's joining with the 2nd Corps d'Armee at Celorico, General Hill had marched by the route of Thomar and joined us at Ponte Murcella; he was left at the Ponte. The brigade moved at daylight, the Hussars two or three leagues in our rear. We crossed the Mondego by a good, though rather deep ford, and halted at dark, within a league of Mortiagua. I was on baggage-guard. The march was not more than five leagues, but through crossing the ford and halting for the Heavy Brigade in our front, we were on horseback the whole day.

Sept. 22nd. We assembled at daylight on the Mortiagua plain, where we found the Light Division with General Pack's Portuguese brigade. The heavy cavalry had been doing the outpost duty for the last three days since the approach of the enemy from Vizeu, and part of Pack's brigade had an affair in the town of Santa Combadao, in which they behaved very well.

The three light regiments—14th, 16th, and 1st Hussars—were ordered to relieve them. Our squadron of the 16th went on duty. Our piquets were along the banks of the Cris, and the bridges destroyed. I remained with the inlying piquet in front of Mortiagua. The enemy made several movements towards our piquets, but not across the river. We were on the alert the whole day. At night all was quiet.

Sept. 23rd. Every one expected the enemy to move on this morning. At daylight all was quiet, and the piquets being relieved, we returned to our camp ground on the plain. About 3, the enemy drove back our piquets near to the village of Mortiagua, which General Crawford wished to dispute. Sir Stapleton ordered him out to the rear of the plain, forming the three light regiments as a covering party to him. The enemy contented themselves with the heights above the village, and at night we retired, leaving a squadron from each regiment with the Light Division.

Sept. 24th. We were the whole of last night in passing the Sierra of Bosoac about two leagues, through the artillery waggons overturning on our front. There are two divisions near us, occupying the heights, and the remaining ones not far off. Every one talks of our not standing, some of the army (viz., the 1st Division) having gone back as far as Coimbra. The brigade went in the evening to some villages near Bosoac, the headquarters of brigade and regiment, to Moito; Captain Cocks' troop to Val de Mo, a little in advance. Lord Wellington has his headquarters in the convent of Bosoac, where he has been since the 21st.

Sept. 26th. At 2 p.m. we returned to the ground we had before occupied at the foot of Bosoac. The whole army was in position along the Sierra, and General Hill moved across this day from his ground at the Ponte Murcella. The enemy have closed up their whole force to the hills in front of the position, and a general action is expected. From the nature of our position, I cannot think the enemy will make any serious attack. The descent in places is so steep and great that a person alone cannot, without holding and choosing his ground, get down. I cannot think they will be so imprudent as to make it a general affair. We have 52,000 men, and their superiority is by no means equal to the advantage we have from position. They may calculate that the Portuguese troops, of which the greater part of the army is composed, will run away. I think we have rather above 20,000 English, the remainder Portuguese. The army ran from right to left as follows:—

2nd Division: Lieutenant-General Hill.
5th Division: Major-General Leith's Corps.
3rd Division: Major-General Picton.
1st Division: Lieutenant-General Sir Brent Spencer.
Light Division: Brigadier-General Crawford.
4th Division: Major-General Cole.

General Anson found one squadron for duty with the Light Division, and the Heavy Brigade one in rear of the 1st Division. All were ordered to stand to their arms before daylight, the troops bivouacked as they stood in position, with their generals at the heads of divisions and brigades. Lord Wellington remained in the wood near the convent in the centre of the line. Every one expected and wished a general attack at daylight. The army is in most beautiful order, and the Portuguese as fine-looking men and as steady under arms as any in the world. The only doubt rests with them; if they do their duty, and the business becomes general, there can be no doubt of success.

The 16th, at night, retired a short way for forage, no baggage allowed on the hill, but sent to the rear near Malhada.

Sept. 27th. The troops at daylight were all under arms, anxiously waiting the enemy's attack. All was quiet for some time, and as there was nothing to delay the enemy that we were aware of, Lord W. ordered patrols to our left, from General Anson's brigade. I was sent on one, and about 9 a.m. got on the hills lineable with our position. I there saw the attack on the Light Division; and on ascertaining that no troops had moved to the left, I returned to the regiment, which I found in the old ground where I had left it.

The enemy made two attacks—one on the left on the Light Division, and the other on the right on the 3rd. That on the left consisted of an advance of about 5,000 men, with a large support in its rear.

The troops came up the hill in the best order possible, suffering a great deal from our light infantry. On their gaining the top, the Light Division stood up, and the 43rd and 52nd moved forward to the charge. The enemy did not stand one moment, and were pushed down in the greatest confusion. The general of brigade, Simon, who led the attack, was taken with 150 men. Their columns suffered much from our artillery during their advance and retreat. Massena saw the attack could not succeed, and halted the support at the foot of the hill.

During this the enemy made another on the 3rd Division; their troops here gained the hill, in considerable numbers, and were charged by General Mackinnon's brigade, consisting of the 74th and 88th. As in the other attack, they fled in all directions, but from having gained the hill they suffered more in retreat.

Very few prisoners were taken, and 700 buried on the spot. The Portuguese brigade of the division was, at first, rather unsteady; but seeing the British move forward, they advanced too, and behaved extremely well. With the Light Division the Cacadores did well, and the day gave the Portuguese confidence in themselves and with the army in general.

These were their two attacks, which completely failed, and in which their loss from our artillery, and their columns being exposed on their advance to our tirailleurs, was great. The remainder of the day was employed by a sharp fire, kept up from the light troops on each side. The enemy said the troops they were engaged with, dressed in blue, were British troops in Portuguese clothing. I have some hopes they will have to continue this notion, and will find the colour of the jacket make no difference in the courage of the soldier. The Portuguese wore blue of the same make as British soldiers.

Sept. 28th. The enemy renewed his attack with light troops only at 12 a.m.; their columns were seen moving to our left. At 2 p.m. the army was ordered to cook, and General Anson's brigade to the left to watch the Boialva road. The Heavies were still farther to the left; we bivouacked at night in front of Moita.

The Heavies were on the Boialva road, and we on the one crossing the Sierra to Moita.

Sept. 29th. We returned at daylight to the ground we had left yesterday near Bosoac; the whole army had moved away in the night, and not a straggler to be seen. General Crawford remained on the hill with a few piquets from his division. The whole of the enemy's force had moved on Boialva, and not a man excepting their wounded to be seen.

From the numbers killed and not buried, and their wounded left on the field, their loss was calculated at 8,000, and by some as many as 10,000. Crawford thought the latter; but from what we afterwards learnt, I conceive 4,000 the outside of their losses. 2,000 wounded were left on the field to the mercy of the peasants. Some were brought by General Crawford to the convent of Bosoac, and the remainder left to the mercy of the inhabitants, and no doubt would be murdered when we left; 2,000 were left dead on the field, the greatest number from artillery.

The enemy pushed on by Boialva, driving back the Heavy Brigade. We retired in consequence near to Mulliada, where the Boialva road and Bosoac join.

The retreat of the Heavy Brigade was made in dreadful confusion; Captain Cocks was present when the enemy advanced.

Return of killed and wounded at Bosoac:-

	Officers	Men	
British Loss	5	104	killed
	35	458	wounded
	1	30	missing
Portuguese Loss	6	84	killed
	25	487	wounded
		20	missing
	72	1183	
		72	
		1255	Total loss

After Bosoac (or Busaco) the Portuguese said the English were for the sea, but the Portuguese for land. *Los Ingleses por mar, los Portugeses por terra.*

Sept. 30th. The Heavy Brigade on the Boialva road mistook some bushes for the enemy, and fired at them for half an hour. We marched through Malliada, and formed with General Slade's brigade in its rear. Here we halted some time, and then moved on to Fornos, in front of which we bivouacked for the night; the two other brigades moved to the rear, and bivouacked on the large plain near Coimbra. The infantry this day passed the Mondego, marching on Leiria. General Hill with his corps passed the Mondego by the ford near Bosoac, and retired on Thomar. The enemy pushed a strong advanced guard close to us; we remained bridled up the whole night in a very unpleasant situation. We ought to have been in its rear, and then men might have rested, and horses been feeding the whole night.

We were in a very improper position, and might easily have been surprised.

Oct. 1st. We formed at daylight in front of Fornos, and Sir Stapleton ordered General Anson to keep his post until attacked by infantry. I was sent to report to him that it was the case; he delayed some time before he came up, and when he did he found us in such a situation as to order our retreat instantly. The country is as much enclosed as possible, only one road to retire by; the enemy's cavalry and infantry close up engaged with our skirmishers. We first walked, then trotted, and at last galloped, and this rate went through the village of Fornos, and half a mile further, on to the plain of Coimbra. Our rear was much pressed, and obliged to halt and charge in the lane. We lost two or three men from the fire of their infantry, and Captain Krauchenburgh of the Hussars wounded above the hip, though not dangerously. Nothing ever appeared worse, both to ourselves and the enemy, as they must have seen our confusion.

We then formed on the great Coimbra plain. Our brigade advanced, supported by the other two; viz., Colonel de Grey's and General Slade's. In our front ran a large drain cut across the plain, and impassable, excepting at the bridge in our front. The horse artillery, under Captain Bull, fired at their advance; but on perceiving our situation, they did not move from the enclosures. At 10 a.m., the whole moved off— the Heavy Brigade by a ford a league below ours, General Slade's and ours (which remained to the last) by a ford a league below Coimbra. On seeing us move off, the enemy followed, and their advance came up to the ford just after we got over. They attempted to cross, and were charged back by a squadron of the 16th, with the skirmishers; they then kept up a sharp fire from their dismounted dragoons from the other side, and all of ours having got off, the troops retired to Soure, four leagues from Coimbra. I remained with a troop in the rear, and marched in two hours after the brigade to Soure.

We were a little surprised, at passing the Mondego, to find all our baggage in a village close to its banks, and nearly taken by the enemy. The fact was, it had been forgot; and though sent out of the way fifty times when not necessary and wanted by officers, yet here, when it was known in the morning that we were to retire on Soure, the baggage was delayed so long that it scarcely got there before the troops, and was nearly taken.

From the short notice the people had received from Lord Wellington's proclamation, which was only issued after the retreat from Bosoac was determined on, and could not have been sooner made known, they had not time to remove one half, and many not any of their property. Many cars had been pressed by us for the conveyance of sick and stores, and those people were in consequence left without any mode of conveyance. The whole road was covered with families of the first rank in Coimbra, walking on foot with bundles on their heads. I went into one or two houses, which the people had only left in the morning. We found sheep, turkeys, geese, and fowls in greatest abundance, and table linen, shirts, with every other kind of thing, were left in the houses for the enemy. Not an inhabitant remained behind. A person in Coimbra went back to fetch some gold chains left behind in mistake, and never again saw her family. The enemy did not pass the Mondego, excepting with a few patrols; they occupied and plundered Coimbra. Headquarters this night in Pombal; considerable stores were destroyed in Condatia and some in Coimbra.

This could not have been avoided; for without them, had we thoroughly beat them at Bosoac, and advanced, we should have starved, and there was not time to get them away. They were not collected to any great extent. Those at Condatia were stores, etc., for the artillery, and might have been issued to the passing troops. In Coimbra, biscuit, etc., for the troops, but not three days in the whole.

Oct. 2nd. Soure, like all other places, is deserted by its inhabitants. The manufactory of hats is left full. Tea, sugar, wine, rum, etc., all left in the houses. It was said the Heavy Brigade got a new set out of Portuguese *chapeos* (hats). Singularity of Foxall in packing tea in a pair of nankeen small clothes, tying up the legs, and carrying them filled round his neck to bring it to the bivouac. He was one of the best men in action in the regiment, and killed in my troop in charging infantry at Vitoria.

We marched two leagues towards Leiria, encamping; the enemy are a long way in our rear, and have remained near Coimbra, plundering and collecting supplies. Headquarters moved to Leiria.

Oct. 3rd. Marched three leagues, bivouacking on the Rio de Manda Nilla, two short leagues in front of Leiria, on the main road. The infantry were only passing when we got to our ground, and the Light Division remained near us till evening, when they moved off, leaving the cavalry on the river.

Oct. 4th. We halted on the ground we occupied yesterday. The infantry continued their march to the rear. A man of the 11th Infantry and Portuguese Infantry, also two of 4th Dragoons, were this day hung in Leiria for plundering. In the evening the enemy advanced to Pombal, and the troops in consequence turned out, though not necessary, and through Major Archer having mistaken the orders sent him. The two men of the 4th Dragoons who were hung in Leiria this day were caught in a chapel plundering by Lord Wellington.

Oct. 5th. Our piquets were this morning driven in, and a good deal of skirmishing took place on the open ground between our camp ground and Pombal. The enemy came on very rapidly, and gave our piquets and the left squadron of the 16th, under Captain Murray, frequent opportunities of charging. We attacked them several times, taking two officers and ten men. Lieutenant Penrice of the 16th behaved particularly well. He rode close up to a French officer, and so much in advance of his men that the Frenchman thought he was going to surrender, and dropped his sword, when Penrice gave him a wipe over his head. The brigade, on turning out, formed in front of the Rio de Manda Nilla, and, on the enemy's advance, retired through a defile on the other side, leaving the left centre squadron, under Captain Swetenham, to cover our retreat. The enemy pressed hard on our rear, and Captain Swetenham received a slight wound in the thigh. Our squadron, with one of the Hussars, was sent to the left of the road to secure that flank, and were obliged to make good our own retreat out of the road. We came to a defile which was almost impracticable, with the enemy close at hand, firing as we passed. Fortunately all got over, and the enemy being checked by the guns, did not advance through the country towards Leiria without infantry, and we retired to the town by a road to our left. Before our troops passed the Rio de Manda Nilla, the enemy brought up two light guns and killed two men of the 16th. In the course of the day we lost twenty men (our whole loss) in killed, wounded, and prisoners. Amongst the last was Lieutenant Carden, of the Royals, who had got into a scrape when near Celorico through admitting flags of truce into our lines, and was anxious to do away with any stigma on his character by his conduct on this day. He was the first in one of the charges, and his horse being shot, was taken. We withdrew everything through Leiria, which was completely plundered by our soldiers, and deserted by its inhabitants. I only saw one person, and that an old woman. (Circumstance of Lieutenant Weyland, 16th, thrashing his farrier, Mic. Mullen, for getting drunk, with the flat of his sword.)

Two Portuguese stragglers this day fell into the enemy's hands; they are the first I have seen on the whole retreat.

The brigade was halted close to the town, and the enemy occupying it with his advanced guard, pushed strong piquets of both infantry and cavalry so close to us that we were obliged to move. We had been hard at it the whole day, and at night our squadron went on piquet. Headquarters this day left Leiria for Alcobassa. The army here marched by two routes, part moving by the Alcobassa and Chaldas roads, and the other by Rio Mayor direct on the Tagus. The Heavy Brigade moved with the Alcobassa column, General Anson's and Slade's by Rio Mayor, Sir Stapleton with the latter. (General Slade providing wine for the Royal Dragoons, saying, "You must not touch this; it is all for the Royals,"— there being enough for half the army.)

Oct. 6th. Soon after daylight our piquets retired, and being relieved marched three leagues to the rear, encamping to the left of the main road, a league in rear of Cavalhos. Towards evening the enemy drove in our piquets with some skirmishing, and

Hay was the officer on piquet on the 3rd; and when he turned out, the enemy coming on, his second man had a turkey on one side of his cloak, two chickens on the other, haversack full of other provisions, and so he attempted to skirmish; he soon found he must part with his livestock.

Oct. 7th. Major-General Slade took the rear guard, and General Anson's brigade marched to the rear of Rio Mayor.

We had a false alarm in the evening; the men threw away their dinners, and baggage was sent off. They had not cooked anything regularly for two days.

Oct. 8th. It rained nearly the whole night. In the morning the troops moved off for Alquentre in the heaviest rain I ever experienced. The left squadron of the 16th was left in Rio Mayor as a rear guard. We marched and encamped in the rear of Alquentre, two leagues. Generals Cotton, Slade, and Anson, with the troop of horse artillery, were in the village, with the two brigades in its rear. About 2 we heard some shots fired near the village, and Captain Cocks' squadron, being the first for duty, moved down as quickly as possible with the first mounted dragoons we could collect, in all not fifty men. On our way down we met five of the guns coming up in the greatest confusion, some with four, some with six horses to them, having got away how they could. On the other side the village ran a considerable brook, which was not passable excepting at the bridge on the entrance into the town. The enemy had two regiments of cavalry close up, and Captain Murray's people were all withdrawn over the bridge. Our party formed up ready to charge down the street. There was a howitzer and two ammunition waggons without a horse to them, commissariat mules and men in the street in the greatest confusion. The enemy did not long remain idle, and detached two squadrons from the 14th Dragoons into the village; they passed the bridge, driving in Captain Murray's people, and came half-way up the street to where we were formed. The enemy's two squadrons were close to each other, in sixes, completely filling up the street. From the bridge to where we were formed the street makes a right angle; the head of the column passed the turning, the other squadron in the rear, not seeing how we were formed. In this situation they halted, when we charged them; they instantly went about and wished to retire. There was the greatest noise and confusion with the enemy, their front wishing to get away, and their rear, not seeing what was going on, stood still. They got so close together that it was impossible to get well at them. We took twelve and killed six, driving them over the bridge again, and by this means allowing time for what remained in the town to get clear away. The enemy dismounted their dragoons, and we retired through the town, forming on the heights on the other side. The cavalry retired to Quinta de Toro. Our squadron remained skirmishing with the enemy till dark, and then retired half a league in front of Quinta de Toro, where it remained on piquet, with Captain Linsingen's of the Hussars in our front.

We lost one horse and man wounded in skirmishing after the enemy passed Alquentre, though not one in the affair in the town. The enemy expected to find nothing in the town, and when attacked, made not the least resistance, each striving to get the fastest out of the way.

Much was said on the day's work, and Sir Stapleton was to blame for not attending to the reports sent in by Captain Murray of the enemy's advance, as he had ordered him to retire watching the enemy, but not to skirmish.

It was a dead surprise; and had the French dashed into the town without waiting a moment, they would certainly have got the two guns and some part of the general's baggage.

Lord Tweeddale (quarter-master general to the cavalry) put us in rear of the town, and Sir Stapleton (or some of his staff) allowed the artillery to take their harness to pieces to clean it.

Rather a new style of war to place guns in a village, and the troops protecting them a mile in its rear.

Oct. 9th. It rained nearly incessantly from the time we yesterday left Rio Mayor. We lay down in the middle of the road, it raining nearly the whole night. The enemy did not move till late this day. Nearly the whole way from the Quinta de Toro to Alquentre, the country is open with ravines and bogs running at right angles to the road.

Captain Cocks' squadron was on piquet behind me, and Captain Linsingen's two miles in our front. At 2 p.m. they attacked Captain Linsingen with two regiments of cavalry; they were aware that we had nothing up to support the piquet, and it was their intention to take it. In his rear he had a bit of very bad road to pass, and charged two or three times their advance on the road, to secure his retreat. In these charges he lost nineteen men taken, and several wounded, he himself cut in the arm in different parts, though not severely. They drove him in on our squadron, which was formed behind the bridge nearest the Quinta, and seeing it was his intention to pass, pressed him hard, in hopes of taking more of his men. We just allowed the Hussars to pass and then charged, driving them back over the bridge. Farther we could not go, as on getting in the open ground the enemy had people on each of our flanks. We then retired, expecting the Hussars would have been ready to have covered us, as we did them. They could not form in the time, having been so scattered, and on our retiring, the enemy followed in very good style close at our heels; we again charged them, and drove them on the bridge. Again we retired close to the bridge immediately below the Quinta de Toro, and passed the defile over the bridge, forming on the plain beyond, with the remainder of the brigade. In both the charges we took some prisoners, but could only get one away. We lost one man of Captain Belli's troop killed, with four horses from the squadron. The regiment with which we were engaged was the 3rd Hussars, and I never saw their cavalry behave so well.

In retiring the second time I caught my bradoon rein in the appointments of a French Hussar who was dismounted lying on the ground, and cut it just as they were about to make me prisoner. My horse's head was held down to the ground, being caught in his appointments; they were not five yards from me when I cut it. I spurred my horse two or three times in hopes he would break it; this he did not, and I was fortunate in catching the rein fair the first cut, and going through it. I will take care not to go into action with a loose bradoon rein.

On the ground near Quinta de Toro, Sir Stapleton intended

to check the enemy, there being only one pass up to it by the bridge and causeway on the main road. This he did for some time with the guns firing a few shots at their cavalry; but their infantry coming up, and getting through the bog up the bank near where we were formed, he was obliged to retire. Had this not been the case, an order which he received from Lord Wellington would have brought us back at night. Our squadron was so much knocked up from the two days' duty, that we were sent to the rear, the horses scarcely able to get along.

On our troops retiring, the enemy passed the Quinta, and were about posting their piquets for the night, when Sir Stapleton ordered Captain Cocks (who had remained behind) to attack an advanced party of about forty chasseurs, which was supported by a squadron in its rear. His attack was supported by Captain Ally's squadron of the Hussars.

The enemy did not expect it, and on seeing our troops move forward, their advance retired on the squadron; and the squadron, seeing ours advance, retired likewise, each down the road in no small confusion. The advanced party under Cocks only consisted of twenty men. In his pursuit he secured one lieutenant and twenty-five chasseurs.

The squadron of Hussars that supported him was bringing back the prisoners, and was mistaken by the Royals for the enemy pursuing our men; they charged, and going too far, got into the fire of the enemy's infantry, losing three men killed, and one of the 16th wounded. In the confusion eight men of the Royals got thrown from their horses, and they being loose went to the last camp they had occupied, and therefore fell into the enemy's hands.

The whole was withdrawn at night to Carrigada, which was occupied by Sir Stapleton and Hussars with two squadrons on duty in front. The 16th went about a mile to its rear, and encamped in an olive grove up to the horses' knees in mud; it raining incessantly the whole night, most of the officers got into a wine vault.

One of the men of the Royals, in getting some wine out of the vat, fell in. The grapes were just pressed, and left in that state.

In this state the men drank it. The dragoon got into it in the night, was half smothered, and caused great confusion. He, or some other, stole a ham from Colonel Archer, which when the colonel perceived, he made a great row; and what with loss of ham, and dragoon in the vat, we had not a very tranquil night.

On arriving at our bivouac, I saw some Portuguese officers and soldiers in a shed at the back of the wine vault. I gave the alarm that the French were expected, when they turned out in an instant, marched away, and I put myself and horses into the place. My old dragoon (Robinson) had got me a turkey out of a house he passed on the march. We had plucked it coming along, and on my return from seeing the men I found him holding it in the flame of the fire, by legs and wings at a time. He had no wood at hand, and broke up and burnt some cane-bottomed chairs, for the purpose of making a fire, which the Portuguese had brought from an adjacent Quinta to sit upon. I rather reproached him, and the only answer I got was that I should find the turkey very good; we soon finished it.

The rain continued, and from the dreadful night and bad camp the regiment was in a sad state. We got under cover in Carrigada, and at 12 a.m. there arrived an order for us to retire within the infantry. We marched to Povoa, passing the right of our position at Alhandra. One squadron, the left centre, remained piquet outside the lines. It rained incessantly the whole day; and thus, for the first time since we left Rio Mayor, was there an opportunity of getting on dry clothes.

Oct. 11th. Marched this morning to Mafra, three long leagues to the left nearer the sea. From the constant fag on our retreat, the horses were in a low state, and the regiment much in want of shoeing and a little rest.

The whole of the infantry were now in our lines for the protection of Lisbon. They extend from Alhandra on the right to Torres Vedras on the left, and so on to the sea. Headquarters are at Pero Negro. In the rear of the first line there are two others, one in rear of Mafra, and the third close on Lisbon. The greatest part of the army are under canvas, and the weakest point at Sobral is protected by a regular fort in which there is General

Pack's brigade of 2,500 Portuguese. Should the enemy carry the first line, he is to keep his fort; the men have cover and a certain stock of provisions. The heavy guns from Fort San Julian have been all brought up with many others (which were at Lisbon) of British. The whole line from left to right is as strong as possible, and all wish for an attack.

The whole brigade with headquarters of the cavalry were in Mafra, and held the whole well. The greatest part of the 16th were put up in the stables and cloisters of the convent. It is an immense pile of building, and erected to surpass in size the Escurial near Madrid. That is the only thing thought of by the Portuguese in all their buildings, and the convent of Mafra fully exemplifies it. There is a good library well stocked with books; and though the French army retired through the town after the battle of Vimiera, the building was not in the least injured. The monks say they are indebted to Louison for this, who would not allow the soldiery to injure anything.

On the 18th I went with Bence to Lisbon, remained there one day, and returned back on the 20th. The town was as full as possible with the inhabitants from the part which the enemy now possess, and many have passed over to Estremadura Portuguese, south of the Tagus. They all seem to think they have done the best for themselves in leaving their houses; and though most of them are ruined, yet they prefer this to remaining for the enemy. It is a great sacrifice, and much good should result from so great a loss.

The Spaniards from the neighbourhood of Badajos this day passed the Tagus into Lisbon; they are under the Marquis Romana, and come to assist us in the defence of the lines. They are about 12,000 men, regularly armed with English muskets, and clothed by us.

Many of the first people in Lisbon have sent away their property to the Brazils, some have gone themselves, and more are going. All wish to get their valuables on board, and should the first line be carried, they will get themselves on board and leave Portugal with the English; the French have their party, but at present they keep quite unknown. I question if their party was ever to be feared, indeed much doubt if they ever had any.

Oct. 22nd. The route arrived yesterday for the brigade to march and relieve the Heavy Brigade stationed in front of the lines near Torres Vedras. We marched to that place, passed the lines to Ramalhial and Amiel, one league in front. The Heavy Brigade moved to some villages to the left of Torres Vedras, and we took the duty, occupying the two villages.

The enemy's whole force is on the right and centre of our position, and our army opposite. Torres Vedras is very strong with a Portuguese brigade in the town and port. On the right of the town to the ground occupied by our army the country is nearly inaccessible, and Lord W. calculates that from the notice we shall give him, he can move before they can get troops sufficient to gain any considerable advantage. Should they pass a detachment for the purpose of getting in the pass and town of Torres Vedras before troops could arrive, I conceive the brigade now in the place sufficient to defend it until reinforcements arrive to occupy the place, as it should be for its permanent defence.*

Between our outposts and the enemy there is a large Sierra, very steep and the roads bad. To pass artillery over will be no small undertaking; and before any considerable body can march from their present camps to our left, we shall have time sufficient to move how and where we like.

We had one officer's piquet from the brigade on the Cadaval road, one sergeant looking to the road up the Sierra (or hills), and one more to our left on the Obides road. The enemy's plundering parties come constantly over the Sierra to the villages near us. Our patrols go up the hills, and for a league on their tops, to ascertain that their camps are in the place they have for some time occupied, and that no considerable body passes our way.

The headquarters of the French are at Alenquer, a town nearly in front of Sobral. The deserters say Massena was employed for the first three days he came down in reconnoitring our position, and considered us too strong to attack. He may think so, and yet not like to give the thing up until he can hear from the Emperor.

* *The 16th are looking better than they have done the whole campaign, and turn out near 400 effective men and horses.—Captain Cocks' Journal.*

A day or two after we got to Ramalhial, I went with four men on the patrol over the Sierra. I had not got half a league on its top, when I met a plundering party of 200 infantry with about four file of cavalry. The infantry had half of them arms, the other without to carry provisions. They followed me down to the village of Mashul at the foot of the Sierra, three miles from Ramalhial, where they remained for plunder.

A regiment of the Spanish army had been placed under General Anson; he sent 200 of them to drive the enemy from the village, and the cavalry piquet at the same time went down the road, whilst they moved through the enclosures to the right. Had they not shown themselves so soon, we might have got some prisoners; but they gave the enemy notice, and allowed them time to get away. A few shots were exchanged as the enemy left the village and on ascending the hills. The Spaniards killed one and took another wounded. All the Spanish officers excepting one boy remained behind; and had the men been properly commanded, more might have been done. The Spaniards were the next day relieved by two companies of Portuguese Caçadores and the Militia of Torres Vedras. We were glad of the change.

One troop from each of the regiments were sent to Obidos, four leagues from Ramalhial. They were to assist the recruits at Peneche and Obidos in checking the enemy's plundering parties. The two troops were under Captain Linsingen of the Hussars.

The enemy's parties now not only come to the village at the foot of the Sierra, but likewise pass over the plain in our front towards the sea. We have deserters in occasionally, all agreeing that their troops begin to feel the want of supplies, and arc becoming sickly from being encamped without tents in the dreadful weather we have lately had. I am sorry to say desertion is not confined to the French, and since we have been in the lines, many of our infantry have passed over. Whether they think the enemy will gain Lisbon, and that they shall have their share in the plunder, or what is the reason, scarcely any one knows. Seven from the Fuzileers went off in one night, and these from one of the best regiments in the service.

Nov. 6th. Captain Linsingen of the Hussars being obliged to go to the rear through ill-health, Captain Cocks was sent to relieve him this day with his troop, the one of the 16th detached from the first being the troop in his squadron. He found the detachment in Moito, a village two leagues on this side Obidos, and it was optional in him whether to occupy one place or the other; and finding Moito unsafe for one squadron to occupy, he moved the following day to Obidos.

I was detained at Ramalhial on a court-martial until the 12th, when I joined my troop at Obidos. The town is surrounded by an old wall, extremely high, without a ditch, and perfectly safe against any of the enemy's parties that come for plunder. Major Fenwick (a lieutenant in the 3rd Buffs) has the command of the place, with 250 recruits from the depot at Peneche, as its garrison. On the advance of the enemy to the lines, the place was destroyed and the guns spiked.

With no small degree of labour he has got the guns up, unspiked them, made platforms, and put the place in a state of defence against any plundering party. We, at night, shut the gates, and have not a dragoon on duty. Major Fenwick has been very successful in taking many of the enemy's plundering parties, and with the French arms has armed many of the peasantry. Through these things he gets most capital information of all that passes, and not a party can come anywhere near Obidos without his knowing of it. The country is full of grain and almost every other supply, which we get in for two or three days at a time.

Nov. 14th. With 50 dragoons and 200 infantry we went after a plundering party of the enemy's. It had left the village before we got there, and we returned to Obidos in the evening. On the night of the 15th we received an order to be in readiness, and during the night another order arrived to march on the Quinta de Terro. The enemy left the lines on the night of the 12th, and the whole army is on the move up.

Nov. 16th. Marched this morning from Obidos to Alquentre, four leagues. The brigade came up to Quinta de Torre, and the enemy having left Alquentre, we put up in the sheds of a tanyard for the night, and were glad of this, as it rained almost incessantly. We took five French infantry, who told us the enemy have retired on Santarem. The parties out had not notice of the move, and numbers are straggling all over the country. (Circumstance of Major Archer and some officers of the 16th sleeping in a room at the Quinta de Torre with a dead Frenchman.)

Nov. 17th. The brigade came up soon after daylight, marching on the Santarem road from Alquentre, our squadron forming the advance guard. In two leagues we fell in with a sergeant and eight French infantry, who laid down their arms. On passing the village of Almustal we were ordered to halt, and sent out parties right and left after the plundering parties of the enemy. I went with twelve men to the left, and Captain Cocks with as many nearly in the same direction. I fell in at first with five infantry, with a flock of goats and nine asses. On our coming up they surrendered, and I forwarded them with two men to the brigade. I then fell in with thirteen infantry under a sergeant, escorting two mules with some asses laden with Indian corn. They at first seemed inclined to fire, cocking their muskets; but on our riding up, laid them down without a shot. Captain Cocks took twenty. Sergeant Liddle of Captain Belli's troop, belonging to Cocks' squadron, was sent from Alquentre with four men on patrol round by Rio Mayor. He fell in with an officer and fifteen French infantry, and having followed them for some way, attacked them, when they all surrendered.

Sergeant Baxter was sent on patrol from the brigade with four men to the left. He met with an infantry piquet of the enemy's, stationed in a house with their arms piled in front, and got so near unobserved that he thought he might get to the arms before they could take them up. He galloped forward; they had time to turn out, gave him a volley, wounding one of his men. It was too late to turn back; he persisted in his charge, rode up to the enemy, who laid down their arms, he killing one man. In all, forty-one men and an officer, which number he marched in. It was a most gallant thing; but though he succeeded, he was not justified in attacking them.

Sergeant Nichols, of Captain Cocks' troop, took sixteen infantry with six men, on the right,—though I think they were glad to find an English party to save them from the peasantry.

Sergeant Blood, of Captain Cocks' troop, was sent on patrol to our front, in the direction of Santarem. He got within the enemy's line of piquets, and was surrounded by a troop of dragoons; he cut his way through them, losing Storer, of Captain Cocks' troop, who was made prisoner. We were ordered to march to Santarem, and, should the enemy have left it, to occupy the town. These were the orders in the morning, and on coming up to Almustal we found the enemy in considerable force a little in advance.

On the main Lisbon road to Santarem on the banks of the Tagus, the enemy were followed by the Light Division, and General Slade's brigade. On the division's coming in front of Cortaxo, General Crawford found three regiments of infantry with two of cavalry formed up in front of the bridge, or rather with the bridge to their rear, over the river to Santarem, covering the retreat of their baggage. He waited a short time for our coming up on his left, having given his directions to the troops. During this, Lord Wellington came up and countermanded the whole; and it was said, had the thing taken place, most of those five regiments would have been prisoners, and that Lord W. did not remember the bridge and long causeway in their rear.

We bivouacked on the ground near Almustal. The officers got under cover; the men in camp in most dreadful rainy weather.

Nov. 18th. Turned out at daylight, waiting in front of the village nearly the whole day. The enemy have withdrawn all their force over the river, defending the bridge with its long causeway with sixteen field pieces. The day was employed in bringing up the infantry on the main road. We bivouacked on the same ground. The weather was very bad. Nov. 19th. An order arrived during the night for the brigade to move at 4 a.m. this morning to our left. We passed the Santarem River at a bridge near Coyembrogia, and on coming into the Rio Mayor road to Santarem, turned to our right, passing a branch of the same river at the bridge of Calares, and on passing the high ground and defiles on the other side, formed up about a mile and a half in front of the bridge. We were now within six miles of Santarem, and not one from the enemy's outposts.

The orders sent to General Anson were to make with his brigade and General Pack's brigade of Portuguese infantry, which was on its march to join us, a sharp demonstration on the Rio Mayor road, at the same time that the infantry attacked the bridge on the main road. A gun was to be the signal for the troops to move.

We waited until 2 p.m., when an officer from the Heavy Brigade was sent to say the attack on the right was all ready, and that we should move on immediately. General Pack was ready to cross the river; but since morning so much rain had fallen that even the bridge was impassable by which we had crossed in the morning. The 1st Division was to have attacked the main causeway, which had been barricadoed, so that only one man could have got over at a time. The hills opposite were lined by troops and artillery, and the division formed up, ready to move on. The gun was fired, and before the troops could move off their ground, all was countermanded. It was said at the time to be through the delay of a brigade of Portuguese guns—there must have been other reasons; and from what one could afterwards learn it was fortunate the business did not take place. The prisoners and deserters taken said Massena was extremely vexed when he saw it was not our intention to attack. His headquarters were in Santarem with the whole of the 2nd Corps d'Armee.

We took two or three small plundering parties of the enemy's, and with one, three horses and two mules belonging to General de Brigade Saverey. No orders reached us of the attack being put off, and we waited on the same ground till dark, when we retired across the bridge of Calares, encamping for the night in an olive grove close to the bridge. It rained the whole of the day.

Nov. 20th. General Pack, with his brigade, passed the river higher up, and occupied the village of Cozembrigera with a strong piquet in front of the Calares bridge and one in its rear. One squadron of the brigade was on duty on the heights in front. This was a mistake, as the troops were only intended to support the infantry, and should not have passed the bridge.

In the evening the left squadron, 16th, and centre moved to

the left into the village of Malhiaquaso for the night, the other two remaining encamped at the bridge. The men had been without bread for three days, and procuring as much wine as they wished in the villages, many got drunk. We, this evening, got half a pound per man. It rained incessantly. Nov. 21st. The enemy drove in our piquets in front of the Calares bridge. We barricaded the bridge, establishing our line of posts on the river. General Anson, with two squadrons of the brigade, moved to San Juan de Rebiera.

Nov. 22nd. All idea of any further attack on the enemy was given up, and orders came for the cantonment of the brigade.

Headquarters brigade, with one squadron from each regiment,

Captain Ally's squadron, Hussars: San Juan de Rebiera.

Cocks', 16th: Malhiaquaso

Captain Murray's, 16th: Rio Mayor.

Captain Ashworth's, 16th: Entre Portas.

Captain Gruben's, Hussars: Village on Calares bridge.

The fourth squadron of Hussars was detached near Cortaxo with the Light Division.

Headquarters of the army are established at Cortaxo, with the whole army (excepting the 5th Division left at Torres Vedras) in the adjacent villages. From the reinforcements which joined the army in the lines, a 6th Division has been added and given to Major-General Campbell.

When at the Ponte de Calares, the men, in an adjacent Quinta, found out some wine, and after drinking nearly to the bottom of one of the large casks, holding three or four pipes of wine, they looked into it and saw a dead peasant, who had been put in by the French. The large casks are cleaned by a person getting into them through a large bung-hole left for that purpose, through which he had been put. We all had some of the wine.

Massena placed his headquarters at Gallega, on the Tagus, but shortly moved them to Torres Novas. Santarem, the key to his position, is occupied by nearly the whole of the 2nd Corps d'Armee. Regnier has his headquarters in Santarem.

The 8th Corps, with Junot's headquarters at Pernes, extends

from that to Alkanadie. The 6th is in the rear at Torres Novas and Thomar. The 2nd in Santarem.

The enemy entirely subsist from the country they are in, which obliges them to cover as much space as possible. They have no regular communication with Spain, and their only means of sending despatches is through strong escorts of from 400 to 500 men. These must subsist on the country, and will find each village deserted by its inhabitants.

Colonel Trant, with the Militia of the north, attacked the enemy in Coimbra, where they had left a small guard under the idea of preserving that place as a depot for their sick. The enemy had no notice of his approach until he appeared before the town. Their piquet fired a few shots and ran back to the town, when a small body of Portuguese cavalry (twenty to thirty) galloped through, forming on the bridge over the Mondego. The enemy finding their retreat cut off, their effective men laid down their arms. In all, 5,400 prisoners were marched to Oporto. The 5,000 were all sick, and those fit for duty were no more than convalescents. By this, we gain the whole country north of Mondego; and with the force Trant has, I should hope he will prevent any parties crossing that river. Those for plunder he may prevent, but not anybody marching as an advance to the army or to any station.

Dec. 15th. The enemy, this day, drove in our piquets in front of Rio Mayor, and having plundered the villages, withdrew in the evening. The following day they showed about 1,000 infantry on the heights near Calares bridge. The French officers took off their swords and came down to speak to us, saying their object was only foraging, and that we need not put ourselves to any inconvenience, as they should soon withdraw. They complained much of the way they were going on, and hoped to put an end to the business one way or other. They did not appear to think things went on well for them. They invited us to a play in Santarem they had got up, and we them to horse-races, football, and dog-hunts. The communication was put a stop to by a general order.

The Marquis Romana (commanding the Spanish force with

this army) died at Cortaxo. He was a true friend to the cause and to his country; should the time ever come for our again joining the Spaniards, his loss will be much felt.

I went with twenty men from the squadron for forage in front of our piquets, and fell in with a party of the enemy's infantry that was come out for the same purpose.

On seeing my party they made off, and after a chase of two miles we came up with them, when they surrendered without the least resistance—in all, twenty men, belonging to the 15th Voltigeurs. They were native French, and the finest men I have seen. They were so blown with running as scarcely to be able to move.

Dec. 17th. The squadron of Hussars that had been with General Crawford had joined the brigade, and was stationed at Rio Mayor, and this day Captain Ally's squadron was sent from Malhiaquaso to that post. Two companies of Portuguese Caçadores were likewise sent to Rio Mayor from Alquentre, to which place the 5th Division had moved from Torres Vedras.

Rio Mayor was never safe without infantry, being only two short leagues from Alhinadie, which the enemy occupied in force (when an army does nothing on a large scale, we should always guard against their petty warfare, as the account fills up a despatch), the troops at the time lying idle; and from the time posts have been taken up in these cantonments, the enemy may, and no doubt have gained certain information of everything. Posts should always be moved, as by remaining exactly in the same place the facility of taking them is much increased.

In consequence of the squadron going away, Captain Hay's troop, under Lieutenant Persse, was sent to Malhiaquaso.

Captain Cocks went with thirty men to cut off a party of the enemy's cavalry that had been in the habit of coming for straw to a quinta near As Cabus. They discovered him in time to get away, and he returned unsuccessful.

Jan. 1st, 1811. Heard of General Drouet's arrival from France with a considerable reinforcement. He entered Spain, according to the deserters' account, with from 25,000 to 30,000; but with the detachments he has made and the men lost on so long a march, I should doubt his having more than 10,000. His numbers on entering have probably been exaggerated. No cavalry came with him. He is stationed at Leiria, and will materially assist the enemy's provisioning, having a good command of the rich country from Leiria to the sea. Sir Stapleton Cotton, Major-General Anson, Brigadier-General Crawford left the army for England.

Jan. 6th. Captain Cocks was ordered by Lord Wellington to occupy As Caldas de la Reyna with his own squadron and one of Hussars. We this day marched to Rio Mayor, two leagues on our route.

Jan. 7th. We, this day, with our squadron and Lieutenant Dekin's of Hussars, marched to Caldas, three leagues to the left of Rio Mayor.

Brigadier-General Blunt, in the Portuguese service, was in our front at Alfeseron, a village a long league in front of Caldas, on the Alcabaça road. He had near 700 recruits, from his depot at Peniche, employed in driving in the cattle, and transporting the corn to the rear.

From Leiria to Alcabaça is four leagues, and four on to Caldas. The enemy have posts three leagues in advance of Leiria, and generally a party in Alcabaça, not stationary, being only sent out for provisions. Our object is to watch this force at Leiria, and take care that early information is sent of any demonstration on this road. From Caldas to Torres Vedras is only six leagues; and if the enemy make a rapid advance, there will be, I should conceive, scarcely time to get our advance in front of Cortaxo clear off. We have constant information by peasants coming in from the enemy's lines, and I have no doubt shall hear of any advance the enemy may attempt on this road, as before it can take place troops must move from Thomar or vicinity to strengthen those now at Leiria.

A short time after we left Obidos, Major Fenwick moved up to Alcabaça, and was very successful in taking many of the enemy's parties. A party of eighty of the enemy's coming to Evora, a league from Alcabaça, he sent an officer with 100 men to attack them. On his arrival, he found they had posted themselves in a house ready to receive him. He placed his men so as to prevent their coming out, with sentries watching them, and reported back to Fenwick, who, on hearing the circumstance, set out with 100 more men to his assistance. When a quarter of a mile from Evora, he found the enemy had sallied out, and were skirmishing with the men first sent. He ran forward, ordering his men to follow as quickly as possible. On coming up, he seized a musket, calling on the men to charge. He had got within five yards of them, when one man turned round and shot him through the body; and here the affair ended. He was taken back to Alcabaça, and so on to Caldas, but died before he arrived there. He was buried in the chapel at Caldas by his own desire. Lord Wellington, in speaking of the business, paid him a high compliment in his despatch. There is not a man hereabouts who does not lament his loss, and the enemy have got rid of a most troublesome neighbour.

Jan. 9th. Captain Cocks went up to near Alcabaça with a patrol, and found a party of infantry plundering the villages, and took them. Their detachment had come all the way from Santarem, and were far from any support. Lord Wellington may not like to detach so far merely to prevent plundering, by which the enemy entirely subsist; yet had two squadrons come to Caldas at the first, much might have been done in preventing the enemy's carrying away so much. Now that Leiria is occupied in force, I fear they will detach parties too strong for us.

The enemy have become so expert at finding where the inhabitants hide their grain that they flood all around the houses (where it is possible), and then dig where the water sinks, which it generally does where the corn is buried. They likewise measure the outside of the house, and if the inside measure does not correspond with the outside they are satisfied (on its being less) that there is some secret hiding-place within, which throughout Portugal is very common. From the system of their own government, and exorbitant demands of the priests, they have always some secret hiding-place for grain, wine, oil, etc.

A deserter came in from Leiria belonging to the reinforcement lately arrived. He says it is the 9th Corps d'Armee, under the command of General Drouet, Count d'Erlon. They marched from France 36,000 bayonets; and he conceives the whole force, from sickness, and some few lost in two affairs in the north with the Militia of the north, under Silviera, near Pinhel and Celorico, to be reduced to 30,000 effective. They left strong detachments in Upper Biera, and have not brought down above 10,000 infantry, and had only sufficient cavalry to do their orderly duties.

Jan. 11th. We sent a daily patrol on the Alcabaça road. I went this day with eight men, and on coming to the village of Sella, three leagues from Caldas, I found the enemy in the village, with the small sergeant's piquet retired to this side. I reported to General Blunt, at Alfeseron, and, in consequence, he retired to Obidos. The enemy's object was only plunder; they followed me until I passed the bridge at Sharnais, and leaving a small body of cavalry to watch the road, plundered the villages about Sella. I remained at the bridge till dark, when the enemy retired. I placed a sergeant on piquet at the bridge, and went to Caldas. Two hundred of General Blunt's recruits were left in Caldas for the night. The sergeant I left on piquet patrolled through Sella in the morning. The enemy had gone back to Alcabaça. It was a strong detachment, consisting of a regiment of infantry and one of cavalry.

Jan. 17th. I patrolled this day to the right of the bridge of Sharnais, sending two men to the pass at the bridge, to remain there until I returned from the right. I had scarcely passed the river, when I heard two shots fired by them, on which I returned and found that two companies of infantry had passed the bridge, and were plundering the village of Vallada. They remained about an hour in the village, and then retired to the place they had marched from in the morning.

Jan. 18th. In consequence of the small party that passed the bridge of Sharnais yesterday, Captain Cocks applied to General Blunt for some of the garrison of Obidos to be stationed at Caldas. They marched in at daylight, about 300, and these, with part of the two squadrons, went up the hill towards the Ponte Sharnais. The patrol in their front fell in with a party of the enemy, which they thought would pass the bridge, as yesterday, and so made for it. The enemy did not, and they saw nothing of them. I was the officer of the day, and remained in Caldas. About 2, on visiting the piquets, I saw all the peasants running in towards Caldas, and learnt that the enemy were advancing on the road near the sea. At the same instant, two French dragoons appeared in front of Rayengo, about a league from Caldas. I took two men to the village, by way of a patrol, and could see nothing until I entered the village, when I saw two dragoon horses in the street, with their riders in a house plundering. A little farther down there were five dismounted. I passed the two, and charged the five; they drew their swords, but on our riding up, made very little resistance (I was wounded slightly on the right hand), running into the houses. We only secured one man and three horses; their infantry were so near that I was obliged to get out of the village as fast as I could. He belonged to the 6th Dragoons. They lay down, and we could not get them up to march away.

Captain Cocks, hearing the enemy were on the left, passed down into the plain, and I met him on my coming out of Rayengo. During this the enemy had completed their plundering in the Sierra de Bura on the sea, and were withdrawing. Lieutenant Hilton of the Hussars followed their rear, and took four infantry. Captain Cocks, in front of Rayengo, made some prisoners, and the patrol to Fossa took two cavalry. In all we took fourteen men and thirteen horses. The enemy's party consisted of 1,000 men, half cavalry, under Colonel Le Fevre, and had come from Santarem. From the careless way they scattered, they had not the least idea they were near an enemy; and if, instead of directing our attention to the bridge of Sharnais, we had been aware of this party, many more prisoners would have been taken.

The recruits from Obidos retired there at night, leaving a strong piquet at Caldas. The enemy withdrew to the rear of Alfeseron.

From the little affair I had in Rayengo, I received a slight thrust in the right hand with a sabre. The three horses sold for 256 dollars, or £64.

Cavalry Division Orders.
Quinta De Chavans, *January 22nd, 1811.*

Major-General Slade has derived great satisfaction from the report made him, by Major-General Anson, of the gallant conduct of Lieutenant Tomkinson, 16th Light Dragoons, who, with two men, attacked seven of the enemy's cavalry, dispersed them and captured one man and three horses (18th January).* Major-General Anson will be pleased to convey to Lieutenant Tomkinson and the two men concerned the Major-General's best thanks for the gallantry shown by them on the occasion, and to assure them of the pleasure he will receive in reporting the same to the Commander of the Forces.

Signed, J. ELLEY,
Lieut-Colonel and Assistant Adjt.-General.

Jan. 19th. From what the deserters yesterday told us, Captain Cocks supposed the enemy would continue their foraging as yesterday. Lieutenant Hilton of the Hussars was sent to the heights above Alfeseron to report if the enemy were in motion; in the place of which he descended the hills to pursue a few of the enemy's infantry advanced from Alfeseron. On seeing him they made back, and he came up with them just as they were entering the wood close to the village. One of them turned round and shot Williams, of Captain Cocks' troop, through the shoulder. The man was so near him as to injure his face with the powder. We waited in Caldas for Hilton's report, and on going to the height he had left, saw the enemy in the plain just in the careless manner they were yesterday. It was now too late to do anything, and a good chance of making some prisoners was gone by. It was a great error in Hilton leaving the height. Williams got quite well, and was in the regiment many years afterwards.

Captain Cocks again applied to General Blunt for infantry. 400 marched in at 3 a.m.

I went to the heights above Alfeseron, and the troops moved out for the purpose of taking the enemy's parties in the valley, should they be in motion as yesterday. The enemy must have

---
* *His twenty-first birthday.*

heard of infantry having come to Caldas, as in one hour after they marched in, they left Alfeseron for Alcabaça. A small plundering party of fifteen infantry came to Alfeseron, but did not belong to the other detachment. The enemy have injured the convent of Alcabaça, with several houses in the town.

Lieutenant Bishop of the 16th on the daily patrol to Alcabaça fell in with 20 French chasseurs of the Hanoverian Regiment. His patrol was six men; he, with two men, was going down the street to the left in Viseterea, and four down the one to the right. The four men fell in with the party, and agreed to fire one shot, and, if the enemy got into confusion, to charge. They were loading their horses with Indian corn, and half were mounted and half not yet ready. The thing succeeded. The men charged, and Bishop coming up with the other two men secured eight men and twelve horses, which he marched into Caldas. Many of the enemy got into the houses, and he, having so few men, could not spare any to look for them. As it was, he had scarcely sufficient to bring off what he took. The horses, as in the case of all captures, were sold, each man's share amounting to 92 dollars, or £23.

The spirit of capturing and attacking the enemy's parties is very great, and the only fear is of not falling in with them —the men not regarding their numbers. A sergeant and two dragoons took eighteen infantry.

Jan. 25th. I patrolled this day to the hill above Alcabaça. The peasants said they had seen nothing of the enemy for several days, and thought some change had taken place in their cantonments.

In consequence of this, Captain Cocks sent Cornet Cordoman of the Hussars with a patrol of eighteen men up to Alcabaça, with orders, in case he heard nothing of them, to remain for the night in some adjacent village. The enemy's not having appeared in the neighbourhood for some days was through a change of parties, and he found them plundering a small village to the left of Viseterea. About forty infantry was their strength, and on his sending six men to see what they were about, they left the village, and he made two prisoners, with forty-five asses, besides a number of mules they left hamstrung in the village. They were in such confusion that had the whole patrol of six men gone on with two men of the 16th, they all would have surrendered. Our men complained much of the Hussars. The patrol returned at night to Caldas.

Jan. 31st. Lieutenant Bishop, on another patrol to Alcabaça, went down to the town, and there found two of the enemy's infantry. They ran over some stone walls, and he dismounted to catch them. They were too quick for him, and a party of more infantry coming into the town from Algiberota, he had only just time to mount his horse. On leaving the square for the street leading to Caldas, he found fifteen infantry formed up on the bridge. He had nothing for it but to charge these, which he did, and they fortunately fired at him before he was quite round the corner. On giving their volley, they made into the houses, and he took the last of them before he could get in. He got the man out of the town, who, on seeing the other party come in, refused to go any further, saying he would rather be shot than taken prisoner. A man of the 16th took his musket from him, and ran the bayonet into his back; all to no effect, he still refused to proceed— when one of the Hussars took out his pistol and shot him dead. I conceive he was perfectly right in so doing, though I should not have liked to have done it myself.

Bishop has proved himself a very dashing fellow, and having now established that character, I hope he will acquire one for steadiness, as this sort of thing will not do. He, this time, got out of the scrape well; but had those fifteen infantry remained in the houses and given him a steady fire (as he must have passed up the street), he probably would have lost two or three men and horses out of the six.

Captain Kilshaw of the 77th Infantry (major in the Portuguese service) came to be stationed with 400 recruits at Caldas. The squadron of Hussars returned to Rio Mayor.

Junot, Duc d'Abrantes, conceiving there was a large store at Rio Mayor, advanced with three regiments of cavalry and two of infantry to carry away whatever he could find. Our troops retired without firing a shot; and the enemy, after searching the place, retired in the evening back to Alhinadie, and our troops took up their former posts.

In retiring there was a little skirmishing, and Junot, coming to the front, got a hit with a ball in the nose. At the time, our people perceived a great crowd round him, but did not know it was so great a personage. He was not long absent from duty.

Report of Major Otto, 1st Hussars, of this affair: "He ordered the infantry into the digs (ditches), and the cavalry to make everlasting skirmish."

We have had a corps for some time on the south of the Tagus, at first under Lieutenant-General Hill, and on his going to England (through sickness) the command devolved on the Hon. Major-General William Stewart. He plagued Lord Wellington with so many plans for foolish attacks, etc., that Marshal Beresford is now there. The enemy have collected a number of boats on the Tagus, sufficient to pass a bridge, though, with the force under the Marshal of 8,000 on that side, with Lord W. on this, after they have finished their bridge, the completing the passing of their whole army in the face of our troops will be no easy thing.

All the deserters (as well as peasants) agree that the enemy are in a dreadful state for want of regular supplies. They must move soon, either behind the Mondego or cross the Tagus, as I conceive it out of the question their subsisting much longer in these quarters. We hear of reinforcements from England.

General Foy left the French army a short time after they left the lines, and is expected back from Paris in a short time. He, probably, will bring something that will decide the business; though, had they ever been able to attack, they would have done it before this. Soult has come down to Badajos with 13,000 men, and besieged the place. The Spaniards who were with us in the lines moved back to that neighbourhood, and the town has now a garrison of 11,000 men. With that force, and no bribery or unfair work, the place ought to hold out as long as their provisions last.

A party of peasants have collected on our right at Santa Catherena, two leagues from Caldas. They annoy the enemy's foraging parties a good deal, and make some prisoners. They brought in here the other day seven horses with four men, and said they killed eight at the same time.

Feb. 17th. The enemy having been for some days past in considerable force near Vallada, and having pushed a patrol every morning over the bridge of Perenera towards San Martineo, the whole of the troops left Caldas this evening on a plan of Captain Cocks' to take this daily patrol. He, with 25 cavalry and 250 infantry under Major Kilshaw, went to San Martineo. I went to Alfeseron with sixteen dragoons, and was joined in the night by 160 infantry from Obidos, under an English sergeant-major, lieutenant in the Portuguese. My orders were to be at Familecon before daylight, and on hearing the firing on the hills to make for the bridge of Perenera, which, if the recruits would keep, the enemy's retreat was cut off.

At daylight I was concealed in the woods near Familecon, and the other party on the hills to my left. We waited till 2 p.m., and then returned to Caldas. Their patrol had generally consisted of 150 infantry, with a squadron of cavalry, but did not appear this morning. The party on the hills patrolled up to the bridge, and found four dragoons foraging on this side the river near the sea. Their retreat to the bridge was cut off, and Lockhart was near coming up with them, but they managed to get away over the river by no ford nor place at which any person had ever before passed.

Had the enemy's patrol consisted of 150 infantry with a squadron, and had not been hard pressed by the party on the hills, I think I should have looked rather foolish in their rear with my sixteen dragoons and the 160 recruits from Obidos— and they under a man who had no idea of what he was to do.

Thirty of the enemy's dragoons had passed the river and been foraging on the left. Had we been aware of this, we might have cut them off.

Cornet Steriwitz of the 1st Hussars patrolled from our old quarters at Malhiaquaso two or three times near Alhinadie, and having ascertained the situation of the enemy's piquet, and reason to believe from peasants that they were little on the alert, went with eighteen men from Malhiaquaso at night for the purpose of attacking them. He had eighteen men, half Hussars and half 16th. He got in rear of their double vidette, and secured the two dragoons without the least alarm being given to the enemy's piquet. By this means he got close up to the piquet, and charged into the middle of them. They were in the most negligent order possible; no one thought of the least resistance, all making into the woods as fast as possible. Their infantry piquet, a little behind the cavalry, turned out, which he charged and took one or two, and a third piquet of infantry in its rear ran away. The business succeeded, and he returned to Malhiaquaso with an officer of cavalry and twelve prisoners. Steriwitz had formerly been in the French service, which enabled him to answer some questions put to him by the videttes in a manner that made them believe he was of their army. He was thanked in cavalry orders for the business.

A few days after, the aid-de-camp belonging to the French general officer at Alhinadie was sent with some men to take a patrol of ours in the habit of coming daily towards Alhinadie, and it so happened that Steriwitz was the officer with the patrol, half Hussars, half 16th Dragoons. He got upon the French detachment, which were all infantry, before they were aware, and took the greatest number, with the aid-de-camp, who, however, made a most desperate defence, and was wounded dreadfully before he would surrender. It was particularly fortunate that the very people sent to play us a trick in return for the affair of the piquet should meet with such a reception.

Steriwitz is a dashing fellow, and I have no doubt will get something for these two things.

Ridiculous circumstance of six peasants, escorted by two dragoons of the 16th as prisoners, crossing a stream being tied together.

Feb. 23rd. The enemy this morning pushed two squadrons of their light cavalry over the bridge of Salles de Porta, and marched towards Fos, foraging in the *quintas*, etc., on the plain.

On hearing of it, the squadron and the infantry turned out and marched on the bridge, but were too late, the enemy's rear being just in the act of passing as we got up. The bridge had been nearly rendered impassable, and only one dragoon at a time could get over. We sent an advanced guard over the bridge, and going too far, the enemy shot Connolly's horse of I troop, and made him prisoner. Three French chasseurs, who had remained behind, were cut off, and surrendered at the bridge. Sergeant Blood of B troop, and Liddle of I troop, were sent on patrol on the first report coming in, towards the sea road, and charged the enemy's rear as they were making back for the bridge. They took nine men and horses and one mule. The enemy's party went back as far as Vallada. In all, we had one horse killed, one dragoon prisoner, and took twelve horses, a mule, twelve men and a boy.

The boy remained a servant to Lieutenant Lockhart, and for many years afterwards was with the regiment; he came to England in 1814.

I went on the 25th to Peneche, four leagues from Caldas, in the rear of Obidos. It is the depot of the recruits for the Portuguese army. It is closed in by a sand wall, on the land side with a ditch and sort of glacis. The sea at high tides flows across the front, and frequently carries away part of the wall. We have expended 70,000 dollars alone in carrying sand to the works, and the sea in one tide frequently undoes what has been the labour of 100 hands for a month. There is a certain supply for troops, of biscuit and corn, perhaps a fortnight for the army. I returned to Caldas the 26th.

On the 27th Captain Cocks received a letter from England, informing him of the death of his grandfather, which obliged him (much against his inclination) to leave the army for England; which he did this day. Though Lord Wellington had refused so many officers leave, yet, on receiving a line from Lord Somers stating the necessity, he granted Cocks leave without his making any application himself: and the first intimation he received of the business was from Lord W. granting him leave to proceed to England.

We daily hear reports that the enemy are preparing for a move; some of the peasants go so far as to say their sick have already left Leiria.

All the people, who at first remained in their houses, have been so pressed by the enemy, and ill-treated, to show where provisions, etc., are hid, that they have all left and flocked to this place. Those families that have not men with them able to go back in the nights to their villages for corn are in a most dreadful state, and die in great numbers. Whole families are lying in one room in the most miserable state. There is a dreadful fever in the town, which has communicated itself to the soldiers. The average of burials in a day is from twenty-five to thirty. We have formed a sort of hospital in the public hospital at this place; and from only giving the poor people soup and Indian corn bread once a day, many are walking about who, before, had not strength to move. The scenes of misery are beyond anything I ever saw; and if the enemy continue long in their present position, half the poor of the country will be in their graves. There are here three and four children belonging to the same family whose fathers and mothers are dead, and have no one in the world to look to for a bit of bread. Instance of a poor girl of ten years old, her brother about twelve, who died, and a sister of little more than a year old, who likewise died of starvation. The girl was saved.

On marching from Caldas, I left my Portuguese boy ill with the fever. He said the deaths were far greater after our departure, and that sixty-five died one day. I never heard a complaint against us, nor a wish that they had remained quietly in their houses. The sacrifice is a great one; yet I really think they would again make it, with the hope of getting rid of the enemy. They are the most patient people in the world. Many of the dragoons have boys to assist them, who live with them; and the women, English as well as Portuguese, attached to the army have a boy to assist them.

March 5th. The enemy's outposts were this night withdrawn on their line from Alhinadie to Santarem.

March 6th. The Light Dragoons moved on to Santarem, and General Anson's brigade moved to Alhinadie. The whole army is on the move. The remounts for the cavalry have joined, and eight regiments of infantry have landed at Lisbon.

March 7th. Received an order this morning from Sir William

Erskine to march on Leiria, and to cross the mountains to Ourem, there to join the army. We marched to Algiberota, one league beyond Alcabaça. The convent of Alcabaça exceeded anything I ever saw as a work of destruction. They had burnt what they could, and destroyed the remainder with an immense deal of trouble. The embalmed kings and queens were taken out of their tombs, and I saw them lying in as great preservation as the day they were interred.* The fine tesselated pavement, from the entrance to the altar, was picked up, the facings to the stone pillars were destroyed nearly to the top, scaffolding having been erected for that purpose. In short, regular working parties must have been constantly employed in a work of so much time and labour. No man, for mischief, would bestow so much time.

An orderly book found near the place showed that regular parties had been ordered for the purpose.

March 8th. The peasantry had given us to suppose the enemy had left Leiria, and we were marching on with that idea. We soon found that the place was still held in considerable force, and that their piquets had only this morning been withdrawn,—their fires were still burning. We were obliged to proceed cautiously, and the 250 Portuguese infantry, under Major Kilshaw, were halted. We did not see anything of the enemy before we arrived at the hill immediately above Leiria, about a mile from the town, when their piquet showed itself, and retired towards the town. Leiria was in flames, and fresh houses set on fire every moment. We supposed the piquet was all the force they had of cavalry, and were going to charge them, when a squadron turned out of the town, and came down to their support. We retired for the night a league back, to a large *quinta*, and Major Kilshaw came up with his infantry.

March 9th. The enemy evacuated Leiria last night, marching by the main road on Pombal. We moved at daylight, and passed the town, when Major Kilshaw's detachment returned to Caldas. We met an aid-de-camp of General Slade's, who told us the army was moving on Pombal, and that he supposed our advance

---

* *Pedro el Cruel and Innes de Castra were, I believe, the two I saw.*

to be near that place. We marched on the main road and fell in with a piquet of the enemy's at the Rio do Mandanilla, the place we had been engaged with them on the retreat. Weyland, with Captain Belli's troop, charged, ordering me to support with Captain Cocks'.

The enemy, on seeing us advance, made off, and at first we could not gain much on them. On ascending the hill, after passing the river, we came up with them and made the whole prisoners, excepting one man who got away into the woods and he was afterwards brought in. They consisted of a sergeant, two corporals, and twenty-two men of the 6th Dragoons, the horses in excellent order, and picked for the occasion. Their other cavalry is in bad order. The enemy turned out two squadrons on the top of the hill, and were advancing upon us; but the Hussars and Royals showing themselves in their rear on the Pombal plain, these troops were obliged to retire. This was a favourable diversion for us, being so far advanced, and with so few dragoons, that we should have found some difficulty in getting our prisoners away. By this means we got all safe, and having sent the prisoners to the rear, followed the enemy's rear to the plain of Pombal.

We followed the enemy's rear up to the Pombal plain, where they showed eight squadrons, formed on the heath in front and their whole cavalry in two lines in rear, with their infantry and artillery in support of them. The Hussars, seeing us come up the Leiria road, mistook us for the enemy, and some delay took place in consequence. At length they advanced one squadron in front, supported by the other three; on which the enemy's skirmishers retired, and their whole eight squadrons began to withdraw. We passed the defile in our front, and came up in time to join the advanced squadron of Hussars in their charge. We first broke one squadron of the enemy, drove that on the second; so on, until the whole eight were altogether in the greatest confusion, when we drove them on their main support. We wounded several, and took a few prisoners, and should have made more, only they were so thick that we could not get into them.

The French officers called on their men composing the support to advance; but not a man moved. The Royals were halted on the plain; and had they come on, there is no saying what might not have been done. The enemy kept their piquets on the heath, withdrawing their main body towards Pombal. The Light Division came up to-day, and the whole army will be near to-morrow.

Strict orders have been found relating to straggling, and none are seen from the enemy's ranks. They start with twelve days' biscuit, nearly which quantity we found on the prisoners we took. An orderly book of the enemy's, found near the convent of Battalia, gives the number of infantry daily employed in the destruction of the building. They either burn or destroy every town and village they pass through, and we daily see poor wretches of inhabitants in the most miserable state. They kill many, whose bodies we see in each day's march.

Major-General Slade, in the absence of Sir Stapleton, commands the cavalry.

March 10th. Major-General Picton, with the 3rd Division, and Major-General Dunlop (in the absence of Lieutenant-General Leith, commanding the 5th) will be to-day at Leiria. The 1st, 4th, 6th, and cavalry are following the Light Division, which moved by Thomar, and will all be up to-morrow.

Marshal Beresford, with the corps south of the Tagus, has moved on Thomar. The reinforcements of eight regiments of infantry from England are on their march to join us.

March 11th. The enemy withdrew his piquets this morning, and a regiment of Caçadores, with four companies from 95th supported by Captain Ross's guns, and the two regiments of cavalry, with our squadron, pushed their advance into the town of Pombal.

The enemy press the peasants as guides, and when at the end of their day's march, shoot them to prevent them giving us information. We have seen their bodies in many instances.

One or two prisoners were taken, who happened to be wounded by our light infantry. The infantry ran quick enough to keep the cavalry and guns in a trot the whole way. They pushed the enemy through the town of Pombal, which was in flames, and took a little baggage.

The enemy, seeing we had only one regiment of infantry and the four companies from the 95th up in the town, pushed them back from the furthest part, obliging our troops to shelter themselves in the walls, etc., on this side. The enemy occupied the heights on the Coimbra road with 7,000 infantry and two guns. The Light Division came up, halting in the road half a mile from Pombal. The 14th and 16th came this day and joined the army from the Pombal road. We were now brigaded with the 14th, the Hussars having marched with the Royals. It is only a temporary arrangement, and the brigades are to be as before. Colonel Hawker of the 14th commands the brigade, Major Pelly the 16th, Lieutenant-Colonel Archer being sick at Lisbon. The remounts from England have joined, and the regiments are very strong and in good order.

The cavalry moved to the left of Pombal, and there halted, the enemy keeping their position on the heights. Excepting a few shots from the enemy's guns, there was no firing the whole day, after the skirmish in Pombal had ceased. The 3rd Division came up to the place we occupied, and took up a position in our front. An order for attack was given out, but before the divisions could get in their places it was too late. The 3rd Division bivouacked in our front, and the whole army near Pombal. It rained a good deal during the night.

The skirmish in the town of Pombal was very sharp. The Caçadores behaved well. We lost—

Eleven rank and file killed.

Two ensigns, two sergeants, sixteen rank and file, wounded.

Sir William Erskine commands the advance, consisting of Light Division and cavalry.

March 12th. The enemy were aware that we yesterday made our dispositions for attack, and had he remained on the ground he had occupied, his rear could not have got off without an affair. He moved in the night, and at daylight not a man was to be seen.

The Hussars went on in front with the Light Division,

and the remainder of the cavalry formed in an open piece of ground near the road, about half a league in front of Pombal. The enemy held a position with their rear guard in front of Redinha, and the divisions moved up as fast as possible to attack. We were moved to the left of the line, and there halted some time to allow the rear divisions to come up. About 2 p.m. the line was formed, and the whole moved forward. Our right marched at the foot of the hills that flank the main road, our left extending into the plain, flanked by the cavalry. The enemy fired a few shots from four-pounders, which did no harm. The cavalry moved at a quick trot, the infantry running in line as fast as they could. The instant we moved, the enemy did the same, and our troops gained the hill as fast as they could inarch there. Their light infantry held a wood close to Redinha, from which they were driven by the Light Division, and in which we suffered a little. The fire was sharp, but, on our side, always advancing. The enemy drew back near two leagues from Redinha on the Coimbra road. We bivouacked near his rear.

The advance over the plain in line was one of the finest things I ever saw; and had they attempted to stop us, the thing would have been complete. Pombal, Redinha, and every other place on their route, has been burnt down. We see two or three poor wretches of inhabitants left dying in every village. The 6th Division marched in the evening to Soure, three leagues on the left. One squadron from the Heavy Brigade went with them. From this I am afraid Lord Wellington thinks there is some chance of their passing the Mondego, though the bridge at Coimbra is blown up, and Colonel Frant, with the Militia of the north, in the place. If they pass, I think they can find provisions for some time, and may perhaps be able to hold that position; if not, they will have to retreat through a barren country by the Ponte Murcella, which they must get over as fast as they can. There will be nothing to be found for an army on that road.

Return of casualties on the 12th March:—

Staff	Captains	Lieutenants	Ensigns	Sergeants	Rank & File	Horses	
-	-	-	-	-	17	3	killed
1	3	5	3	7	153	4	wounded

By letters since received from home, I heard of the death of an old friend. She died on the 12th March, aged above eighty.

March 13th. The enemy in the night withdrew their piquets, and in the morning we pushed forward to the heights, two miles from Condatia. The enemy had taken up a position in Condatia, forming abattis on the causeway up to the town, with a breastwork on each side the road. It was too strong to attack, and Major-General Picton, with the 3rd Division, was detached to the right over the hills. They, finding we were pushing on in this direction, abandoned their ground, and the whole army having closed up, we moved forward and bivouacked close to the town. The Light Division, with cavalry piquets, was in front. To conceal their movement, the enemy set fire to the town, and scarcely a single house escaped.

The 6th Division joined the army again. The enemy have all retired on the Ponte Murcella, and not a man has crossed the Mondego. This is a great point gained, as we save the whole of the fruitful country north of the Mondego, and oblige the enemy to retreat through one affording nothing. Also to the poor inhabitants of this distressed and impoverished country.

We returned to our old regiment, the Hussars, to be brigaded. Lieutenant-Colonel Arenchildt of that regiment commanded, and the 14th Light Dragoons returned to their former brigade, commanded by Colonel Hawker, in General Slade's absence in command of the cavalry.

March 14th. The roads are bad, and the enemy is obliged to keep his rear as near us as possible, to allow time for artillery and baggage to get off. We fell in with their piquets, within a league of Condatia, which were driven in by the Light Division with a sharp fire. The ground is particularly strong, hill after hill running at right angles to the road. One of these the enemy's rearguard occupied, and the Light Division, supported by the

6th, moved forward to attack them, whilst the 3rd marched on the right. We found one squadron per regiment with the guns of the Light Division. Captain Swetenham took the command of ours, and this day went to cover the guns. I was sent on patrol to look out for the infantry on the right. The enemy held their ground as long as they could, and then retired to another ridge of high ground in their rear. Our artillery rather cut them up as they withdrew, and a sharp fire was kept up on either side through the day. From the nature of the ground, it could only be an affair of light troops, and much ammunition was expended to little use. The 3rd Division kept moving on their left, which obliged them, at 2 p.m., to withdraw to the heights near Miranda de Corvo. We took up our ground with the infantry about a league in rear of Miranda de Corvo; it was after dark before we got to it.

The wounded are all sent back to Coimbra. Our loss was—

Majors	Captains	Lieutenants	Ensigns	Sergeants	Rank & File	Horses	
-	-	1	-	-	14	-	killed
1	5	4	1	12	112	-	wounded
-	-	-	-	-	4		missing

Major Stewart of the 95th was the one wounded; he died in consequence. Two of the captains are Napiers—brothers to Major Napier of the 50th, who was wounded and taken at Corunna, and again wounded at Bosoac.

The 4th Division and Heavy Brigade this day left the army to strengthen Marshal Beresford in the south.

Soult is besieging Badajos, and it is hoped the town will hold out until it is relieved by the Marshal.

March 15th. The morning was so foggy that the army could not move till late. The whole had been closed up the night before, and Lord W. was said to be much disappointed, as he intended to have attacked them, and, from the nature of the ground, much might have been done.

The Light Division formed the advance, and passed Miranda de Corvo before we arrived. The distressed state the enemy were in began to show itself. Two waggons were left in the village, and the hill on the other side covered with dead mules and asses. The enemy's rearguard had halted in front of the river at Foz d'Aronce, the bridge over which was destroyed. They were attacked late in the day by the Light Division, assisted by the two troops of horse artillery belonging to Captains Bull and Ross. The enemy made some stand, wishing to cover the retreat of some baggage through the ford. It was too late, and 3rd Division moving down the road, they left all behind them. The Light Division got into their camp, securing some plunder and all their dinners left on the fire. The enemy destroyed 200 asses which they could not get through, leaving them hamstrung on this side the water.

The affair was a very gallant one for the division; but had the day been favourable, and the whole army moved forward at daylight, in the place of coming up with their rearguard only, we should have found half their army on this side.

Dreadful cruelty on the part of the enemy to a peasant girl told to me by Assistant-Surgeon Evans, who attended her.

Return of casualties this day:—

Lieutenants	Ensigns	Sergeants	Rank & File	
2	-	1	6	killed
1	1	1	59	wounded

The enemy's bodies were seen floating down the Mondego for some days afterwards. Some time afterwards I saw them as low down as Coimbra. I conceive they suffered a good deal.

Assistant-Surgeon Evans appointed to the 16th.

March 16th. The army, on leaving Cortaxo, had started with ten days' supply, which was out, and the divisions now began to be short of bread. The Portuguese troops had already been some days without. They are supplied by their own commissariat, which is much inferior to ours. The British, from being very bad, is now getting into a better system, and is very tolerable; Lord Wellington looks well after them.

The army halted this day. It rained considerably last night and nearly the whole of this day.

We have heard of the fall of Badajos, which surrendered to a force very little superior to its garrison, and at the time they knew our troops, under Marshal Beresford, were on their march to relieve the place.

The governor had been killed in a sortie, and the lieutenant-governor had been bribed by the enemy. Lord Wellington, in his dispatches, much censured the thing, saying it speaks for itself; they were aware our troops would soon be up, as, on his leaving Cortaxo, he had informed them of Massena's retreat, and of Marshal Beresford's march.

March 17th. The Light and Sixth Division, with the two brigades of cavalry, this morning passed the river at Foz d'Aronce and marched about a league on, encamping two miles short of the Ponte Murcella. The enemy's rear-guard had passed the Alva, leaving a small piquet on this side. Sir W. Erskine had the command of this force. We saw nothing of the enemy excepting their piquet. It rained considerably during the day. The enemy leave mules and other baggage animals dead all along the road.

March 18th. We pushed on to the hill above the Ponte Murcella. The enemy's small infantry piquet was driven across by a detachment from the Light Division. The place is very strong either way, and the enemy hold the opposite banks with the whole of their 6th Corps d'Armee. Our nine-pounders came up to the nearest ground they could to the river and fired a few shots, and, although at their utmost range, the enemy moved off, not intending to keep it longer than was necessary to get everything away. Major-General Picton had crossed a ford to the right, and was marching on Gallices, which the enemy were aware of. In the evening our squadron was ordered for piquet near the bridge, pushing an officer's piquet on the opposite side (Cornet Cust was the officer).* The Staff Corps were at work all night in constructing a bridge over the Alva, which in the morning was passable for infantry only. The river was fordable close to it for everything.

March 19th. Lieutenant-Colonel Arenchildt was at the

---

* *Afterwards General Sir Edwd. Cust, K.C.H., Colonel of the 16th Lancers.*

Alva this morning by daylight, and his brigade, with the Light Division, passed the river, halting as soon as we gained the opposite bank. The enemy had now an open country to pass; and had the cavalry with the two troops of artillery gone on, many prisoners would have been made. Captain Hay's squadron had been detached to the left, and came into the main road in our front; they, alone, took a number of prisoners and sheep. At length a squadron from each regiment was sent on, and made many prisoners, chiefly their sick and wounded—in all, I should think, 200. About 2 p.m. orders came from Lord Wellington to march on; after two leagues we were taking up our ground, when another order came to proceed another league, and we encamped for the night. Our biscuit was out, and neither officers nor men had any this day. Meat in abundance taken from the enemy, both sheep and oxen.

March 20th. The cavalry and Light Division marched on to Gallices, where the infantry, excepting one regiment of Caçadores, halted. These, with the cavalry and Ball's guns, went on, and came up with the enemy's piquets about two leagues from Gallices. We had a trifling skirmish in driving in their piquet, which withdrew to a sergeant and twelve of the 16th, and allowed us to overlook a plain they were passing with two battalions of infantry and a regiment of cavalry. General Slade (who commanded) went up, hesitated for half an hour, and then, on every one saying what a fine opportunity we were losing, sent me back for Lieutenant-Colonel Arenchildt's brigade and guns. These were two miles in the rear; and before they could get up, although he ordered them to come as quickly as possible, the enemy got clear away. The regiment of Caçadores likewise moved on, and we encamped within a short league of Coã, on the main road. This was the second day without bread and third without corn, and we had marched nearly five leagues. In the evening General Slade ordered piquets of officers and thirty men where half would have done. I suppose he thought we had not enough to do. Every one talked loudly of his conduct through the day.

March 21st. We marched a league to Penhancos, encamping

in the fir grove, a mile in its front. The Light Division came up to Penhancos. We sent one squadron from the brigade in front to the convent of Venho, and remained quiet through the day. The officers, in the evening, got three pounds of biscuit each and the men a pound and a half of rice. Wanting bread is the greatest of all privations (water excepted), and therefore the biscuit this day was a great treat. We got some Indian corn out of the villages for our horses, and some wine. This, with the halt, quite set us up again. We could not eat meat by itself after the first day; all I had was a little tea. The men had nothing, but did not complain.

The enemy's piquets are in Villa Cortes.

March 22nd. We marched to the plain near Mello, and, having waited some time, the 16th occupied the three small villages near the convent of Coto. Colonel Arenchildt preferred the camp with the Hussars, and remained on the heath. General Slade went into Villa Cortes with the Royals and 14th Light Dragoons. The enemy occupy Celorico in considerable force, with their piquets a league and a half in its front.

March 23rd. Halted this day. The peasants from the villages had all fled to the mountains, on the enemy's retreat; and on seeing us they came down, baked bread for the troops, and gave us whatever they had left. The villages had suffered a good deal, though from the time their troops had been passing, they could not discover all the corn, etc., concealed by the peasants. All the principal houses in the villages had been burnt, and those left a good deal destroyed.

March 24th. The two brigades assembled this morning at Villa Cortes, and, having waited till 2 p.m., were ordered into camp near Liniares; the Royals, with General Slade, went on to Celorico, which place the enemy's piquets had left this morning. The Light Division came up to Mello, and the whole army is moving up by easy marches. They are detained for want of bread. It was one of the coldest nights and days I was out in.

March 25th. Remained quiet in our camp the whole day, and just before dark were ordered into Liniares. It just held the whole brigade.

March 26th. The two brigades were ordered to be at Celorico by daylight; and though General Slade had been in the place the whole of yesterday, he had not the least idea where the enemy had retired to.

Patrols went out from our brigade towards Alverca, and we moved up and occupied Marshal de Chaõ and Barracol, our squadron to the latter. Colonel Hawker's brigade went to Lagioso, on the Guarda road, a short league from Celorico.

Lieutenant Persse of the 16th, on patrol near Alveria, took an officer and eighteen infantry men after some resistance in which they had one wounded.

March 28th. Lord Wellington came up to Celorico. The Light Division moved to Barracol, and our squadron—to make room for them—to the village of Frasches to the left. The whole army was this day assembled near Celorico. The 3rd Division moved by the Prados road, and was this day near that place.

March 29th. The Light Division and cavalry were ordered to assemble this morning at Marshal de Chaõ. We moved about a league on the Alverca road, and then turned to our right, marching on Guarda. The 3rd Division came up from the Prados road on the right of Guarda; and the enemy, seeing us move in the bottom at the same time, retired from their position without a shot. Their troops took the Sabugal road, and a squadron from each of the regiments in the brigade (ours of the 16th) was ordered to watch them, at the same time that a squadron of the Royals and 14th Light Dragoons moved through Guarda. The enemy did not expect to have been obliged so soon to abandon Guarda, and had all their parties out in the villages about. Their rearguard that we came up with consisted of three battalions of infantry, with but few cavalry. These withdrew as fast as possible, and a party of their stragglers appearing so far from them as to be unable to join, I was ordered, with a sergeant and twelve men, to cut them off.

I came up with them in an open piece of ground, and on charging, the greatest part laid down their arms. One or two made some resistance, and attempted to join their comrades in the line of march; they were too far off, and we secured them all. They amounted to sixty-four infantry detached to Vahe. One of the enemy took up his musket and levelled it at me when about a yard distant; it either missed fire or a dragoon knocked it out of the man's hand. The dragoon had his pistol in his hand, and said, "Lieutenant, shall I shoot him?" I said, "No," though he ought to have shot him: it was a narrow escape. We followed the enemy until dark, taking from them 150 sheep with twenty oxen. The Hussars had one or two men hit in skirmishing. We occupied a small village for the night, and the remainder of the brigade came down to us. The Light Division, with Colonel Hawker's brigade, bivouacked in front of Guarda.

March 30th. The infantry halted this day. Lieutenant-Colonel Arenchildt followed the enemy's rear with his brigade and two troops of horse artillery on the Sabugal road. Colonel Hawker with his moved to Rapoullia de Coã, watching the passes over the Coã on our left. We came up with the enemy's rear at Pega, consisting of six regiments of infantry with a piquet of thirty cavalry. In the rear of Pega, there is a plain of two miles, which the enemy had to pass; and from where we stood above Pega, had the guns come up immediately, we might have fired into their very camp. As usual, we looked at them for half an hour; and when the enemy began to move off, the guns were ordered up, and in the place of firing at their main body, could only get within range of the piquets and a few flankers. The enemy, as soon as they saw we had guns up, abandoned the village of Pega, and we followed them over the plain on the other side. Here, had the guns come on, we might have fired into their columns at 300 yards; but, as usual, they were behind. Two, however, contrary to the orders of General Slade, were brought up and fired a few shots. They were so provoked at the fine opportunity they had lost that Lieutenant Stanhope, of Captain Bull's troop, did not make the best of practice, or the enemy carried off their wounded, as only one was left dead. We continued to follow them; and although they had no cavalry, yet our general was afraid to go into the plain with his, to get the guns within range of their infantry. The enemy, of course, got clear off, and placed their rear in the woods, a league in front of Sabugal. The 16th left a squadron in piquet, and the brigade returned to a camp the enemy had left close to Pega.

When we came up with the enemy in the morning, their band was playing in the village; they continued to do so for some time, and did not cease playing until our advance made them move off. There is considerable advantage frequently gained by putting the best face on an affair.

We had scarcely taken the bridles out of our horses' mouths, when a report came in that the enemy had sent a small patrol of cavalry a short way in front of their posts.

Though only a patrol, our wise general had us all out again on the hills in front with two guns. There we remained for an hour, and then took possession of the same camp. When he has us out, and there is a chance of doing something, he allows the business to go by, and harasses both men and horses on the most trivial occasions, when there is no chance of meeting an enemy.

The peasants, a day or two before we came up, caught a French infantry man, took him to a high piece of ground near Pega, and buried him alive.

March 31st. This was intended to have been a halting day for us, but our wise general marched us up to look at the enemy's posts half a league on this side Sabugal and one and a half from Pega. After remaining about an hour in the rain, we returned and took possession of the village of Pega for the night, and the Hussars occupied Val de Morisco, half a league in our front.

Lieutenant-Colonel Archer, this day, joined and took the command of the 16th.

April 1st. We, this day, again marched up to the enemy's posts, and found them, as yesterday, in front of the Coã. I went on patrol to the right, and took fourteen infantry and an officer's baggage, belonging to the adjutant of the Irish battalion in the French service.[*] The enemy had kept a considerable force in this direction, which had withdrawn this morning at daylight over the Coã. I found their piquets a mile in front of the river. On returning, I found the brigade on the ground I left it, and

---

[*] *His commission from the Emperor, now in my possession, runs as follows.*
1ere Division.   LEGION D'HONNEUR.
No- 27633.   PARIS, LE 29 MAI, 1810.

Colonel Beckwith's brigade in the Light Division had come up to take the outposts with the cavalry. The remainder of the army had moved up, and headquarters came to Marmeliero. We returned to Val Morisco for the night, which not holding us all, our squadron went to a small village a little to the right. Not an inhabitant to be seen, having all fled to the mountains.

April 2nd. The whole army, this day, closed up to the hills near Sabugal on the left bank of the Coã. The enemy had only a small piquet on our side, which withdrew on our sending a patrol to drive it over. Our outposts were on the Coã; and if the enemy in the morning holds the position he has to-day, we shall attack. The brigade bivouacked. We have had some wet for the last four days. Our men and horses stand the duty well. We find a little forage in the villages as we pass, and by being the advance, have the first chance in the leavings of the enemy.

April 3rd. The enemy appear as yesterday, and the following orders are given to the different general officers:-

Sir Wm. Erskine with the Light Division and cavalry (Colonel Hawker's brigade joined from the left this morning) is to pass by a ford on the right, moving round the enemy's left flank, and so taking post on a hill near the road by which they (the enemy) will retire to Alfiates (the point is marked by a single tree).

The 3rd Division to pass by another ford more to the left, nearer Sabugal, and the 5th Division with the 1st and 6th to

---

LE GRAND CHANCELIER, MINISTRE D'ETAT, A MONSIEUR PERRY, *Membre de la Legion d'honneur, Adjudant Major dans le 2e Bataillon du Regiment Irlandais.*

L'Empereur et Roi, en Grand-Conseil, vient de vous nommer Membre de la Legion d'honneur.

Je m'empresse et je me felicite vivement, Monsieur, de vous annoncer ce temoignage de la bienveillance de Sa Majeste Imperiale et Royale, et de la reconnoissance de la Nation.

b. g. et. Ae. de Lacepede.

P.S. - Je vous invite a preter, devant le President de la Cour ou du Tribunal les plus voisins, le Serment prescrit par la Loi, ou a m'envoyer, signe de vous, celui dont je joins ici la formule.

make an attack on the town of Sabugal, but not to force it until the enemy are withdrawing through, the other two divisions being on their flank and rear. The Light Division and cavalry got across with little difficulty, and in the place of their marching to the appointed hill, they attacked the enemy, keeping along the right bank of the Coã.

Much was said of the impropriety of the division crossing left in front. As it attacked immediately on passing, it was correct; had it marched, as intended, some distance before it met an enemy, it ought to have moved by its right, and so would have been ready on the march to form line in a moment.

Colonel Beckwith with his brigade was in front, and had a sharp affair with the enemy. They saw we were weak, attacked him, and drove him back a little. The other brigade coming up, the 43rd Regiment charged and took a howitzer, driving the enemy back. At this moment, the head of the 3rd Division appeared, when the enemy began to draw off.

It was a most gallant affair for the Light Division, which beat three times its numbers. We were sent far away to the right at the time; a squadron of the enemy was annoying our infantry. Sergeant Proctor of the 16th, with two men, saved an officer of the 52nd from being taken. The enemy withdrew to Alfiates, after having their 2nd Corps d'Armee well thrashed; and had the Light Division obeyed its orders, or rather had Sir W. Erskine obeyed his, not many of that corps would have got away. As it was, their rear had scarcely time to clear off, and some baggage was taken by a detached squadron of Hussars—that of General Soult, nephew to the Marshal, was taken.

Lieutenant-Colonel Beckwith with his brigade gained great credit. He was hit by a musket-ball on the outside bone of the right eye; he kept going on through the affair, it did not keep him a day from his duty. Headquarters of the army this day in Sabugal.

Return of casualties:—

BRITISH LOSS.

Genl. Staff	Majors	Captns.	Lieuts.	Ensigns.	Sergts.	Drms.	Rank & File	Horses	
1	-	-	2	-	1	-	15	8	killed
1	1	2	5	2	8	2	117	11	wounded

PORTUGUESE.
Rank and File.
1 killed.
9 wounded.

In consequence of the reinforcements from England, a 7th Division has been formed.

A report came to Lord Wellington that the 8th Corps d'Armee was in motion; he conceived them to be on the march to support their advance, in the place of which they were moving to the rear, and at the time the reporter sent word it was not known which way they were going. It was much to be lamented, as, bad as the business was, their advance would have been made prisoners.

April 4th. The advanced guard of the army assembled this morning at Alfiates, and the Hussars marched with the Light Division and occupied Albergarea, the first village in Spain. The 16th went to Alamadelia, a short league to the left. We were now in Spain, and the whole of the enemy's army, excepting a small force near Almeida, had left Portugal. The enemy first brought into Portugal 65,000 infantry and 4,000 cavalry, and under Drouet received a reinforcement of 10,000 brought down to Leiria, and as many, or perhaps 15,000 left in the neighbourhood of Guarda and Covilha. They returned about 35,000 infantry fit for duty and about 1000 cavalry.

They have certainly done all the injury possible to the country they passed through, but have paid dear for this by the number of men they have lost.

	Infantry.	Cavalry.
Brought originally into Portugal	65,000	4,000
By a reinforcement to Leiria	10,000	
Left in the towns adjacent to Guarda.	15,000	
	90,000	
	4,000 cavalry.	
	94,000	
Returned	{ 35,000 infantry. 1,000 cavalry.	

The sight of a village with inhabitants in it was a thing we had not seen since we left Mafra, October 22nd—excepting the inhabitants who had taken refuge in Caldas, and were, like ourselves, strangers to the place.

They had not in the least injured these villages, and the people told us the soldiers came rich out of Portugal, and having been for a length of time on a scanty allowance of bread, were glad to pay almost any price for it. They said the French had used them well, and many families from the borders of Portugal had come into these villages for protection. They have learnt such a lesson by forcing a population to leave their houses that they will, for the future, be glad to induce them to remain in their villages.

Headquarters of the army at Alfiates.

April 6th. Colonel Arenchildt's brigade marched a short league to the left to Nava de Aver, and occupied that village. I was sent on piquet towards Gallegos, and had scarcely placed my men when the brigade was ordered to move to Villa Formosa, a long league to the left. It was nearly dark when we got there. The enemy still occupied Almeida, and had posts in San Pedro, not a league from Villa Formosa. We placed three piquets, two officers, and twenty men, one each on the main road to San Pedro, and the other towards La Alameida. A sergeant and twelve were on the left-hand road to Almeida. All was quiet through the night.

April 7th. We turned out at daylight, and remained on our ground for three hours before any orders arrived; we ought, after finding all was quiet, to have been in the village. One squadron (under Lieutenant Weyland*) was left at Villa Formosa to watch the enemy, and the remainder of the brigade moved with the 6th and 5th Divisions towards Almeida, in which place the enemy had left a small garrison and were withdrawing their force. The horse artillery came up with their rear, composed entirely of infantry; and the left squadron of the 16th, led by Colonel Archer, charged their rear of sixty-five infantry. They kept their fire until our men were close, but were broken and all made prisoners, we losing two men wounded, one of whom afterwards died.

Our advance was in Val de la Mula, the enemy retiring on the Agueda.

Lieutenant Lockhart was on piquet with twenty men on the La Alameida road from Villa Formosa, and a patrol of two men sent out by him fell in with some baggage of the enemy's on its march, with an escort of infantry. The advance of the infantry was just getting into La Alameida, and the rearguard coming out of the wood, about a mile below at the foot of the hill crossing the Duas Casas. In the road betwixt the two was a large caravan escorted by some private servants on horseback and drawn by four oxen. The two men rode up, the servants made off, and two Spaniards on foot driving the oxen, being forced by the dragoons, made away quick with it for the bridge leading back to Villa Formosa over the Duas Casas. One company from their infantry towards La Alameida turned back and came up time enough to fire a few shots at the men, which Lieutenant Lockhart heard and advanced with the piquet, when they halted and allowed the dragoons to get clear away with their prize.

It proved to be the waggon belonging to the Marquis de Lerna, the Portuguese general in the French service, with the greater part of his baggage and correspondence with Lisbon. It created much fun, being as large as those used in England for showing wild beasts. The dragoons called those escorting it "show men," and had many jokes: they went by that name for some time.

* *Of Woodeston, Oxford, d. 1864.*

The enemy have left a small garrison in Almeida under Brigadier-General Reniere. If they have sufficiency of provisions, I do not see how we are to take the place, having no battering train nearer than Lisbon. The 6th Division is placed to invest it.

April 9th. After halting yesterday in Villa Formosa, we were ordered this day to occupy our old quarters in Gallegos. Colonel Beckwith's brigade with Captain Ross's guns were put under cover with the 16th. The Hussars and remainder of the Light Division went to the right to Espeja. The enemy have withdrawn their force over the Agueda, leaving a garrison of about 2,000 infantry in Ciudad Rodrigo, with their cavalry encamped under the walls. Their army has marched on Salamanca, sixteen leagues from the Agueda.

We were now in our old quarters. The village, from being one of the nicest I ever saw, had been half unroofed for firewood, and many of the families obliged on that account to leave it. Headquarters came to Villa Formosa.

April 10th. The enemy's cavalry withdrew last night from Ciudad Rodrigo, marching on Salamanca. Thus ended the retreat of Massena from the lines at Santarem. They commenced their retreat on the 4th of March, and our army moved the day following, making in all thirty-six days' march, with only two halts,—one near Foz d'Aronce on the 16th, and the other on the 8th of this month at Villa Formosa. The French army withdrew in a dreadful state, wanting most of the necessaries for an army, yet their retreat was not attended with much loss in men. We took few stragglers, and when pressed they always covered themselves in good style. Marshal Ney had the rearguard with the 6th Corps d'Armee the whole way as far as Celorico, where he and Massena had a dispute, and he left the army for France. The prisoners and deserters told us it was in consequence of Ney's wishing the army to move on Badajos in the south, and that Massena would not hear of it. The 2nd Corps, under Regnier, was then placed in the rear, and had the affair of Sabugal with the Light Division.

Lord Wellington desired Major-General Slade to send two regiments over the Coã, to be nearer our supplies. We have now been without corn since the 4th, and bread has been very scarce for the troops. Officers' horses this day got ten pounds, the troops none at all. Our army has been carried through this desolate, abandoned country in an astonishing manner. It has required the best arrangements in the commissariat to accomplish it.

April 11th. The 1st (Royals) Dragoons and the 16th were the two regiments fixed on to march to the rear. We passed the Coã at the ford below Castel Bom, and halted for the night in Misquitella. It held the whole regiment.

The regiment this day marched to its quarters as follows:—

Musella (Headquarters): Right centre squadron.
Rapullia de Coã: Right squadron.
Sardiera: Left squadron.
Richioso: Left centre.

Major Pelly went with the left centre squadron to Richioso. During our stay at Richioso the horses scarcely received two days' corn, and the men latterly were on half-rations of bread. The regiment subsisted on the green corn, which was dreadful to the inhabitants, and of little use to the horses, when they began to work. We had nothing else, and were obliged to cut their rye.

A mail arrived from England, bringing the melancholy account of the death of an old friend.

I here had an attack of ague, which got ahead from my not knowing what it was.

Lieutenant-General Sir Stapleton Cotton arrived from England and resumed his former command of the cavalry. Major-General Slade returned to his brigade, having lost many opportunities on the advance of raising his name. The things said of him by different officers were so gross that I am certain they would not have been allowed to pass unnoticed had they been applied to any other man in the army.

April 27th. A route arrived during last night for the regiment to move to Alfiates. We marched to that place, which put under cover the whole regiment. It was three short leagues from Richioso. In the evening an order came for us to march on to

Gallegos. We turned out just as it became dark, and marched through Nava de Aver, Villa Formosa, and the left wing of the regiment to Gallegos, with headquarters, and the right, under Major Pelly, to Villa de Puerco. We expected after this night's march to have been engaged, but took possession of the village an hour after daylight, and remained quiet through the day. Lord Wellington has been absent in the south for a short time, with the army under Marshal Beresford, which has besieged Badajos with guns taken from Elvas. He has fortunately returned, as the enemy have collected a considerable force for the relief of Almeida; and if that place is to be covered, it is as well he should do it as Sir Brent Spencer.

On the 29th the enemy brought down a considerable force to Ciudad Rodrigo. Headquarters of the cavalry in the village of Gallegos, with the two brigades in the adjacent villages.

May 1st. The enemy this day drove our posts over the Azava, and the 16th in consequence assembled on the hill in front of Gallegos. They had eight squadrons of cavalry and two battalions of infantry close to Carpeo, which in the evening they withdrew towards Rodrigo, and the 16th occupied Gallegos with their posts on the Azava. I had the ague every other day since I left Richioso, and this day was obliged to leave the regiment for the rear. I went to La Alameida for the night, a league in the rear of Gallegos. In my way I met Captain Cocks, just come from England, much vexed at having missed the advance from Cortaxo. I was so altered from the time we parted at Caldas (27th of February) that at first he did not know me.

May 2nd. The enemy pushed in our advance from Gallegos, and the Light Division with the horse artillery took up their ground in the rear of the Duas Casas, on the hills covering the bridge. I reported myself to Inspector-General Franks at Villa Formosa (headquarters), who ordered me to the rear. I slept at Castel Mendo, a long league from Villa Formosa on the Coâ.

May 3rd. I, this morning, proceeded on to Casteniera, where I found Assistant-Surgeon Rozia belonging to the 16th, and there remained.

Lord Wellington, finding the enemy determined to relieve Almeida, assembled the army behind the Duas Casas, with his left in the wood and rocks towards Fort Conception, his centre in rear of the village of Fuentes de Onoro, with light troops in the village. His right was thrown back towards Frenada, resting on a hill with a tower on it, on the Nava de Aver road to Almeida. The position from Fuentes to the left is strong, but from that to the right is almost in a plain, excepting the hill on the right, on which Major-General Houstoun with the 7th Division is placed, and ordered to keep the hill to the last.

On the enemy's first advance the army was very differently posted, the 7th Division being in the wood to the right near Possa Velha. Our two brigades of cavalry scarcely amounted to 900, and these in bad condition. The enemy had 4,000 fresh cavalry, and were driving ours back on the infantry.

The 7th Division in the wood waited too long, and Lord Wellington thought it was all over with them, the enemy's cavalry being on each of their flanks, and they had ground to pass on which cavalry could act. They, however, got away into the rocks, and the enemy's advance charged up the rising ground on which our horse artillery was posted, and passed two guns of Captain Hull's troop. Their advance was not well supported. Our cavalry came on and took a lieutenant-colonel and some prisoners. The Chasseurs Brittaniques in the 7th Division behaved very well, and checked the enemy by their fire. Their advance obliged the Light Division to throw itself into squares, and retire across the plain.

On their seeing thus, the affair ended, and the remainder of the day was occupied in taking up our position, and the enemy in closing their troops up to the woods near Fuentes.

On the right, before the 7th Division evacuated the Possa Velha wood, Major Myers of the Hussars was in advance with two squadrons—one from the 16th, and one of his own regiment. Captain Belli had joined from England the day before, and taken the command of Captain Cocks' squadron. Cocks commanded the left. Captain Belli's squadron (late Cocks'), with one of the Hussars, was in advance; and the enemy having sent forward two or three squadrons, Major Myers attempted to oppose them in front of a defile. He waited so long and was so indecisive, and the enemy came up so close, that he ordered the squadron of the 16th to charge. The enemy's squadron was about twice their strength, and waited their charge.

This is the only instance I ever met with of two bodies of cavalry coming in opposition, and both standing, as invariably, as I have observed it, one or the other runs away.

Our men rode up and began sabring, but were so outnumbered that they could do nothing, and were obliged to retire across the defile in confusion, the enemy having brought up more troops to that point. Captain Belli was wounded slightly, and taken; Sergeant Taylor, of his own troop, and six men from the squadron, were killed on the spot in attempting to rescue him. The enemy cannonaded the cavalry a good deal in retiring, in which we lost Lieutenant Blake of the 16th. He was hit by a four-pound shot in the thigh, and, through some mistake, the shot was not taken out, and he rode with it to Castel Mendo, where a Portuguese surgeon took it out. Surgeon Robinson of the 16th went in the morning to Castel Mendo and cut his leg off, and in half an hour afterwards he was dead. Had the operation been performed immediately, his life would probably have been saved. From the spot where he received his wound to Castel Mendo is good six miles, and the large bone shattered all to atoms. Had I been with the regiment, I should have been in his place, —or rather, he occupied mine.

On the 5th April the enemy attacked the village of Fuentes de Onoro, and gained possession of it twice. The 88th and 74th from the 3rd Division gained it again, and the 79th a second time carried the village. It was a very sharp thing, costing us, on the 3rd and 5th, 2,000 men. The enemy remained before our position two days, and Lord Wellington thought they would attack the right. They began to draw off, and on the 9th their whole force had recrossed the Agueda, on its route for Salamanca. They lost many more in the attack on Fuentes than ourselves, and completely failed in their attempt to relieve Almeida. They had about 42,000, and to oppose to that we had nearly 40,000.

Marshal Massena here resigned his command, and went to France. He was relieved, when before our position, by Marshal Marmont, Duc de Ragusa.

What the enemy's whole army could not effect was unfortunately accomplished by the garrison of Almeida itself. On the night of the 10th they sallied out, first blowing up the place. They drove back the piquets, and marched over the open plain on Barba del Puerco. The 4th Regiment was to occupy that village, and the order reached Sir Wm. Erskine's quarters at 2 p.m. on the 10th. They took about 150 of their rear, and attempted to follow them to the other side the river, but were driven back with some loss by troops stationed in San Felicis il Grande, which turned out on hearing the fire.

Lord Wellington was much enraged at this, and would never allow the thing to be inquired into, nor admit of any excuse from Colonel Bevan, 4th Regiment, who was the person condemned as having erred. Colonel Bevan of the 4th Regiment was so much hurt at the expression in Lord Wellington's despatch, viz.: "that the Garrison escaped through the 4th Regiment losing its way," that at Portabayre, on the route down to Badajos, he put an end to his existence, though certainly no blame was attached to him. With his regiment he was ordered to watch the passes over the Agueda to the right of Barba del Puerco, where he was the day previous to the escape of the garrison. On the morning they got away, he heard the firing, and had his men under arms to march of his own accord to the point, and that instant the order arrived for him to move to Barba del Puerco; but it was too late, as on his arrival the enemy were passing. The order reached Sir Wm. Erskine at 2 p.m. the preceding day; he put it in his pocket, and did not despatch the letter to Colonel Bevan before midnight, and to cover himself, when required to explain by Lord Wellington, he said that the 4th Regiment unfortunately missed its way, which was not the case.

Major-General Anson joined and took the command of our brigade a few days after the enemy retired.

From the number of sick and wounded that came in to Casteniera, I was obliged to remove on the 7th of May to Celorico.

I here recovered fast, and on the 20th left to join my regiment. I found Captain Cocks' squadron in Gallegos. The headquarters of the regiment, Villa de Puerca. Cavalry headquarters, Sismicro.

Lord Wellington, finding the enemy had given up all operations in the north, moved himself with the 3rd and 7th Divisions to the south, Soult having advanced with the intention of relieving Badajos.

He was too late, Marshal Beresford having sent his artillery over the Guadiana to Elvas, and taken up the position of Albuera. On the 16th May a general action was fought, and the most severe thing that has taken place in the Peninsula. We lost 4,000 men, but gained the day, Soult retiring on Llerina.

Considerable blame was attached to Beresford for the way he fought, having neglected to occupy the key to the position.

The enemy gained the hill on the right, which cost us many fine fellows to carry. The Fuzilier brigade in the 4th Division, 7th and 23rd Infantry, suffered very much, but behaved in the best style. General Cole led this brigade in a manner worthy of the difficulty he had to contend with; he was wounded. Colonel Durban, 2nd Marshal-General to Beresford, was the person who did everything.

The Marshal lost his head when the enemy gained the hill, on which he was for an immediate retreat. Had he done so, with the enemy's superiority of cavalry, and the open country he had to pass, most of the army would probably have been sacrificed. The Polish Lancers got amongst our infantry and did great execution. On his talking of a retreat, Durban immediately represented the danger, and begged the Fuzilier Brigade might advance. The enemy thought a great deal of our success, considering it quite a defeat on their part. It often occurs that a person not having the responsibility on his own shoulders can direct an affair with much more judgment than a principal, who feels everything at stake on his own decision.

Return of Albuera, May 16th, 1811.

GenStaff	Staff	Lieuts. Cols	Majors	Captns.	Lieutenants	Ensigns	Sergants	Drummers	Rank&File	Horses	
British 1		1	1	7	13	9	31	4	315	54	killed
7	6	4	4	43	81	20	132	9	2426	26	wounded
			1	4	3	1	28	10	492	17	missing
Portugese 1	1						2		98	9	killed
1	1	1	1	5	5	2	14	1	230	9	wounded
								1	25		missing
Gen Total 2	1	1	1	7	13	9	33	4	913	63	killed
8	7	5	5	48	86	22	146	10	2656	35	wounded
			1	4	8	1	28	11	517	17	missing

May 25th. Sir Stapleton Cotton, this day, left this army for the south. Captain Cocks went with him as Quarter-Master General, he being obliged to leave his in the north.

Sir Brent Spencer was left in the north with the command of the four divisions, viz, 1st, 6th, Light, and 5th.

On the 27th he moved the Light and 1st a few days' march towards Castel Branco, conceiving they would be ordered down to Badajos. Lord Wellington had again laid siege to that town with the guns of Elvas. The two divisions were ordered back to their former quarters. I went, on the 27th, with a flag of truce to Ciudad Rodrigo, and was allowed to come close to the town.

June 1st. An order arrived last night for the brigade to march to the valley of the Zezere, near Covilha. We moved this day to Alfiates. June 2nd. Marched this morning three leagues, to Sabugal.

June 3rd. The whole regiment with the headquarters of the brigade this day occupied Coria. The Hussars went to Campillia.

The following day the left squadron moved to Quintans, and Captain Cocks' to a miserable village near Caria. It would not hold us, and the following day we moved into Quintans. Captain Belli* being taken, gave Cocks his old squadron.

The siege of Badajos continued, and Soult, finding himself too weak to relieve it, the army of Portugal (the same opposed to us at Fuentes de Onoro) moved on Ciudad Rodrigo, and so on through the Puerta de Banios for the south. They drove in the four divisions, and Sir Brent Spencer, although they never advanced beyond Nava de Aver, thought it right to retire on this side the Coã, taking up a position in rear of Sabugal, at the time the enemy were all moving from Rodrigo on the pass of Banios. General Slade had an affair with the enemy's cavalry in front of Nave A'aver. He waited too long with the Royals, and was nearly in a scrape. He charged and took a few prisoners, but at the time he moved forward, the enemy was advancing on his flank, and he not only could not bring off the prisoners, but lost one or two men from their horses falling, in consequence of this advance. Sir Brent moved with his force to the neighbourhood of Penamacor. (Probably these were his orders from Lord Wellington.)

June 9th. The route this day arrived, and the brigade moved three leagues on the road to Castel Branco. The 16th and General Anson halted in Attalia, the Hussars in a small village a little in our advance. The right squadron, 16th, occupied a small village near Attalia.

June 11th. The brigade moved four leagues this day, to Castel Branco, bivouacking just before we entered the town.

The Light Division came to Escallies de Sima, and the whole force is closing up in its rear.

The weather is uncommonly hot, which obliges us to move at two each morning. From the rest and green forage, the regiment was in very good condition, and moved very efficient. Lieutenant-Colonel Archer here left the regiment through sickness, and shortly after got his leave for England. Major Pelly succeeds him.

* *He was taken at Fuentes, and remained prisoner in France till the peace of 1814.*

June 12th. We marched this day to Villa-Velha, on the banks of the Tagus, five leagues from Castel Branco, and on our arrival received an order to move on to Niza, two long leagues on the other side. The river was to be passed on a floating bridge, taking twenty horses each time. This caused much delay. The troops got to Niza just before dark, and the baggage not before 9 or 10. We encamped close to the town, and found abundance of hay on the ground.

In using the word encamped I ought to say bivouacked, as the army had no tents. The men put one blanket on the ground, lay down in their cloaks, and being two together had another blanket to cover them. The officers did the same, and if it rained we got wet.

The Light Division passed on the 13th, and lost two men from heat in ascending the banks of the Tagus. The esprit of this division is so great, they will suffer anything sooner than leave their ranks on the march; from which spirit the two men in question lost their lives.

We halted two days at Niza, and marched to Portalegre, passing the town to our camp on the Badajos road. We here expected some news from Badajos, but only heard from the peasants that for the last two days there has been no firing, and that they always heard it previous to that.

We halted a few days in our bivouac at Portalegre and moved three leagues to Aronches. We are now in quite a different country to the north. The houses and inhabitants much cleaner and superior, though not so healthy. Ague prevails in almost very place, and if yielded to, as the Portuguese do when they are ill, it is almost impossible to get rid of it.

A remount here joined the 16th from England. The horses come from the 12th Light Dragoons, are heavy, and not likely to answer for Portugal.

June 23rd. We this day marched for the army, three leagues from Aronches, encamped on the banks of the Caya (called the camp of Torre de Mora). The siege of Badajos had been raised some days before, and the whole army withdrawn on this side the Guadiana. Soult and Marmont had united, and should they move on us, it is the intention to take up the position on this side Campo Mayor.

The 11th Light Dragoons, from England, had joined the army a few days previous to our coming up, and having sent a piquet of 50 men, under Captain Lutchens of that regiment, on the road from Elvas to Badajos, the enemy crossed a strong force of cavalry over the Guadiana, on their right, got in their rear, and took every man. The lieutenant on duty was the only person that escaped. The piquet was badly posted, and the ground not explained to Captain Lutchens. It was probably the first piquet he ever mounted, and on seeing enemy's troops on the road he looked to for retreat, had not his wits quite about him.

Captain Cocks joined his regiment, commanding the same squadron as before.

Headquarters of the army were in the Quinta San Juan, near Elvas.

Several officers got brevet rank for their services in the Peninsula, and Captain Cocks, not the least deserving, received his of a brevet majority.

Major-General Picton, with the 3rd and 7th Divisions, is encamped near Campo Mayor, and at night occupies the town with his own division. Lord Wellington intends, from the orders issued, to fight in the position of Campo Mayor. There are certain signals appointed to be made on the enemy's showing himself in any force on this side the Guadiana, and on infantry appearing in force, the whole army is to move into position. Lieutenant-General Hill, with the 2nd, 4th, and Major-General Hamilton's Portuguese division, is to occupy the right; Major-General Picton, with the 3rd and 7th, the centre; and Lieutenant-General Sir Brent Spencer the left (should the enemy move to the left of Campo Mayor), with the 1st, 5th and 6th. The Light Division on the left of the whole.

General Hill is called by the men "Daddy Hill," from his attention to them, being much esteemed by all ranks.

The position is very extensive, and should they attack on the right, before their troops can assemble in any force, we, being on the inner line, shall have time to move. The cavalry is to be distributed through the line, and Major-General De Grey's Heavy Brigade, with Anson's, are to move wherever the attack is made. It is the same position mentioned by La Lippe as a good one for covering Elvas from the Spanish frontier, though I conceive the left in that case would entirely rest on Campo Mayor, with the right more brought forward on the right bank of the Caya.

Lord Wellington rises at six every morning, and employs himself to nine (the breakfast hour) in writing. After breakfast, he sees the heads of departments, viz. Quarter-Master and Adjutant-General, Commissary-General, Commander of artillery, and any other officers coming to him on business. This occupies until 2 or 3 p.m., and sometimes longer, when he gets on his horse and rides to near six—this, of course, is interfered with when the troops are before the enemy. At nine he retires to write again, or employs himself until twelve, when he retires for the night. His correspondence with England, and the Spanish and Portuguese government, is very extensive.

I cannot think Soult will fight, having gained his object in the relief of Badajos; and should he gain a victory, he cannot push on for the conquest of Portugal. His force is not sufficient to render him by any means certain of success, and if he cannot beat us, and is beaten, I conceive we take Badajos. Our annihilation can be his only object, and after the lesson we taught him at Albuera, he will not again attempt that.

It is said the observation he made on that day was, "There is no beating these fellows, in spite of their Generals. I always thought them bad soldiers, and now I am sure of it; for I turned their right flank, penetrated their centre; they were completely beat and the day mine, but yet they would not run."

July 1st. It was the intention to make a reconnaissance on the 2nd towards Badajos, and orders came late this evening for Major Cocks, with his own troop and 34 men under Lieutenant Deakin of the Hussars, to move on the left by La Roca to secure that flank. We left our camp about sunset, and the brigade at the same time moved for the night to ground appointed for them in front of Campo Mayor. We marched about six leagues, within one of La Roca, and halted for about two hours at 2 a.m., on the morning of the 2nd. At daylight we proceeded on to La Roca, and Cocks, with Deakin, patrolled on towards Montejo, finding the enemy's piquets a league in front of the place, which, from peasants' reports, was occupied by 2,000 men. I remained at La Roca, and on the return of Cocks we marched to the rear of Valla del Rey, encamping in rear of the Albagarvena for the night. Major Cocks marched fifteen leagues. I not much less, being on my horse nearly the whole time he was absent.

July 3rd. We, this day, marched to Albuquerque, three leagues, encamping on the foot of the hill on which the town stands. The reconnaissance made by our cavalry in front of Campo Mayor did not gain much information, returning to their camp-ground as wise as when they left it.

The enemy's troops are all employed in threshing wheat for the provisioning of Badajos, which they intend to complete for four months. The Spanish force has left the army for Seville, and it is calculated that if they march quick, and the enemy does not gain very early information, they can arrive there before Soult can get down, and by destroying their works and depot, may much retard, if not altogether put a stop to, the siege of Cadiz.

The enemy have a foundry at Seville, where they make mortars which throw shells further than was ever before heard of.

On the 5th Major Cocks, with twenty-five men, was ordered up to La Roca; and on the 7th, Lieutenant Deakin, with twenty more, joined him, and with the remainder I marched to my regiment, which I found in their old camp at Torre de Mora, on the Caya. Our long march and fatigue had brought back a return of my ague, and I was obliged to get into a small house near the camp. The diversion made by the Spaniards obliged Soult to move on Seville, and the intention of the Spaniards was entirely lost, he arriving at Seville before they got half-way.

This left Marmont with 25,000 infantry, and thirty-two squadrons of cavalry. Soult took with him that force of infantry, and about half the number of cavalry.

July 12th. The enemy, this day, began their retreat, marching in Truxillo for Talavera de la Reigna, so passing the Tagus for

Palentia. One division of the army of Portugal remained south of the Tagus.

July 18th. The 3rd and 6th Divisions, with Major-General Slade's brigade of cavalry, began their march, under Major-General Picton, for Castello Branco; and on the 23rd, headquarters of the army moved to Portalegre. The same day the right wing of the 16th moved to Monte Porte, and the left to Barbecena, headquarters of the regiment to the latter place. Cavalry headquarters came to Mont Forte. The weather is dreadfully hot, and the army very sickly; they say more than 20,000 in hospital. During our stay at Torre de Mora camp, we had scarcely a sick man, and the instant we got into quarters, and the troops received money we had some in hospital, though compared to other regiments the 16th was very healthy.

Since the assembling of the army on the Caya, the cavalry has been divided into two divisions—the 1st under Lieutenant-General Sir S. Cotton: and the 2nd under Major-General Sir Wm. Erskine. Sir Stapleton commanded the whole when together.

The infantry are all cantoned in and about Portalegre, and on the right towards Elvas.

The following arrangement took place on the troops leaving their camp ground:-

1st Division of Cavalry, under Lieut-General Sir Stapleton Cotton;

1st (Royal) Dragoons 12th Light Dragoons	Major-General Slade's brigade.
13th Light Dragoons 16th Light Dragoons	Major-General Anson.
11th Light Dragoons 1st (Hussars) K.G.L.	Major-General Alten.

Brigadier-General Madden's Portuguese Division.

2nd Division, under Major-General Sir Wm. Erskine:

3rd Dragoon Guards 4th Dragoons	Major-General de Grey's brigade.

14th Light Dragoons   } Major-General Long.
2nd Hussars, K.G.L.   }
9th Light Dragoons, not yet joined from England.
Brigadier-General Otway's Portuguese brigade.

The weather during our stay at Mont Forte was excessively hot, and, excepting early in the morning and at night, it was impossible to move out.

The army became so sickly that Marmont having moved to Palentia, Lord Wellington determined to move into Upper Biera, which, at this time of the year, is much cooler, and at all times more healthy. On the 1st, he left Portalegre for the North, and put the whole army in motion for the other side the Tagus, leaving General Hill at Portalegre with 2nd Division of Infantry, Major-General Hamilton's Portuguese Division, and Major-General Long's brigade of cavalry, and all the Portuguese cavalry. On moving from the South the 14th Light Dragoons were ordered to Major-General Anson's brigade, and the 13th to General Long's. The 16th Light Dragoons made the following marches:—

August 1st. Assumar, one long league. Encamped, the 13th being in the town.

2nd. Portalegre;   occupied the town.   Three leagues.
3rd. Alpalliao.   Three leagues.
4th. Halt.
5th. Niza.   Two leagues.
6th. Villa Velha;   encamped on the right bank of the Tagus.
7th. Castello Branco; encamped on the old ground on going to the South.   Five leagues.

August 8th. The brigade, this day, moved into quarters. Captain Hay, with the left centre squadron, occupied Idanha Nova, with an advance on the Zarza la Mayor road leading to Palentia, the enemy occupying the former place. The other three squadrons moved to Lonza, two short leagues from Castello Branco, and the day following the right squadron occupied Escalhos de Baixo. Headquarters of the brigade were at Lonza. The 14th

Light Dragoons occupied S. Miguel de Arche and adjacents.

Headquarters of the army were at Castello des Flores, a short distance in rear of Fuente Guinaldo, in Spain, and shortly moved up to that place.

Our advance is towards the Puerta de Banos, leading to Palentia. Ciudad Rodrigo is said to be in great want of supplies, and that it is Lord W.'s intention not to allow Marmont to throw any in.

We were now in the most miserable, sickly place I was ever in. Scarcely a single officer enjoyed his health, and the men were becoming daily more sickly. I had my ague nearly every other day; and Major Pelly removed, in consequence of ill health, to Escalhos de Baixo.

August 31st. We received a route to move this day, and the regiment marched to Silleguel d'Arche, two leagues on the Sabugal road. The 14th Light Dragoons marched two leagues in our front.

Sept 1st. Marched four leagues to Penamacor, a good town which held the whole regiment; and though the 2nd Corps d'Armee was here some time before Massena's advance place is by no means much injured.

Sept 2nd. As we were to be cantoned in the villages in front of Guarda, we, this day, left the main road and marched near five leagues to small villages on the ground we encamped the night before the affair of Sabugal.

Sept 3rd. Headquarters of the brigade and regiment moved to Musella, Captain Cocks' squadron to Richioso, our old quarter. The 14th occupied the villages on the Coã near Castel Mando. On the 4th our squadron moved up to a small village near Misquitella, and the following day were obliged to march back to Richioso, the village being so small it would not hold us.

Sept 7th. The brigade, this day, moved up to the villages in Spain, situated on the Agueda, to the left of Gallegos, viz.:

Villa de Yegua: Headquarters brigade and regiment. Three squadrons 16th.

Sismeira: Headquarters cavalry, Major Cocks' squadron, 16th.

The 14th Light Dragoons occupied Matillian and adjacents. Major Pelly had been in a bad state of health for some time, and here left the regiment for England. Captain Hay succeeded him. Headquarters of the army were at Fuente Guinaldo, with the whole army closed up between the Coã and Agueda. The Light Division is on the right of Rodrigo, and a squadron of the 16th was sent to San Felices el Chico to look out towards Ladesma. We have parties of cavalry from Major-General Alten's brigade on the road from Rodrigo to Salamanca. The enemy have a considerable force at Salamanca, and likewise one near Palentia. In the former place they have a large convoy ready, which, the peasants say, consists of 300 cars and as many mules.

During our whole march we thought and heard Lord Wellington was about to besiege the place, and that our battering train had moved up the Douro, and so to Almeida, for the purpose.

On the 22nd September, our patrols met the enemy's advance on the road to Salamanca, and that night they were within five leagues of Ciudad Rodrigo.

They advanced by three roads, each party the same distance from the town. Their troops in the neighbourhood of Palentia made a similar movement on Rodrigo. The infantry to our left all marched this night towards Guinaldo and Espeja. The whole was concentrated near those points.

Sept 23rd. The brigade moved to Espeja, two short leagues from Cismeiro and encamped in front of the town. Lieutenant-General Graham had joined the army from Cadiz, and relieved Sir Brent Spencer in his command as second to Lord Wellington. We were happy in the change.

Lieutenant-General Graham was here placed with the 1st and 6th Divisions, the remainder of the army near and in front of Fuente Guinaldo. The enemy did not, this day, advance before evening to Rodrigo, and then only sent about sixty cavalry up to the gates. Their advance was halted two leagues from the place, and they do not like to bring up the convoy before their troops are well closed up. Our piquets arc on the high ground to the front of the Azava, and on the right in front of Elbodon.

Sept. 24th. The enemy, this day, moved a considerable force into Rodrigo, and pushed a few cavalry in front of the place. Our piquets, at night, retired in rear of the Azava, the enemy withdrawing in rear of the Agueda.

Sept. 25th. From the high ground our piquets held, we could overlook the whole of what they brought into Rodrigo; and this morning about eight, they advanced, driving our posts over the Azava. To Carpeo (the road on which we were) they came with fourteen squadrons of cavalry, leaving six near the village, and crossed the remainder over the Azava at the ford below the village. Major Cocks, with his own squadron and one of the 14th Light Dragoons, was sent down into the wood leading down to the Azava; and the brigade turned out in the open ground which extends a mile in front of Espeja. The two divisions were all ready to stand to their arms in the woods near Espeja.

With the two squadrons we found the piquets retiring a short distance on this side the Azava, and fell back a little to form in an open space in the wood sufficient for two squadrons. Major Cocks commanding the two, his squadron fell to me. The wood is sufficiently open to ride through, and we remained skirmishing for some time.

The enemy brought up their eight squadrons, and we retired through the wood on the brigade. In the open ground, a little in front of the Azava, they halted four of their squadrons, and with the remainder, two of Lancers and two of Hussars, they pushed forward up the wood. We let them come to just the edge of the wood near the plain, and the squadron of the 14th, with the piquets, charged and drove them back. They again rallied, and came back upon us, and we again fell back on the brigade. During this, the Light Companies from General Nulse's brigade in the 6th Division viz., 11th, 61st and 53rd, were ordered to the edge of the wood by General Graham, and the enemy pushed up most gallantly. We got out of the way of the infantry fire; they gave them a volley, and whilst they were firing, the two advanced squadrons, under Cocks, and two squadrons from the 16th, moved to charge. The enemy did not wait a moment, and we drove them two miles down the wood, taking every man the infantry hit, and several besides (in all about thirty), killing ten on the spot, with their commanding officer, Chief d'Escadron O'Flyn, an Irishman.

O'Flyn was taken prisoner, and whether from unwillingness to go to the rear, or from finding out that he was an Irishman, he was shot by Fitz-Patrick, a dragoon in the 16th, afterwards in my troop. This I had from Fitz-Patrick himself. The fellow said he was an Irishman, which the dragoon could not hear and allow him to escape alive. I never saw an affair in which a small force retired more regularly, and kept the eight squadrons from pressing on them; and when the time came to attack, Cocks led on his men most gallantly, and though not a third of the enemy in strength, our success was complete. It was a very well arranged affair.

They did not again attempt to come on, but withdrew to the other side the Azava, remaining for some time on the Carpeo high ground, and in the evening withdrew altogether, and our piquets occupied the line of the Azava. They took thirty-two men and five officers, badly wounded, through Carpeo. The Lancers looked well and formidable before they were broken and closed to by our men, and then their lances were an encumbrance. We asked the Lancers where they last marched from; they said, the Vistula, having come through France, without remaining any time.*

We had only one person (Lieutenant Hull, of the 14th) hurt with a lance, and when retiring, they got on the ground, caught in the appointments of other men, and pulled more dragoons off their horses than anything else.

Observations on seeing the prisoners we made, being so cut by those in the rear. The infantry said it was a shame to cut them so. On the right the enemy pushed on in much greater force over the plain to Fuente Guinaldo. The 3rd Division was in Elbodon, a league in front of Guinaldo, and not being withdrawn in time, one brigade, viz., Major-General Colville's of that division, and one regiment of Portuguese (21st), with three squadrons of the 11th Light Dragoons, and two of the 1st Hussars, were obliged

---

* *This was, I believe, the first occasion on which our cavalry came into contact with Lancers.*

to make a stand on the high ground to the front of Guinaldo covering the junction of the road from Elbodon.

The infantry took post on the hills covering the road, to ascend which the enemy's troops had a very steep ascent. The cavalry were formed ready to charge on the plain on which you enter on ascending, and the six guns from the division were placed on the hills raking the road. The enemy sent an immense body of cavalry, when compared to our few, about twenty squadrons, and charged up the hill in a most gallant manner. They passed the guns, and the 5th Regiment, lying down behind the brow of the hill, jumped up, charged the cavalry after giving them a volley, and drove them back.

Their troops on ascending the top were in confusion, but it is the first time I ever heard of infantry charging cavalry.

Their fire probably stopped them, and then seeing our troops advance they retired.

This check did not stop them, and they gained the hill to the left, obliging our infantry to go into square to cross the plain. During this some hard fighting took place, our cavalry charged the enemy's advance repeatedly—then got too far, and being so few fell back on the infantry. The 11th were particularly steady, and the whole got off with very little loss. Lord Wellington was there, and aware of the critical situation they were in. Our infantry behaved in their usual cool way, and the conduct of the 21st Portuguese was much spoken of.

Captain Childers of the 11th* was the officer who particularly exerted himself, to which the safety of the detachment is to be considerably ascribed. He charged bodies three times their number, rode at them with the greatest determination, and always succeeded. The conduct of the 11th Light Dragoons was such as must stamp them as soldiers doing their duty in a critical situation. Very flattering orders to the troops came out.

The enemy had crossed a considerable force over the Agueda,

---

* *Captain Michael Childers, younger son of Mr. Childers of Cantley, and great-uncle of the Right Hon. Hugh C. Childers, first Lord of the Admiralty 1868-74, and Chancellor of the Exchequer 1880-5. He was on the Duke's staff at Waterloo, and afterwards commanded the 11th Hussars.*

and some redoubts being thrown up near Guinaldo, Marmont thought we should stand there.

Sept. 26th. The infantry marched last night from Espeja to Nave de Aver, and on the right Lord Wellington evacuated Fuente Guinaldo, marching on Aldea de Ponte, in Portugal. We this morning retired to the Quinta de Agueda, two miles in front of Nave de Aver, and encamped in the wood.

Marmont yesterday got in the whole of his convoy for Rodrigo, and the very time Lord Wellington was marching from Fuente Guinaldo he was moving back to Rodrigo, it not being his object to fight, having gained his end. For this, however, he was obliged to collect 60,000 men, and some came all the way from Madrid for the sole object of throwing in the convoy. Our piquets remained on the Azava, and withdrew in the course of the day to the high ground in front of Espeja.

Circumstance of two privates of the Light Division being drunk, and when ordered to march off by one of Lord Wellington's staff, said they knew who it was that ordered them- "It was that long-nosed beggar that licks the French."

Sept. 27th. Marmont, finding that Lord Wellington had left Guinaldo, in order to have to say he had driven him into Portugal, countermanded his retreat, and advanced with this whole force on Guinaldo.

The wing of the army under Lieutenant-General Graham retired to the right of Villa Mayor, a league in rear of Nava d'Aver, and Lord Wellington, with the remainder, took up a position in rear of Aldea de Ponte. The enemy's advance came into that place, but their main force never advanced beyond Guinaldo. They had an affair in Aldea de Ponte in which they lost a good many from our artillery, and we too from the Fuzilier Brigade (7th and 23rd) in the 4th Division.

On burying an officer of the Fuzilier Brigade, there was no Prayer-Book to read the service from. Lieutenant George Brown, of the 23rd Regiment, stepped forward and repeated the service from recollection, and with exactness.

Headquarters quarters of the army were at Quadrasayes. Lieutenant-Colonel Graham, with his wing of the army, moved about midnight from his ground in front of Villa Mayor to his right in the rear of the position Lord Wellington had taken up.

Sept. 28th. We encamped a short distance in front of the Coã, and the move of last night proved useless; the enemy, after their affair in Aldea de Ponte, retired on Guinaldo and so across the Agueda on Salamanca.

Sept. 29th. Orders this day came out for the cantonment of the army. The Light Division, with Major-General Alten's brigade of cavalry, moved up to Guinaldo and adjacents, and the 4th to Gallegos and the adjoining villages.

Sept. 30th. The brigade this day marched on its route for cantonments near Freixedas, four leagues in rear of Almeida. The 16th halted in Villa Fernando this night.

October 1st. Major Bull's troop of horse artillery was attached to the brigade, which this day took up its cantonments occupying as follows, viz.:-

    Freixedas: Brigade headquarters, Captain Cocks' squadron. 16th Light Dragoons, Major Bull's guns.
    Souripere: Headquarters, 16th left centre squadron.
    Ervas Tendras: Right centre.
    Rigadinhea: Right squadron.
    Cavalry headquarters, Alverea, with Major-General de Grey's Heavy Brigade.

Headquarters of the army on the 30th moved to Richioso, where I believe they halted one day, and from thence moved up to Treneda, on the right bank of the Coã. The army was cantoned as follows:-

1st Division,		Lagioso, etc.
3rd	"	Aburgaria, etc.
4th	"	Gallegos, etc.
5th	"	Guarda, etc.
6th	"	The villages close in front of Freixedas.
7th	"	Pena Macor.
Light	"	Fuente Guinaldo.

The English battering train has arrived near Lamego from Oporto, on its way to Almeida, in which the guns are to be placed.

The whole of the cavalry was here reduced to three squadrons per regiment, and A and I troops of the 16th were ordered to England, the former belonging to Captain Macintosh and the latter to Captain Belli.

The right squadron moved from Rigadinhea to Ervas Tendras.

During our stay at Freixedas, the regiment did not receive its complement of corn, and latterly long forage became rather scarce. (Long forage means straw, hay is any other kind.)

Don Julian took Renaut, the Governor of Ciudad Rodrigo, and the enemy sending down a fresh one from Salamanca, Lord Wellington wished to shut the escort up in the place, and the troops from these quarters moved in consequence. It was too late, and their troops got safe back again.

One brigade of cavalry was upon the Agueda, doing the outpost duty round Rodrigo, and each remained there one month. Major-General Alten had been relieved by Major General Slade's, and it was now Anson's turn to move up.

The brigade this day moved from its quarters. The 16th marched to Castello Mendo, and Misquitella, our squadron to the latter place, three short leagues from Freixedas.

We, this day, moved to the villages we were to occupy.

Since the two troops had been sent home, Captain Macintosh

Had joined with a remount from England and took G troop. The following arrangement of squadrons was ordered.

We occupied

Gallegos: Headquarters brigade and regiment.
  Right squadron, G and D.
Espeja: Centre squadron, K and E.
Thuro: Left squadron, B.F., Major Cocks.

The 14th went to Elboden and adjacents. The 12th Light Dragoons had been in Thuro; we met them on their march to the rear, and never were horses in such a state. We found very few men for duty. The garrison of Rodrigo was all we had to watch, and they only 2,000. The infantry took nearly the whole of the duty at night, and in the day from Stuero we only found one vidette.

We, this day, moved to Puebla de Azava, and the whole of the infantry closed up to near Guinaldo, to which place headquarters moved from Frineda. It was with the idea that the enemy were preparing another convoy, and had it been so, it was Lord Wellington's intention to prevent them. The other two squadrons of the 16th came to Castellejo, a little on our left.

Headquarters this day left Guinaldo for Frineda, and the whole army moved back to its former post. Cavalry headquarters up from Alverea to Stuero, and moved from thence to Covilha, in the valley of the Zezere.

The Light, 3rd and 4th Divisions were ordered to make fascines and gabions, and at headquarters the siege of Ciudad Rodrigo is talked of. Every one says that it is only to make Marmont collect his forces and prevent his detaching. The engineers say that it cannot be for besieging Rodrigo, as the fascines are made so far from the place that we have not transport to carry them there. The time of year is another objection. The staff corps are throwing a bridge over the Agueda at Molleno de Floris.

Major-General Anson left the brigade for England. The weather was extremely severe. The horses got nothing by way of long forage but the long grass which the men cut themselves from out of the woods, for which they daily went a league. We were frequently eight and nine days without corn, and in consequence lost many horses.

There was no straw in the country, and from the horses being so starved, they eat the withered grass with so much avidity that they swallowed many of the stones at the roots, and died in consequence.

Stuero, January 1st, 1812. The brigade having remained up in the country round Ciudad Rodrigo the appointed time, this day began its march to the rear, being relieved by three squadrons only from Major-General de Grey's Brigade, it being found that they could do all the duty, and that it was only (by sending a whole brigade) destroying the troops. This should have been done at the first, and some hundreds of horses would have been saved. We marched as follows:—

    1st. Caste Mendo and Misquitella one squadron to the latter, three leagues.
    2nd. Alverea, three leagues.
    3rd. Soure and adjacents, two leagues.
    4th. Gouvea and adjacents, our squadron Valla Cortes.
    5th. Coã and adjacents.

Lieutenant-Colonel Harvey commanded the brigade and was quartered at Villa Nova, the 16th occupied the following villages, and through Captain Murray's joining from England the squadrons were changed.

Right squadron, headquarters.

K, Captain Hay
E, Captain Ashworth, England
} Moimento

Centre squadron

B, Major Cocks'
D, Captain Swetenham
} Coã

Left squadron.

F, Captain Murray
G, Captain Macintosh
} Santa Marinha

After our arrival at Coã we lost a number of horses, Major Cocks' troop six, and all the others in the same proportion.

After our mules had time to go to the Mondego for supplies, we got our ten pounds of corn a day, and the Juis de Fora,

In all the villages where the troops were cantoned, supplied them with straw without sending out for it with the horses.

Major Cocks, after our march from Stuero on the 1st, remained at headquarters of the army for one night and joined again at Alverea. From him we heard that Ciudad Rodrigo was to be besieged, and on the 7th that ground was to be broken before the place. The 5th and 6th Divisions had been for some time back in the neighbourhood of Olivera de Hospital, and moved up from thence to cover the siege of Rodrigo.

We expected, from having been so lately sent down, not to have been called up, but on the night of the 12th January, the route arrived—

January 13th. Headquarters regiment, Liniares.
     Major Cocks' squadron, Valla Cortes.
" *14th.* Liniares, the whole regiment assembled.
" *15th.* Freixedas, seven leagues, 14th to Alverea.

Major Cocks left on the 13th to see the siege. His leave came from Lord Wellington, and I had made a similar application to cavalry headquarters.

We left the greatest number of our bad horses at Coã, and found more forage in Freixedas and neighbourhood than I should have thought.

Siege of Ciudad Rodrigo, taken by Lord Viscount Wellington, 19th January, 1812.

The garrison on paper was 2,000 men, 1,500 or rather more fit for duty, with Baron Barrier, General de Brigade, as Governor. The artillery were two companies, 100 each, and excellent. The remainder of the garrison was said to be in a bad, sickly state.

Headquarters of Lord Wellington moved from Frineda to Gallegos, and the following troops were employed in the siege.

     Light Division.
     1st Division.
     4th Division.
     3rd Division.

One Division came on duty daily, and in the above rotation. They found working parties and everything; the General of the Division had the direction for the twenty-four hours.

They were all cantoned in the adjacent villages, so that, excepting on duty, they were under cover in quarters. The 5th and 6th Divisions crossed the Coã and were cantoned near Almeida, and the 7th came up from Penamacor, near Fuente Guinaldo.

Thirty 24-pounders and eighteen 18-pounders were moved from Almeida, crossed the Agueda at the bridge constructed by the army at Molleno de Floris, and were employed in the siege.

January 8th. A detachment from the Light Division this night attacked the detached work of San Francisco. The detachment was commanded by Lieutenant-Colonel Colborne, of the 52nd Regiment. They were provided with ladders, and on leaping into the ditch over the palisades, attempted to get up the wall of the fort by their ladders. They were made from the rails of a Spanish car and all gave way, when they stuck their bayonets into the sod wall and by that means carried the work. The enemy on seeing our men get into their work all retired into a small guard house in the centre of the fort, and there surrendered—in all, two officers and fifty men. The garrison, on hearing the fire, turned out, but too late to do anything, our people being in full possession of the place. Ground was broken the same night, within 300 toises of the body of the place. The fort, being open in its gorge towards the town, was not tenable, and destroyed as soon as we took it.

On the evening of the 14th January, three batteries were ready, and twenty-four guns opened their fire at 550 yards from the town. On the right and left of the approaches are two convents; and that on the right, Santa Crux, was taken by the German Legion on the 13th, on the left the 40th Regiment from the 4th Division carried the one of San Fransisco. In the latter the enemy had two howitzers, which completely enfiladed our approaches, and from which we lost Captain Ross, one of the best engineers in the service.

On the night of the 15th our approaches were pushed in front of the first parallel, and a battery placed on the left in advance of the second parallel. It consisted of seven guns, and opened on the morning of the 18th, about one hundred yards nearer than the first batteries.

The town is surrounded by an old wall, which is so much

above the glacis that from the hill of San Francisco the place is to be breached. The glacis itself is so steep that the crest of it was battered in. There is no covered way, nor regular bastions, and only one raveline, which the French, since they took the place, have added at the turn of the wall.

From the 13th to the 19th the second parallel was completed, and some advance made from it to the crest of the glacis.

On the 19th two practicable breaches were made; and orders were issued for the 3rd and Light Divisions to storm, the Light on the left by the small breach formed by the 7-Gun Battery, and the 3rd by the main breach on the right formed from the first guns that opened.

About an hour after dark the divisions moved from the trenches, and in half an hour after the attack was made the place was in our possession, the garrison surrendering, with its governor, prisoners of war. We took Baron Barrier, General de Bogade, Governor, 78 officers, 1700 rank and file.

The garrison consisted of one weak regiment of French infantry, one German, one Italian—the last as strong as the other two. The artillery (two companies) were the only good part of the whole, and did all they could to prolong its defence.

The governor at the time we stormed was going to dinner, and had not made his appearance for the last two days in the ramparts. He behaved very ill, but with his weak garrison could not have held out until Marmont could arrive. We lost Major-General MacKinnon, of the 3rd Division, and Major-General Robert Crawford, who died of the wounds he received at the head of his division; the former was blown up by the explosion of a powder magazine, by which we lost 150 men killed and wounded. In General Crawford the army has sustained a great loss; he was hot in his temper, but knew when duty was done, and did it himself. He was the best outpost officer in the army; he was killed urging a man of the Light Division on up the breach.

Our loss in the whole is 900, out of which 300 are trifling cases. Our troops plundered the town, and it was not before daylight on the 20th that any order could be restored. Three or four houses were burnt through accident.

Lieutenant Wheeler* and I left Freixedas on the 19th; slept that night at Almeida, on the following day proceeded to Gallegos, and on the 21st visited the town and works of Rodrigo. We returned to our regiment on the 23rd.

At Gallegos, the report ran that the army was to be closed down by degrees to the Tagus, and that under idea of the troops receiving their clothing and camp equipage, the divisions were to move on their route to besiege Badajos. The 5th Division was put into Rodrigo to repair the works and destroy our approaches.

Marmont made some show of relieving Rodrigo, and the Governor said that it was promised that he would be at Rodrigo on the 25th of January.

After the siege, the army remained on the Coã until Marmont had heard the place had fallen and cantoned his troops. During the siege the weather was particularly favourable, the frost continued the whole time. This made the trenches dry and the men work hard to keep themselves warm. Some of the Portuguese lost their fingers through cold.

January 30th. A route arrived this day for the brigade to move back to its former quarters, near Coã; we marched:—

January 30th.	Soure and Lagioso,	2 leagues.
January 31st.	Millo and adjacents,	4 leagues.
February 1st.	Coã and adjacents,	2 leagues.

The headquarters of the brigade went to Seixo, the 12th Light Dragoons being placed to the brigade; Lieutenant-Colonel Ponsonby, being senior to Lieutenant-Colonel Harvey, took the command. The brigades of cavalry are now all nine squadrons, excepting Major-General Alten's. The 16th occupied as follows:—

Coã (headquarters)	Right squadron.
Santa Marinha	Centre squadron.
Moimento	Left squadron.

* *Afterwards Sir Trevor Wheeler, d. 1869.*

A day after our arrival Captain Swetenham's troop, from the centre squadron, and Captain Macintosh's troop, from the right, were ordered to occupy San Rosnan. This gave a squadron to Swetenham, who was not entitled to one, and took squadrons from two officers, viz.: Captain Murray and Major Cocks, both his senior, and permanently commanding their squadrons in the regiment. Our Colonel is uncle to Swetenham.

Major Stanhope was gazetted out of the 16th to the 17th Light Dragoons as Lieutenant-Colonel, in reward for the long campaign he has had in Bond Street since the time he left the 16th in July, 1810. Captain Hay got the majority, Lieutenant Persse the troop.

The regiment in these quarters received its full allowance of corn; the horses in better spirits, and will do well till the grass comes; but after the starvation they have endured they will never thoroughly come about before spring.

February 16th. We, this day, set off, viz.: Major Cocks, Swetenham, Lieutenant Foster, 14th Light Dragoons, and myself to a hall at Covilha, cavalry headquarters. We had to pass the Sierra de Estrella, on the other side of which Covilha is situated. We, this day, walked three leagues over the steepest and highest hills I ever passed, and halted at Montegas, in the very centre of the Sierra. Montegas is the place where all the people in this part of Portugal went on Massena's advance and retreat, and now all their valuables arc deposited in the place. It is situated at the mouth of the Zezere, and surrounded on all sides by the most inaccessible steep mountains; before descending to it from Santa Marinha, it looked about a mile off, and took us one hour to get down.

Lieutenant-Colonel Ponsonby had gone through the day before, and an orderly man went after him with a route for the brigade, which obliged us to return the following day to Santa Marinha. Headquarters of the army still remained at Frineda; some of the infantry had moved for the Tagus. The 1st Division has gone down to Abrantis, to receive its clothing. The 12th Light Dragoons moved on the route with ourselves; the 14th more to the right by the Ponte Murcella.

Route for the march of the 16th Light Dragoons from Coã to Thomar:-

February 18th.	{ Captain Murray's troop.	Iorrogella.
	{ Major Cocks' troop	Failadoza, 2 leagues
February 19th.	{ Right squadron	Avon (headquarters)
	{ Left squadron	Venda de Porco
	D troop	Gallens.
	B.	
February 20th.	{ Right and Left squadrons	Arganil.
	{ Centre squadron	Boidiera.
" 21st.		
" 22nd.		
" 23rd.	Espinhel	Left squadron detached as yesterday
" 24th.	{ Cabaces.	Centre squadron at Alfiazue. Captain Macintosh's troop at a Quinta near Cabaces.
" 25th.	Thomar	the whole regiment.

The 16th occupied the convent, which held the whole regiment at the top of the hill; the 12th and 14th Light Dragoons were put up in the town.

Thomar is the third best town I have seen in Portugal, and although the 6th Corps d'Armee was in it the whole time the French were in their cantonments near Santarem, it is not in the least destroyed; the people are by no means averse to the French, and saved their houses by remaining in them.

Chapter Three
Winter of 1811 and Spring of 1812.

The procuring of forage through this winter for the horses was attended with the greatest difficulty, both to men and horses.

The detachments left their quarters soon after daylight, and were absent from six to eight hours generally, and frequently until dark. The peasants hid their straw with the greatest care, being the only chance they had of keeping what few oxen remained to them, for the purpose of agriculture, alive until the spring. They hid their straw behind stores of wood laid by for fuel, which two or three dragoons would remove with several hours' work, and possibly not find three or four days' supply for three or four horses. The carrying it away was always attended with the complaints and lamentations of the women, who followed us out of the place saying then their oxen must now die. The officers always sent their baggage mules and bat-men for forage, and each dragoon brought back what he procured for the use of his own horse. Nothing but this would have induced them to exert themselves as they did; and on the return home of the party, which was always under the command of a subaltern officer, it was amusing to hear the different tales one dragoon to another of the success he had met with and the plans of the inhabitants to save their straw. It was frequently found under their beds. The scarcity towards the last was so great, we took it out of the beds they lay upon. The dragoons were at last so knowing, and got to find out every place likely to have straw in it, that nearly every bit through the country was used, and I do not think we could have stayed another month without half of the horses dying of hunger. When we entered a village, most of the men hid themselves, from being afraid of our taking them as guides, or threatening them in some way to oblige them to point out where the straw was hid. The women exerted themselves in doing all they could to mislead us; and on our finding any, assailed us with cries and entreaties to leave some for their oxen. These were always directed to the officer of the party. We have frequently gone four and five leagues from our quarters.

February 26th. The 16th marched this day to Torres Novas, three long leagues. The 14th remained in Thomar. The 12th moved to a village near Abrantis.

Captain Swetenham left the regiment for England, being placed on the strength of the depot. In consequence of his departure I was appointed to the command of his troop, and left Cocks after having been with him for nearly two years. I before refused the command of a troop out of his squadron, and would not have taken this had it been out of the one under his command.

Torres Novas was the headquarters of the French the time they kept the position of Santarem. Many of the best houses were preserved, from having general officers in them, and Massena's just in the state in which he left it. The inhabitants, like those of Thomar, remained in their houses, for which some have since been taken up. We were the first British that entered since the retreat, and they were anxious to show us they had quite forgotten their former friends.

Lord Wellington, for the taking of Ciudad Rodrigo and for the last campaign, was made an Earl.

The day after our arrival we received the following route and marched agreeably to it.

March 3rd.	Tunhete and Saucos, headquarters, former, Major Cocks' squadron, Saucos, three leagues.
March 4th.	Abrantis, three leagues
March 5th.	Ponte de Lor, Alentigo, five leagues.
March 6th.	Avis and adjacents.

The 12th and 14th marched in our advance one day, and the 14th occupied Frontura. Headquarters of the brigade, with the 12th, were at Souzel. The right and centre squadrons, 16th, occupied Avis; the left went to Ervidal, a long league on the Estremos road.

We here began to use the green forage, which we got in great abundance. The barley was just fit to cut, and improved the horses a good deal. From the starvation in the winter most of the horses threw out mange, and there was scarcely a dollar in the regiment to buy medicines. Had not a druggist in Avis given some, on promise of payment, I do not know what we would have done. In Avis, the inhabitants have never before seen English troops, and expected you to subsist without eating their corn or burning their wood for cooking. They are extremely uncivil, with all the parade of the old Portuguese; promise you rations of green forage at 10 in the morning, which are not ready before 4 p.m., and then do not give you full weight. They tell the colonel that if he allows the troops to cut it, they will report him to Lord Wellington, and he is fool enough to be determined by what they say. The consequence was, that the horses did not improve so fast as they should have done.

The whole army has crossed the Tagus, and assembled in the neighbourhood of Portalegre. Lieutenant-General Sir Rowland Hill is up at Albuquerque, in Spain, with the 2nd, and Major-General Hamilton's Portuguese Division. He pushed on to Merida, where General Drouet (Count d'Erlon) was quartered with 5,000 men, and had thrown up some field works in front of the place.

On our troops moving up, he retired. Our advance from the 9th Light Dragoons had a trifling affair with their rear.

A mail steamer arrived from England bringing the appointment of Major Cocks to a majority in the 79th (Highland) Regiment.

1st March, 1812.
Statement Of The Allied British And Portuguese Army, Under The Earl Of Wellington.

First Division.
Lieutenant-General Sir Thomas Graham, Second in Command.
Major-General Stopford's Brigade.
2nd and 3rd Guards, one Battalion each.
1 Company, 60th Regiment, Rifle.

Major-General Lowe's Brigade.
3 Battalions, King's German Legion.
Major-General Wheatley's Brigade,—Highland.
22nd Regiment, 1st and 2nd Battalion, 79th Regiment.

SECOND DIVISION.
LIEUTENANT-GENERAL SIR ROWLAND HILL.
Major-General Howarth's Brigade.
50th, 71st, and 92nd Regiments.
Colonel Ashworth's Portuguese Brigade.
6th and 18th Regiments.
Major-General Lumley's Brigade.
Three Provisional Battalions, 28th, 34th and 39th Regiments.

THIRD DIVISION.
LIEUTENANT-GENERAL PICTON.—TEMPORARY RANK.
Major-General Kemp's Brigade-late MacKinnon's.
45th, 74th and 88th Regiments.
Lieutenant-Colonel Sutton's Portuguese Brigade.
9th and 21st Regiments.
Major-General Colville's Brigade.
5th, 77th, 83rd and 94th Regiments.

FOURTH DIVISION.
LIEUTENANT-GENERAL COLE.-TEMPORARY RANK
Major-General Kimmi's Brigade.
27th, 40th, and 97th Regiments. Brigadier-General Harvey's Portuguese Brigade. 11th and 23rd. One Battalion Lusitanian Legion.
Major-General Bower's Brigade.
7th, 23rd and 48th Regiments.

FIFTH DIVISION.
LIEUTENANT-GENERAL LEITH.-TEMPORARY RANK.
Major-General Hay's Brigade.
1st, 9th and 38th Regiments.
Portuguese Brigade.
Major-General Walker's Brigade.
4th, 30th and 44th Regiments.

SIXTH DIVISION.
MAJOR-GENERAL CLINTON.
Major-General Burne's Brigade.
2nd, 32nd and 36th Regiments.
Brigadier-General Baron Eaten's Portuguese Brigade.
8th and 12th Regiments.
Major-General Hulse's Brigade.
11th, 53rd and 61st Regiments.

SEVENTH DIVISION.
MAJOR-GENERAL HOUSTON.—ABSENT IN ENGLAND.
Major-General Soutag's Brigade.
51st, 85th and Chasseurs Brittaniques.
68th and Brunswick, afterwards added to the 1st Brigade, 85th, went home.
Major-General Baron Alten's Brigade.
Two Light Battalions, K.G.L. In command of Division.
Light Division, vacant by the death of Major-General Robert Crawford.
Major-General Baron Alten appointed to it after the siege of Badajos.
Colonel Beckwith's Brigade.
43rd, 3rd Portuguese Cacadores, half-Battalion, 95th Regiment.
Major-General Vandeleur's Brigade.
52nd half-Battalion, 95th, 1st Portuguese Cacadores.
MAJOR-GENERAL HAMILTON'S PORTUGUESE DIVISION OF INFANTRY.
Two independent Brigades not attached to Divisions.
Portuguese. Brigadier   General Pack's.
1st, 16th Regiments, one Battalion Cacadores.
Brigadier-General Bradford's.

CAVALRY.
LIEUTENANT-GENERAL STAPLETON COTTON, BART.
Major-General Le Merchant's Brigade, 9 Squadrons Heavy.
3rd Dragoons, 4th Dragoons, 5th Dragoon Guards.
Major-General Bock's Brigade, 6 Squadrons Heavy.
1st and 2nd Dragoons, K. G. Legion.
Major-General Anson's Brigade, 9 Squadrons Light,
12th, 14th and 16th Light Dragoons.
Major-General Alten's Brigade, 6 Squadrons Light.

11th Light Dragoons, 1st Hussars, K. G. Legion.
Cavalry, with Lieutenant-General Sir William Erskine in the south, under Sir Rowland Hill, Second Division.

Major-General Slade's Brigade, 9 Squadrons Heavy.
1st (Royals) Dragoons, 3rd Dragoon Guards, 4th Dragoon Guards. Portuguese Cavalry very weak; some with Sir William Erskine, and some in the north.

Major-General Long's Brigade, 9 Squadrons Light.
9th Light Dragoons, 13th Light Dragoons, 2nd Hussars, K. G. L.

Cant names in the army for the Divisions:—

Light Division.	The Division.
1st Division.	The Gentlemen's Sons.
2nd Division.	The Observing Division.
3rd Division.	The Fighting Division.
4th Division.	The Supporting Division. After the affair in the Pyrenees, they were called the Enthusiastics.
5th Division.	The Pioneers.
6th Division.	The Marching Division.
7th Division.	They tell us there is a 7th, but we have never seen them.

Headquarters of the army arrived from Freneda on the 11th, at Elvas, and on the 15th a route arrived for our brigade to move up nearer Elvas. The 16th marched.

March 16th.	Canno and Sousel, three troops to each three leagues.
March 17th.	Estremas, two leagues.
March 18th.	Villa Vicosia, three leagues.

The 12th and 14th arrived the two preceding days; the former was in one of the adjacent villages, and the latter, with the 16th, occupied the town of Villa Vicosia. It held both regiments with the greatest ease. It is one of the best towns in Portugal. Before the revolution, it had been the summer residence of the court. The palace, like all their other buildings, was a large place made without the least plan, one room leading out of another. It had long been destroyed by the different troops that were quartered in the place, and occupied by us as a barrack for the men. Close to the town there is a large park stocked with deer, and after the campaign of 1809, the 16th were quartered a long time in Villa Vicosia, and then shot as many deer as they pleased. Now no one is allowed to shoot without an order from Lord Wellington or the Regency.

The whole army had now assembled near Badajos, excepting the 1st Hussars, K.G.L., which was left with Major-General Alten up in front of Ciudad Rodrigo, watching the French force at Salamanca, under Marmont.

The siege of Badajos commenced on the 17th, when ground was broken before the place, and Lord Wellington, the following day, came and encamped with the troops employed. The following divisions were fixed on, and had tents issued to them for the siege; 3rd and 4th and Light, Sir Thomas Graham, with 23,000 men, has moved up to Villa Franca and adjacents to cover the siege. Sir Rowland, with the 2nd and Portuguese Divisions, is at Merida. During our stay at Villa Vicosia I went with Penrice to see the siege of Badajos, and arrived there on the 25th; remained that night and saw the Fort Piquerena taken. Returned to Villa Vicosia on the 26th.

March 29th. The brigade marched from Villa Vicosia; the 16th to Villa Biere, two leagues.

March 30th. Marched this morning by Elvas down to the pontoon bridge over the Guadiana. The whole brigade halted in Olivenza; marched 6 leagues.

March 31st. Olivenza. The Brigade of Heavy Germans, under Major-General Baron Bock, this day crossed the Guadiana for Olivenza. We had now five regiments in the town, with the exception of the left squadron of the 16th Light Dragoons, which had moved the day after our arrival to Aldea de George, one league from Olivenza. The place was as full as it could be, but at this time of year it does not signify where a horse stands. The grazing near the town was excellent, and the horses through it improved much.

The Heavy Germans are fine regiments, though they will not, I think, stand this country. Their men are full-sized for their horses, which have been shaken by the English system of quick field days, nor are they the first regiments that have suffered from the same cause. We do everything so quickly that it is impossible men can understand what they are about. They have enough to do to sit their horse and keep in the ranks, without giving their attention to any sudden order. Before the enemy, excepting in charging, I never saw troops go beyond a trot, though in some cases it might be required, and therefore in some movements they should be taught to gallop.*These are few, such as moving to a flank in open column of divisions or half squadrons, wheeling into line and charging without a halt. In England I never saw nor heard of cavalry taught to charge, disperse and form, which, if I only taught a regiment one thing, I think it should be that. To attempt giving men or officers any idea in England of outpost duty was considered absurd, and when they came abroad, they had all this to learn. The fact was, there was no one to teach them. Sir Stapleton Cotton tried, at Woodbridge in Suffolk, with the 14th and 16th Light Dragoons, and got the enemy's vedettes and his own looking the same way. There is much to be learnt in service which cannot be done at home, though I do not mean to say nothing can be taught in England.

 The bridge of pontoons over the Guadiana having once failed, Lord Wellington was determined that all his troops should

---

* 1819. *This was an established option in Spain, and yet on our return to English duty we continue the old system, each regiment estimating its merit by the celerity of movement. I do not think one idea has been suggested since our return from service by the experience we there gained, and in five years we shall have all to commence again on going abroad. We never teach our men to disperse and form again, which of all things, before an enemy, is the most essential. Inclining in line left and right is very useful, and this is scarcely ever practised. Moving quick to a flank in a column of divisions is also very useful, and we might nearly limit any quick pace to this and charging. In the latter there is more to be taught men than is generally considered worthy of service. They should be kept extremely well together until the squadron officer commences his hurra, and then, in England, they should be taught to disperse as if in pursuit of a broken enemy, with as much confusion as possible, but to form instantly on hearing the bugle, or rather retreat at the sound, and for fear anything should happen to the trumpeter, to return by word. This should be explained; the old soldiers would enter into it for the vanity of instructing those who had never been on service, and so the practice would be continued. But we go on with the old close column and change of position.*

come on this bank, and the Germans were the last over, with the exception of a brigade of Portuguese left near Campo Mayor to watch San Christoval.

The inhabitants of Olivenza are half Spaniards and Portuguese. In the late war it was given up to the former, and Campo Mayor to the latter.

We had a very pleasant halt at Olivenza. The town had many families in it, who had left Badajos in consequence of the siege (many were shut in, through the short notice of our besieging it). We had several balls, and on hearing the guns firing at their houses, they would joke and say that was probably at their house-I knew one family whose house was close to the point we were breaching. They told me they were aware their residence must be destroyed, and therefore knew all that could befal them—they were not in the least vexed or dispirited.

April 3rd. The route arrived last night for the brigade to move up to relieve the heavy brigade, under Major-General Le Marchant, on the outpost duty.

April 4th. The 14th and 16th moved to Villa Alba, three leagues; the 12th to Fuente del Maestro, a league on our right. The wing of the army under Sir Thomas Graham is falling back; the troops this day marched to Santa Martha.

Major Cocks brought with him from the siege of Badajos an order to do duty in the 16th as major, and here joined us.

April 5th. The brigade moved and occupied the following places two leagues in front of Villa Alba:—

12th Light Dragoons, Los Santos—headquarters brigade.
14th Light Dragoons, Villa Franca.
16th Light Dragoons, Do.

Major Cocks was sent with his own squadron, 16th, and Captain Mills of the 14th, to Rebiera, a short league in front of Villa

---

Regular signals should be established throughout the cavalry, so as to be understood by all. In Gallegos, in 1810, we had the following:-

When the enemy appeared, the vidette put his cap on his carbine. When he only saw cavalry, he turned his horse round in a circle to the left; when infantry, to the right. If the enemy advanced quick, he cantered his horse in a circle, and if not noticed, fired his carbine. He held his post until the enemy came close to him, and in retiring kept firing.

Franca. The heavies marched to the rear. Cavalry headquarters were in Villa Franca. Marshal Soult (Duc de Dalmatia) is moving up from Seville to relieve Badajos. His advance patrolled into Bienvenida (four leagues in our front) this day. As yet we have no idea of his force.

Lieutenant-General Sir Thomas Graham this day left Villa Franca with the remainder of the infantry for Albuera, where, should Soult advance, it is the intention to fight.

April 6th. For the time the heavy brigade occupied these quarters the duty had been done by one or two detached parties, under different officers, of ten men each; and now that they had come close to us, instead of a regular chain of posts, the same mode was adopted. This did very well when the enemy had not any troops within eight or ten leagues, but I now think the thing is altered, and if we do not mind, some of our parties will be taken. We are only just come to the country; the enemy have been here for the last two years, and know every lane hereabouts.

If they take a piquet or detachment of ours, half the force will immediately be put on duty, and on the enemy retiring fifty leagues, the same will be observed.

I marched this morning with a party of ten men to relieve an officer of the Royals at Llerena, four leagues from Rebiera, on the left-hand road to the south. Captain Badcock, of the 14th, went with the same detachment on the main road, and was either to remain in Usagre or somewhere near it. The enemy were in both places before we could get there, and I met the officer of the Royals coming back. I halted at Hinioja, two leagues from Rebiera, and Badcock about the same distance on the Usagre road. The detachment of the enemy that entered Llerena was only a flanking party, and left the place when a patrol of mine entered it.

I was ordered by Cocks to join Badcock, and at dark marched a league to the right, to unite with him on the main road. All was quiet through the night.

The system of supplying an army by means of mules in Spain and Portugal is brought to the greatest perfection. There are about sixty mules to every cavalry regiment, for the purpose of supplying bread to the men and corn to the horses. Each mule is hired at the rate of a dollar a day, and the muleteers have each a dollar per diem. There is one muleteer to every five or six mules. Reckoning about sixty mules and ten muleteers,—in all seventy,—and the dollar at 5s, it will amount per diem for each regiment to £17 10s.- equal to £6387 per annum. The dollar was not procured at 5s; government generally paid 6s., and in many instances 6s. 6d., and even at that rate were obliged to have agents in all parts for the purpose of procuring them. The calculation made, at 6s. for the dollar, amounts to £21 per diem, or £7,665 per annum. There were never less than ten regiments of cavalry, which, for the supply of cavalry alone, would come to, the dollar at 5s., £63,870 per annum – the dollar at 6s., to £76,650 per annum. The difficulty in procuring dollars was so great that the army was always six months, and frequently eight months, in arrear, and the muleteers two years and sometimes longer. There were, besides the mules for the cavalry, a certain number to each division of infantry, and a large train attached to the commissary-general, headquarters, etc. The expense of supplying the army was not to be calculated. At one time, during the winter of 1811, it was said a horse's ration cost government, transported to the banks of the Coã, at the rate of 10s. 6d. per diem. Oats and hay came from England, were brought, at an enormous expense, in vessels to the Tagus, and then transported up the country by means of mules or bullock cars at the rate I have stated. The hay from England did not come out in any quantity, being only used for the horses at headquarters and some stationed at Lisbon, etc. There was frequently a considerable supply of specie at Lisbon, and when the muleteers demanded payment, threatening to leave if not paid in part, an order was given them on Lisbon for a certain amount. They had no means of procuring this money, and in many instances agreed to receive a much less sum for their order, it being paid them in ready money. These orders were called *vals*, from the Portuguese verb *valer*—to be worth. The only persons with the army who could buy these *vals* were the commissaries (with the public money), which in many instances they managed to speculate with, giving the muleteers for their *vals* a third, and, in some cases, a fourth less than their value. These vals were sent by them Lisbon; they received the dollars at 5s., when the Paymaster-General gave them an order on the Treasury in England at 6s. per dollar, or at whatever rate government were taking up the dollar—frequently at 6s. 6d. Had any person come out to the army with a large supply of dollars, he might have made cent, per cent.

In the first instance, it was difficult to get any muleteers to serve the army. They were all Spaniards, and probably a large sum was requisite to induce them to enter the service.

If any amount could have been raised to pay them up within six months, I have no doubt much more reasonable terms might have been obtained. A dollar per diem for each mule was an immense allowance. They, however, were quite requisite to the army, and any disturbance with them would have deprived us of supplies and consequently crippled our operations. The system, though expensive, was excellent, and the army continued its operations in countries where there was nothing to be had, and where any other army without mules would not have remained. Our advance from the lines in 1811, through a country completely exhausted, was most wonderful. The enemy were quite astonished how we got on.

April 7th. The brigade, with the two squadrons from Rebiera retired last night, and before morning an order reached us to retire at daylight on Villa Franca. I marched to Rebiera, Captain Badcock remaining with three men to see if the enemy were coming on. They appeared an hour after daylight, and drove him in at a gallop. On his arrival at Rebiera, he ordered me to Villa Franca, in the rear of which place I found the two squadrons under Major Cocks. The enemy advanced on that place, and pushed on between the village and the place where we formed. The squadron of the 14th was ordered by Sir Stapleton to retire on Fuente del Maestro, and that of the 16th on Villa Alba. They drove back the squadrons a mile in rear of Villa Franca, and then the country becoming woody, they did not follow us. I joined Major Cocks, who had retired with the 14th at Fuente del Maestro.

We hear that Badajos was taken by assault last night (see following account). Soult brought 23,000 infantry and 3,500 cavalry. Two divisions had come all the way from Talavera de la Reyna, on the Tagus (where we fought), and a third from Toledo. Suchet was said to be on the march to join with what should make him 40,000, with which he was determined to fight. We could have brought 50,000 without taking a man from the siege.

The people in Villa Franca said that when he heard of the fall of Badajos, he broke all the plates and dishes in the house.

The enemy, at the time they had moved on Villa Franca, pushed another column on Fuente del Maestro, through Los Santos, which at 3 p.m. made its appearance, and pushed on in the rear of the village. The enemy were about placing their piquets when we began to skirmish, which continued till dark, and in which the 14th lost two horses.

The brigade had retired a long mile in rear of the Guadaljore, and there encamped. The squadron of the 16th, detached with Major Cocks, was relieved by one of the 12th. At night he retired in rear of the river, three miles from Fuente del Maestro. The enemy occupied that place in force. Soult came to Villa Franca.

ACCOUNT OF THE SIEGE OF BADAJOS, TAKEN BY THE EARL OF WELLINGTON, 6TH APRIL, 1812.

March 17th, 1812. The 3rd, 4th, and Light Divisions, amounting to 11,500 men, this day marched from Elvas to invest Badajos.

They encamped on the left bank of the Guadiana, on the south of the town. Ground was broken the same night, and the first parallel formed, the right of which was brought within 500 yards of the body of the place.

The garrison consisted of 5,000 infantry and 60 cavalry, with Philippon, their Governor-General of Division in the French service—a rank which he gained by his defence against Marshal Beresford and Lord Wellington in April and June, 1811, being then only General de Brigade. Eighteen guns, 24-pounders, had been left at Lisbon from our train that moved to Oporto, and so up to Almeida to besiege Ciudad Rodrigo. These, with more 24-pounders and 18 taken from the iron guns the Russians left at Lisbon, formed the battering train against Badajos.

They had been brought up and placed in Elvas. The guns from the fortifications of Elvas were not made use of: the inconvenience of brass guns in quick firing is well remembered from the ill success of the former sieges. Though Lord Wellington had not employed mortars against Rodrigo, yet Badajos was so much better garrisoned, and the place itself so much stronger than Rodrigo, that he moved a certain number of 5½-inch howitzers with the train from Elvas. After Rodrigo he said that mortars were not worth the transport, for that all we wanted was a hole in the wall, and that our troops would get in. Lieutenant-General Picton conducted the details in the trenches.

March 25th. I arrived at the camp before Badajos just as the batteries opened against the place. The number of guns brought into fire in the first parallel was 21 and 7 howitzers. They were in six batteries, the four on the right directed against the body of the place, and the two on the left (10 guns in both), against the detached work of Picurena. Our fire was very good, and that from the town very slack. The fort of Picurena had not fired a gun since the first day, being silenced by our musketry, and this day not a man could show his head from the place. The enemy had one howitzer in rear of the work, which was occasionally fired. The four batteries on the right knocked the enemy's defences a good deal about, silencing many of their guns.

At sunset, orders came out for the troops on duty to attack the fort of Picurena. They were principally detachments this night from the 3rd Division, with some of the Light. Major-General Kemp, from the 3rd Division, was the officer of the trenches, and directed the attack.

The fort was garrisoned by 200 men, not including a piquet of 30 outside.

Our troops moved in three columns, two of which were directed to escalade in the front by any point they could get in at, and the third to pass in the rear and enter by the gorge of the work. In all we employed 500 men. The two that were intended to escalade got in with ladders, and the third in the rear entered by the gate, which was broken open, after half the detachment had scrambled over the palisades. After our people got in, the enemy's troops ran into a guard-house, and there kept themselves shut up, and it was impossible for our people to get at them. In this state things remained for about half an hour, when a report got amongst our men that a large body was coming out of the town, and the fort was on the point of being given up. There was some move with our men, and the enemy, thinking we were leaving, came out, when our troops turned round, charged into the place, and took the whole prisoners. General Kemp gained great credit, and had he not exerted himself, the place (after our people gained it) would have been given up. The second parallel was carried from the fort this night and completed. I went through the trenches on the 26th, and into the Picurena. The firing from our batteries had done very little to it to facilitate the escalade. The ditch was 18 feet deep, and the fraise which went all round was not in the least injured.

The Engineers said that the fort should not have been attacked so soon, and that, had they been aware of its strength, the attack would not have been recommended by them.

The troops gained much credit, but being done by detachments, no one division or regiment could claim the thing as their own. The detachment to the gorge was chiefly from the 88th regiment. Men in detachment do not know their officers, nor officers their men. There can be no regimental esprit, and detachment I consider a bad mode of doing duty, particularly for night work, when confusion is more liable to occur; and when men are not well known by officers, they may do anything with impunity. The enemy are erecting a battery under the castle, which will command our works a good deal.

I returned on the 26th from the siege to Villa Viciosa.

During our halt at Olivenza I went once to see the siege, and passed by Badajos from Olivenza on our route for the front.

Before the Picurena was taken (almost in the beginning of the siege), the enemy made one sortie and got into the right of the first parallel. The only harm was carrying away some intrenching tools, and their handful of cavalry galloped into the Engineers' camp on the right, and carried one officer a good way back, but were obliged to leave him. In consequence of this, the 14th Light Dragoons found a strong piquet in rear of the trenches, and on our brigade's moving to Olivenza, the 11th Light Dragoons went to Villaverde, four leagues from Badajos, to furnish the duties.

The bridge of pontoons on the Guadiana was carried away by the floods, and for some days the ammunition was rather short in consequence of the communication being interrupted.

The breaching batteries opened on the 30th of March, and by the 6th of April had formed three practicable breaches, when Lord Wellington determined to assault the place. No summons during the siege was sent, having found in Rodrigo instructions from Bonaparte that any governor surrendering without an assault should be shot.

The 5th Division had been employed on the right bank of the Guadiana in the investment of San Christoval, and moved on the 31st March to Villavendi on the left bank.

On the 6th they marched to the camp of Badajos, and were employed in the assault.

Three breaches had been made, all of which were considered practicable: one in the right flank of the bastion La Trinidad, called the main breach; another in the curtain of La Trinidad, close to its right flank; and the third in the left flank of the bastion Santa Maria.

The four divisions were employed in the assault. The Light Division was to proceed and attack the main breach.

(A false attack was to be made on the Pardaleres by the Portuguese Brigade from the 5th Division. A detachment also attacked and carried the detached Ravelin of San Roque, which was the first thing taken.)

The 4th, the two smaller ones.

The 3rd, to escalade the castle.

The 5th, to escalade the bastion of San Vincente, close to the Guadiana.

About 10 p.m. the troops moved to the attack, and were scarcely in motion before perceived by the enemy, and received by a most tremendous fire.

The Engineer appointed to lead the Light Division was killed before he pointed out the breach, and they clashed with the 4th.

This created a good deal of confusion, and the troops moved up in great disorder to attack. No rush in a body was made at any of the breaches, and the two divisions remained under the wall firing at the enemy, and suffered greatly, being crowded up close to the wall.

Their situation was dreadful--exposed to the enemy's fire from above, scarcely able to return a shot, and suffering very severely.

The ditch in front of the main breach was flooded, but not full of water. Some said they got through it, and others that it was not fordable, though from all accounts I conceive it was to be passed.

The two divisions remained for some time, exposed in the place they stopped at to the enemy's fire, during which the attack on the castle had succeeded, and at 12 p.m. the 3rd Division gained their point, all their general officers being wounded before, or just as they entered: General Picton, on leading up his division, and Kempt just as he entered. The enemy attempted to regain it, but could do nothing. Colonel Sturgeon, of the Staff Corps, was the officer who suggested the escalade on the castle.

All the troops in the castle, about 300, were bayonetted.

The 5th Division, in their attack, had not been idle, and Major-General Walker, with a very few men from his brigade, at first succeeded in gaining possession of the ramparts.

The enemy attacked him and drove him back; he again advanced, and was most severely wounded. This gave time for the whole division to enter, and the enemy, finding we had succeeded, abandoned the breaches and retired into different parts of the town, surrendering in different parties. Our troops (3rd and 4th Divisions) then entered by the breach.

Philippon retired to San Christoval, over the Guadiana, and in the morning, when summoned, said he doubted our having gained the place, the firing was so great. He was soon convinced to the contrary, and delivered up the work.

As soon as the troops entered the town, such a scene that night, and for the whole of the 7th, took place as was never before witnessed. The men got drunk, fired their muskets off in the streets, wounding and killing many people, as well as their own comrades. Every house was plundered, and most of the doors opened by firing at the locks. The people, on our passing through from the south, were in a most wretched state, and said that the soldiers had killed 85 inhabitants. I believe 32 to be the fact.

The men had not the least respect for their officers, and if not of the same regiment, would as soon shoot them as not. All interference on their part was quite out of the question. (Scene with an officer in the artillery, and a family he protected from the soldiers.)

The dead and dying on and about the breach were the most shocking thing ever seen, and perhaps a little plunder was necessary to drown the horror. Badajos had always been very uncivil to the British, and from our passing things over, they thought they could do what they pleased. It could not have happened to fall upon people who deserved it more, though it would have been as well had it not gone so far.*

This is the second siege the Light Division have been employed in, and considering they do all the outpost duty when infantry are employed, and had the advance the whole way from the lines to Rodrigo in 1811, it is not quite fair to employ men on two services which are generally distinct. They are far from complaining, and would have considered it a great loss had they not had their share in the attack on Badajos. After such duty they look upon skirmishing and outpost as amusement. It is not customary to employ the same troops for both duties when others are at hand. These regiments are ready for all duties.

In the town of Badajos, when the troops entered on the night of 6th of April, all the houses were shut. The doors were soon burst open, and the inhabitants fancying our men would be satisfied with getting drunk, generally placed a bottle of spirits (aquadente) on a table with a candle, close to the door on entering. This the men drank, and then, made half mad with liquor, began their plundering. The men got all kinds of plunder, though nothing of great value. They were seen walking about with French soldiers under their arms, giving them drink, and inviting them to join in the plunder. Lord Wellington rode into the town on the 7th.

They saw him, began firing their muskets in the air for joy; but several drunken men, from not knowing what they were about, nearly shot him.

April 8th. The brigade moved at 12 this night to Santa Marta, and halted a short time before daylight in rear of the town. Our piquets kept the line of the Guadaljore, and the two squadrons remained in advance. We had one or two foolish alerts during the day, and for some time remained formed on the hill in rear of Santa Marta. Once we occupied the village, when a report arrived that they were advancing, and the troops turned out (I believe no one ordered it) in no small confusion. The enemy only

---

* *"But the strong desire for glory was, in the British, dashed with a hatred of the citizens on an old grudge, and recent toil and hardship, with much spilling of blood, had made many incredibly savage." – (Napier, "Peninsular War.")*

showed their cavalry on the opposite banks of the Guadaljore, and were the whole day marching to the rear. At night, the brigade bivouacked in rear of Santa Marta, a short league. The infantry had taken up their ground near Albuera, and had sent forward their Light Infantry into the wood; and this through the report of some sergeant.

The weather was dreadfully hot; we were exposed to the sun the whole day.

April 9th. The enemy had been withdrawing the whole of their force both yesterday and this day, and about 12 a.m. their rear left Fuente del Maestro. Lieutenant Alexander, of the 10th Light Dragoons, was the officer on piquet, and did not find it out before Sir Stapleton Cotton, in riding out, heard from the peasants they had retired and went into the town, from whence the Lieutenant-General sent back to the subaltern that, having ascertained for him that all was safe, he ought (had he finished his nap) enter the place.

So much for the alertness of the piquet. The brigade moved up to Fuente del Maestro in the evening. With one sergeant, corporal, and twenty men, I went on piquet to Los Santos, a league in front. The enemy had left all the adjacent places. Their rear was this night in Usagre. I put my piquet up in the town, with vedettes on the main road to Usagre, which was four leagues off.

In the night the Alcalde (magistrate of the place) received information that General Ballesteros had entered Seville with the Spanish army. There was such confusion and firing of pieces that I turned out my piquet, when I was told the cause and turned in again, reporting to Fuente del Maestro, as the firing might have caused an alert.

They rejoiced through the whole of the tenth at Ballesteros' having entered Seville; but not a word was said of our success against Badajos.

The Spaniards did not enter Seville, nor did they, I believe, take any steps likely to effect it. At Zafra they said they would give us a bull-fight, and talked of it with so much assurance that we all expected it. All the windows round the grand square (Plassa) were filled with the ladies of the town. The men congratulated them on Ballesteros' success, telling us we were to see how they would drive the French out of the South, stating at the same time we had nothing like bull-fights in England, and that it was right to show us one. After waiting for more than two hours, we learnt there was no bull to had; indeed, they had never the least idea where to get one. Some officers then asked our commissary to lend a poor foot-sore bullock, which was driven into the Plassa. He had marched several leagues that morning, and had more the appearance of dying than coming to grace so gay a scene. We had now a bull, but no matadors. The poor animal stood in the middle of the square without moving, when one of our farriers, coming past, took off his apron, and began to plague him by throwing it in his face. He was soon joined by two or three dragoons, who, by dint of pushing the animal and other means, made him move about a little. Both parties were soon tired of their sport. The bullock was sent back to the commissary, killed and eaten that night; and so ended our bull-fight.

April 10th. By an order received in the night, I marched at daylight to Zafra, a capital town to the right, two miles from Los Santos—headquarters of the cavalry and the 16th. Came into the town soon after daylight. The whole town had been up through the night, rejoicing on account of the news from Seville. The 12th and 14th occupied Villa Franca and Rebiera, Major Cocks at the latter, with two squadrons from those two regiments. Orders came out in the evening for the brigade to march. The 12th and 14th did move to Usagre, but through the 16th not having rations issued, our march was delayed till midnight. (This was the third night I had been up.) The people gave us a ball, and we danced until we turned out. This gives one some idea of Spanish enthusiasm. They have been rejoicing the whole day for Ballesteros' having entered Seville, and if asked to find five men with arms to garrison it and keep it, they would rather hear of its falling into the enemy's hands than so far inconvenience themselves. They fully delight in any success, but will not undergo privations to prevent disasters. We had a party of observation under Lieutenant Penrice in Bienvenida, to which place Sir Stapleton went in the evening; and on his arrival, the enemy had sent a strong patrol and driven our people back, it served him right for always going so far to the front. He was ashamed to return to Zafra, and went to Los Santos.

The rejoicings which took place at Zafra for the occupation of Seville by Ballesteros were very characteristic of Spanish patriotism and exertion to save their country, and of Spanish rejoicing. Ballesteros marched with a miserable detachment to occupy a town which a couple of French battalions would in half an hour have dispossessed him of. He never made any haste in his march to effect the purpose of it, yet, when he set out from Zafra, under the idea of Seville being the object of his march, the inhabitants rejoiced as if the south of Spain had been freed by the movement.

The regiment moved this morning at 1 a.m.

April 11th. The regiment moved this morning at 4 a.m. on Bienvenida, three leagues from Zafra, and arrived there just at daylight. Sir Stapleton Cotton came up at the same time, and moved the regiment through the town on the Villa Garcia road about half a league, where we dismounted. The 12th and 14th had moved from Usagre a short time before us, and driven the enemy's vedettes off the rising ground in front of Villa Garcia just before we made our appearance from Bienvenida. Major-General Le Marchant's brigade moved in our rear, and was not seen by the enemy.

The two advance squadrons, under Cocks, pushed through Villa Garcia, and were driven back by a considerable force. Lieutenant-Colonel Ponsonby, with the 12th and the 14th, pushed on to support them, and the enemy brought up about 2,000 cavalry to drive them back, conceiving there was nothing up but these six squadrons. (Each regiment of British cavalry was reduced to six troops, forming three squadrons.)

At this instant the 16th moved forward over the hills to the right of Villa Garcia, and came into the plain leading to Llerena on the right of the 12th. (The 12th and 14th were to our left.) Major-General Le Marchant's brigade moved to our right, came down on their left flank, charged at the same time that we advanced, broke five squadrons, throwing the remainder into no small confusion back towards Llerena.

(When we came on the top of the hill, there were the 12th and 14th on our left, close in front of Villa Garcia. The enemy formed a quarter of a mile from them, and a small stone wall betwixt the 16th (our regiment) and the French. We came down the hill in a trot, took the wall in line, and were in the act of charging when the 5th Dragoon Guards came down on our right, charged, and completely upset the left flank of the enemy, and the 12th, 14th and 16th advancing at the same moment, the success was complete. The view of the enemy from the top of the hill, the quickness of the advance on the enemy, with the spirit of the men in leaping the wall, and the charge immediately afterwards, was one of the finest things I ever saw.)

We pursued, and made some prisoners; and in the place of pushing them on, the enemy were allowed to form in rear of a ditch half-way between Villa Garcia and Llerena. Here we delayed a little, when Sir Stapleton ordered the right and left squadrons, 16th (which had got together) down the road, turning the enemy's left flank. They did not halt one instant. The 12th and 14th advanced at the same time, and charged with three squadrons (12th). We drove them quite close to Llerena, and Cookson, of Captain Cocks' troop, was killed in the town. To check us, the enemy fired (from the ground they held with 10,000 infantry close to the left of Llerena) a few cannon shots over our heads, not daring to hit us, being so intermixed with their own people. The Heavies (cavalry) supported us, and, on the cannon opening, we were ordered to withdraw on Villa Garcia. The enemy skirmished a little in front of Llerena, though they never advanced a mile from the place, and in a few hours left it altogether, their infantry and cavalry marching on Seville.

We killed about 53 of the enemy in the charge from Villa Garcia of the 5th Dragoon Guards, and in our pursuit to Llerena took one lieutenant-colonel, 17th Dragoons, two captains, one lieutenant, 132 rank and file, with the same proportion of horses.

(Circumstance of a poodle dog coming to find his master, who was killed.)

The prisoners were dreadfully cut, and some will not recover. A French dragoon had his head nearer cut off than I ever saw before; it was by a sabre cut at the back of the neck.

The day was well managed, and the troops brought up at the same instant in good order, as well as the assembling the three brigades in the morning, Major-General Slade having moved up at the same instant, and ready to support (though not engaged), had it been necessary. The halt on the road to Llerena was the only fault, and could not at the time be avoided; Sir Stapleton having no one to send with the order, was obliged to ride to give it to the whole.

(Sir Stapleton Cotton sent Lieutenant Wheeler of the 16th to Colonel Ponsonby, with the following order from Zafra, which I afterwards saw at Canno:

ZAFRA, APRIL 10TH, 1812.
"Should the enemy not occupy Usagre in force, you will move from your present quarters and occupy it this evening. Should he occupy it, you will bivouack in rear of the town, and advance at daylight the following morning."

"ZAFRA, THE 10TH.
"I wish we had been allowed to follow them this day. I fear it is too late. The enemy have left Villa Garcia. Push Cocks on in the morning to Villa Garcia, and let him send on patrols to feel the enemy, whose rear, I think, he will find in Berlanga.")

The day's affair did him great credit, though, at the time, he blamed Lieutenant-Colonel Ponsonby for advancing so soon from Usagre; but, if he had not, the enemy would have seen us and the Heavies' advance from Bienvenida, and have retired. The Count d'Erlon (Drouet) commanded the whole, and had retired the cavalry from Villa Garcia, when General Allemand, the cavalry officer, thinking the chance of cutting up the six squadrons under Ponsonby a good one, requested to advance, and was moving on when we came over the hills. The whole of their infantry saw the affair from their ground near Llerena.

At Villa Garcia, we heard that the troops from Badajos had moved north to relieve Rodrigo, which was invested with 15,000, under Marmont. The whole of Lord Wellington's force returned north, with the exception of one brigade of cavalry, which was left with Sir Rowland Hill.

In Lord Wellington's letter to Sir Stapleton, he said, "You may have any brigade you please excepting Anson's, 11th, 12th, 16th, which must move with us." He fixed on Major-General Slade's.

In the evening, Major-General Le Marchant's brigade and the 16th returned to Bienvenida, occupying the town. Sir Stapleton came there likewise. The 12th and 14th, under Lieutenant-Colonel Ponsonby, went to Usagre, leaving Cocks in Villa Garcia, with two squadrons.

In the advance on Llerena, in pursuit of the enemy's weathered cavalry, I cut off the half circle of brass formed on the top of the French dragoon's helmet, and it made so great a noise close to the man's head that he conceived himself to be killed, without being in the least injured. He fell off his horse as if a round shot had struck him.

The enemy, from the position they held with their infantry, had full view of the affair.

(Circumstance of Sergeant-Maloney going down the road full gallop past me, showing me the speed of his chestnut mare.)

The desire of General Le Marchant to halt after the charge, my urging the men on, the enemy being in confusion; and his after acknowledgment that I was right.

He said, "Halt, and form your men."

I said "The enemy are in greater confusion."

"You must halt."

"Must I call out 'Halt'?" I asked.

Seeing the general hesitated (he would not give the order), I called to the men to come on, and we drove the enemy a mile, in the greatest confusion, into Llerena.

By an after thought, Sir Stapleton sent an order, by Lieutenant Luard (4th Dragoons), desiring Ponsonby to wait, and to give him a chance, with the troops moving on Bienvenida, to get in rear of the enemy stationed at Usagre. He was angry with Ponsonby for advancing; and yet, by his previous order, he directed him to push on, stating expressly that the enemy had left Villa Garcia, by the rear being at Berlanga. Luard could not overtake Ponsonby, and he never received the order till too late.

Lieutenant-Colonel Archer remained behind at Zafra, through illness, and hearing we were likely to be engaged, set off to join the regiment, and met us on our return to Bienvenida, much mortified. Captain Murray commanded the regiment in the affair of this day.

April 12th. Major-General Le Marchant's brigade marched for Santa Marta and adjacents this day, halting in Los Santos. The 16th, with headquarters of the cavalry, returned to Zafra, the 12th and 14th to Villa Franca, and Major Cocks, with his two squadrons, to Rebiera.

April 14th. The route came yesterday for us to march this day for the north. Sir Stapleton gave a ball, attended by about 100 people. We left the ball-room at daylight, mounted our horses, and marched. During the night a mail arrived from England, bringing my appointment to a company in the 60th foot. Sir Stapleton advised me to apply for leave to England. I marched with the 16th to Fuente del Maestre, two leagues, where they halted, and then proceeded to dine with Sir Stapleton at Santa Marta.

April 15th. The headquarters of the army had gone so far that there was no chance of overtaking them, and I moved to Torre de Almendral, where I expected the regiment, but in consequence of their going to a ford on the Guadajira, which was not passable, they got no further than Santa Marta.

April 16th. Marched to Olivenza, where the 12th and 14th were, but from the fords over the Guadiana not being passable, the 16th halted at Villaverde, being obliged to go round by the bridge of Badajos, and by coming to Olivenza it was only so much out of their way.

April 17th. The brigade halted this day. I went to Badajos, where Major Cocks, with his two squadrons, halted this day. The breaches had been cleared, but the town still in a shocking state.

April 18th. The brigade arrived this morning at Badajos. In consequence of the halt yesterday, we were obliged to march on to Elvas, and in passing the Caya it was so deep that most of the baggage was obliged to go round by the bridge near Campo Mayor. The brigade marched five leagues.

April 19th. Marched to Estremos, six leagues, where we got a supply of corn, which latterly had been rather scarce.

April 20th. Marched to Frontiera, four leagues. For the last two days we have halted within a league from our quarters, and cut enough green forage for the night. This ensures every horse his quantity, and the idlers axe obliged to cut with the others.

The forage thus procured was the green corn, of which barley is the best, wheat the next and rye the last. The horses improve on any, and eat a great deal.

In entering a large town, where the Juis de Fora is to be regularly applied to, the forage never makes its appearance before night, and frequently not at all.

April 21st. 14th and 16th marched to Crato, four leagues; 12th, Flor de Roza, quarter of a league further.

April 22nd. The brigade marched to Niza. The 16th occupied the town, the 12th and 14th the wood near it.

We hear various reports of Marmont; one is that he is standing at Pedrogao, on the other side Castello Branco, and another that he had taken Rodrigo by escalade.

April 23rd. The brigade marched to Sarnadas, three leagues from Niza, and one on the other side the Tagus.

I determined on going to headquarters of the army, and left the regiment with Major Cocks, who was going to see his regiment, the 79th, in the 1st Division. We went to Castello Branco, four leagues on. The 6th Division, with General Le Marchant's Brigade, were in the place, with two of the cavalry regiments encamped near.

April 24th. Marched this morning to Pedrogao, six leagues. Marmont had advanced as far as this himself, and sent 3,000 infantry and a regiment of cavalry on to Castello Branco. He had plundered Covilha and Guarda, which place was shamefully abandoned by the militia on the advance of the French cavalry.

The French force was 15,000 men, and has done us more harm than plundering the towns and villages through which they passed, and which, excepting by burning, were as much destroyed as possible.

The 1st Hussars, under Major-General Alten, had retired across the Tagus before there was any necessity. Lord Wellington, in his despatches, spoke rather severely of his conduct, as well as in a letter on the subject addressed to Sir Stapleton.

The roads in the Peninsula have been so bad that it has been impossible to keep the forge carts, brought from England, at all near the regiments of cavalry, to enable them to use the forges for shoeing the horses. The number of horses killed in transporting them has been very great, and an excellent contrivance has been substituted, in constructing a small anvil and bellows, which are carried on the back of a mule; a second is allowed for carrying charcoal and iron.

These march with the baggage, are always up, and the farriers can make several sets of shoes after each day's march. Had this plan been adopted in the first instance, the troops would always have been well shod, considerable trouble would have been saved, besides a great many horses that were lost in dragging the wheel forge carts already mentioned, through impracticable roads. The invention was Colonel Schovel's, headquarters.

April 25th. Major Cocks left me to see the 79th, which passed through this morning. I marched to Sabugal, six leagues, which was so destroyed that I encamped on the other side the Coa. The 4th Division were encamped close to me.

April 26th. Marched this day to Fuente Guinaldo, where I found headquarters, and arranged with Lord Clinton for his troop in the 16th. I dined at headquarters this day.

At headquarters they spoke very slightingly of Marmont's diversion, and thought he might have done more.

The garrison of Rodrigo consisted of 4,000 Spaniards, under Vives, and had fifteen days' biscuit left when we came up.

Headquarters left Freneda for Badajos, on the 6th March, and for three weeks after their departure he made no movement. He brought 15,000 men, had 4,000 men at Talavera de la

Reyna, on the Tagus. This would have made him 19,000 strong. Immediately after the taking of Rodrigo, the siege of Badajos was spoken of, and had his information been good, he should have known this and likewise that Almeida was not tenable against escalade. On headquarters leaving Freneda, had he made ladders, moved down and taken Almeida (which I think he might), and broken ground before Rodrigo on the 17th, the day we begun at Badajos (in Almeida he would have found our battering train and ammunition), sending a detachment, or by marching Foy's division from Talavera to Palentia, and so on, he might have destroyed the bridge of boats at Villa Velha, which would have made a difference to us in arriving at Rodrigo, of six days. Had we stayed to take Badajos with our whole force, and had we detached before, Soult might have had fair chance of relieving Badajos, and provided we did not, Marmont would have been before Rodrigo more than a month. At all events, destroying the bridge at Villa Velha would have been no small inconvenience to us; but as it is, he has only obliged us to march from Badajos with part of our army, and should we undertake operations in the south it will be moved back again before the other preparations can be ready.

The 3rd, 4th, and 5th Divisions marched to San Juan de Pesqueira, on the Douro, giving up their mules to provision Rodrigo, and Major-General Alten's brigade marched to the same neighbourhood. The 1st and 6th Divisions, with General Le Marchant's and Anson's brigades of cavalry, were ordered to recross the Tagus, the infantry went to Niza and adjacents, the cavalry headquarters to Cabaca de Vide.

Having obtained permission to remain with the 16th, I returned to the south of the Tagus, and marched.

April 27th.   Aldea de Ponte, three leagues.
April 28th.   Pena Macor, eight leagues.
April 29th.   Castello Branco, six leagues.
April 30th.   Niza, seven leagues.
May 1st.   Alter de Chao, four leagues.
May 2nd.   Avis, five leagues, headquarters 16th.

The regiment has scarcely halted a day since they left Olivenza, and is by no means in bad condition. At this time of year horses will do almost any work, but if reduced low before winter, nothing but grass in the spring will recover many. Headquarters of the brigade, with the 12th Light Dragoons, were at Canno, and the 14th Light Dragoons, Frontiera.

Major Cocks had remained at Niza with the 1st Division. His brother James from England had arrived in Portugal as an amateur, and came with me from Alter de Chao to Avis. In a few days Cocks joined us, and intended going to Lisbon to fit out to join the 79th Regiment He left the 16th a week after he came to Avis, and my notification to the 60th having come I went with his brother and himself to Lisbon.

The first day we went to Mora, four long leagues, the second to Benevente, nine, and the following morning embarked for Lisbon on the river on which Benevente is situated, a league from the Tagus, and in five more arrived at Lisbon, about 2p.m.

The remounts from England arrived during our stay at Lisbon. That for the 16th is detained for want of ships.

We have heard of the murder of Mr. Perceval in the House of Commons.

May 26th, Having heard at Lisbon that a movement was likely soon to take place in the army, I, this day, left Lisbon to join the 16th. The move was to be on Salamanca, and the 1st, 6th, and the two brigades of cavalry were to move up to Fuente Guinaldo. I here left Major Cocks (he going to join the 79th), after having been in his troop above two years. He is a great loss to the 16th, and to me in particular.

Our horses not being able to procure rations at Benevente moved to Salvaterra, a league higher up the Tagus.

I went up in a boat eleven leagues; left Lisbon at 11 a.m. and arrived at 7 p.m.

It was the depot for the Portuguese cavalry.

May 27th. Marched four leagues to Cronze.
May 28th. Mora, four leagues.
May 29th. Avis, headquarters 16th.

Lieutenant-Colonel Archer here left the 16th, and the army. Major Pelly got the lieutenant-colonelcy, Captain Lygon* the majority, and Lieutenant Buchanan the troop.

During last night a route arrived for the brigade to march, as follows. The 16th moved on the following route, with the other two regiments close to us each day.

June 1st.   Soda, three leagues.
June 2nd.   Flor de Roza, three leagues.
June 3rd.   Niza, four leagues.
June 4th.   Villa Velha, three leagues.
June 5th.   Castello Branco, four leagues.
June 6th.   Escallies de Baxo, two leagues.
June 7th.   Pedrogao, four leagues.
June 8th.   Memoa, four leagues.
June 9th.   Qudrasayis, four leagues, and crossed the Coa.

June 10th. Marched and encamped on the Azava between Puebla de Azava and Stuero, four leagues from Qudrasayis. The brigade, during the whole march, had encamped most nights. We were the last, and the whole army was this day assembled near Guinaldo, the headquarters of the army.

June 11th. Sir Stapleton Cotton this day asked me to join his staff as extra aid-de-camp until my exchange to the 16th took place. I joined him at Carpeo, where he remained for the night.

Major-General Le Marchant's, Anson's, Bock's and Alten's brigades this day encamped on the Agueda, and the greater part of the infantry moved there at the same time.

On the march from Memoa, Major Hay again broke his arm, in the same place as before.

Captain Murray succeeded him in the command of the regiment

June 12th. Lord Wellington reviewed Le Marchant's and Anson's brigades with the 11th Light Dragoons this day near

---

Son of the first Lord Beauchamp, d. 1860.

Carpeo. The regiments were in fine order, and strong.*

June 13th. Orders came out on the 11th for the army to move the following day, but in consequence of three eighteen-pounders, which were to go with it, not having arrived, the day was put off. The army marched on three roads, as follows:

Left Column.	Centre Column.	Right Column.
11th Light Dragoons.	1st Hussars.	14th Light Dragoons.
3rd Division.	Light Division.	1st Division.
Maj.-Gen. Le Marchant's.	12th and 16th Light Dragoons.	6th Division
Brigade of Cavalry.	5th Division.	7th Division.
Brig.-Gen. Bradford's brigade.	4th Division	
Portuguese Infantry.	Gen. Bock's Brigade Cavalry.	
Brig.-Gen. Pack's Division.	Reserve Ammunition.	

HEADQUARTERS. MILITARY CHEST.

The Light Division and 1st Hussars to form the advanced guard of the army under Major-General Charles Allen, and to proceed to and bivouack on the 13th June at Aldea de Alba. The piquets of the right and left columns will communicate by daily patrols with the Light Division and 1st Hussars.

Lieutenant-General Sir Thomas Graham is requested to direct the details of the right column, and Lieutenant-General Picton the left; and they will be so good as to order detachments of cavalry and infantry to form the advanced guard of the column under their command, and the outposts and piquets of the columns will communicate by daily patrols with the Light Division and 1st Hussars.

---

*Sir Stapleton put them through some movements, contrary to the desire of Lord Wellington, who said he had no wish of the kind. After doing one or two things, the affair got confused, the Peer rode off in the midst of it, expressing what he thought, "What the devil is he about now?"

The general officers commanding columns will fix the order in which the troops and their baggage are to march in column. The troops in the centre and left column will march by their right and the right column by the left.

Signed.—W. DELANCEY,
Deputy Quarter-Master General.

Left Column.	Centre Column.	Right Column.
To pass the River Agueda, and proceed to and bivouack on the river Gavallanes, near the village of Espiritas.	June 13th, 1812. To pass the Agueda, proceed to and bivouack on the river Tenebron, near to Boca Cara.	To pass the Agueda, and proceed to and bivouack on the river Tenebron, near the village of Tenebron.
On the river Huebra, near the village of Munoz.	June 14th. On the river Huebra, near the village of San Munoz.	On the river Huebra, to the left of the road on which it has passed.
On the rivulet between Aldea Huela de la Boveda and Robleya.	June 15th. On the rivulet near to Cayos de Robleya.	On the rivulet near to Villa Alba de Los Santos.

Sir Stapleton marched with the two brigades in the centre column. On the 13th we halted in the hamlet of Boca Cara three leagues from Rodrigo, and left Carpeo the preceding to encamp on the right bank of the Agueda. We turned out at half-past two, and arrived on the encamping ground before the heat of the day. Headquarters of the army left Fuente Guinaldo this day, and this night were at a small village two short leagues in front of Rodrigo.

Copy of a letter from Sir George Anson to Henry Tomkinon Esq. of Dorfold.

9, LOWER GROSVENOR STREET,
19th March, 1812.

Sir,

I am happy to inform you that your son is gazetted to a Company in the 60th Foot, for which he has paid £1,500. The difference to be paid for his exchange to Cavalry is £1,650. Your son will have his Lieutenancy and Cornetcy to sell, amounting to £997 10s. It will be necessary for you to lodge the £1,365 which, added to the £285 now in Collyers' hands, will make the regulated difference of £1,650. I have desired Messrs. Collyers to send you the necessary papers for the exchange for your signature on the part of your son.

I remain, sir, yours faithfully,
G. ANSON.

I confess myself very anxious to secure your son's return to the 16th Light Dragoons.

June 14th. The army advanced four short leagues. Headquarters of the army, Cabrillas; of the cavalry, Sanmunez, a league in advance of Cabrillas.

June 15th. The army marched four leagues. Headquarters, Aldea Huela de la Boveda. Cavalry, H.2, Cayos de la Robliya. The columns were close to each other every day, and, as yet, have seen nothing of the enemy.

June 16th. The three columns continued their march as usual this day, and in two leagues came up with the enemy's outposts, two leagues in front of Salamanca. They had about two squadrons of cavalry overlooking the centre road, which were driven in by the 1st Hussars. They pushed them within a league of Salamanca, and the 11th Light Dragoons coming up from the left column and the 14th from the right, advanced on the plain. The enemy kept a piquet of twenty men on a commanding hill which remained there a considerable time, and had the 14th known of it, and been as forward on the right as the 1st Hussars were on its left, it would have been taken. Major Bull's guns came up and cannonaded their cavalry, and the Hussars, with a detachment of the 14th, charged a small advanced party of three squadrons. The affair was nothing, and contrary to the orders of Lord Wellington. The enemy withdrew over the Tormes. The army bivouacked a league from Salamanca.

June 17th. We moved forward at daylight, the whole assembling on the plain near Salamanca. The enemy left the place last night about 12, and the army crossed, as follows, by different fords, there being a small garrison in the fort which they had constructed on the north-west side of the town, and which commanded the bridge over the Tormes. The left column passed the Tormes at the ford of El Campo, a league below Salamanca. The centre and right at the ford of Santa Marta, the 14th Light Dragoons and the 6th Division forming the advanced guard of this wing, and entered Salamanca with Lord Wellington and Sir Stapleton about 8 a.m.

We were received with shouts and *vivas* in the town. The inhabitants were out of their senses at having got rid of the French, and nearly pulled Lord Wellington off his horse.

The scene in the Plassa was one of the most interesting I ever saw. The troops (6th Division) were there formed, supposed preparatory to an immediate attack. The place was filled with inhabitants, expressing their joy in the most enthusiastic manner. The women were the most violent, many coming up to Lord Wellington and embracing him.

He was writing orders on his sabretash, and was interrupted three or four times by them. What with the scene caused by the joy of the people, and feelings accompanying troops in an attack on a fortress, it was half an hour of suspense and anxiety, and a scene of such interest as I never before witnessed.

Headquarters of the army and cavalry were fixed this day in Salamanca.

The 6th Division invested the fort, and the left wing of the army moved to Villares on the Toro road, a league in front of Salamanca; the right and centre columns encamped on the Tormes, near Santa Marta, on its right bank. Lieutenant-Colonel Ponsonby's brigade followed the enemy, and skirmished with them two leagues in advance of Salamanca. Marmont's headquarters were in Aldea Nueva, four league from Salamanca, on the Toro road.

Our outposts were established two leagues in front of Salamanca. Lieutenant-Colonel Ponsonby's brigade occupied San Christoval and Castalliano, and General Alten's a little more to the left, at Castalliano de Merisco.

Ground was broken this night before the fort by the 6th Division, but not much progress made,

June 18th. We continued our works against the fort, and this day the three eighteen-pounders crossed the Tormes. The enemy remain as yesterday.

In addition to the three eighteen-pounders, six iron howitzers moved up with the army and crossed the Tormes at the same time.

June 19th. The three guns got into battery last night, and opened against the fort this day.

The place is garrisoned by 600 men, and constructed out of the convent of San Francisco, the wall of which is close to the ditch, and by knocking it down it is supposed the ditch will fill up by the ruins falling into it.

The fort is situated close to the town, and a great many houses have been destroyed to prevent an enemy coming quite close to it. As it is, there are houses from which infantry can fire, and our works began at 300 yards from the place. The inhabitants say that each year the enemy pulled down a certain number of houses, and that, had the thing gone on, the whole town would have been destroyed.

The enemy continue as yesterday. Sir Stapleton this evening rode round some heights in front of Salamanca, covering the Toro road, and from that extending to the right towards the Tormes.

June 20th. We left Salamanca this morning for Castalliano, Sir Stapleton being in orders last night to take the command of the outposts, both infantry and cavalry.

Soon after daylight the enemy moved their cavalry and 5,000 infantry to the village of Arsalliano. The four brigades of cavalry were on their alarm posts, Lieutenant-Colonel Ponsonby watching the road from the left, from Aldea Nueva to San Christoval, a league in front of that place, and Major-General Alten's on the right, in front of Castalliano, a short distance. In front of the chain of heights from San Christoval to Morisco the country appears a fine plain, and in most parts covered with wheat. When examined there are a number of watercourses formed by the rain in the wet season and now dry, many of which are impassable, and all would cause great delay to a body of troops moving across them.

The enemy's troops did not advance from Arsalliano before late in the day, and the brigades went back to their camps and quarters about 12 at night.

At 3 p.m. the enemy moved forward in three columns. The brigade turned out, General Alten's on the right, as before, and Colonel Ponsonby's on the left.

The two Heavy Brigades moved up from the Tormes on to the bill, ready to support, and the whole army, as soon as the report went in to Lord Wellington, was put in motion for the positions. By 5, the whole had arrived and taken up their ground, and about the same time the enemy's cavalry marched through Castalliano, forming in its front. They drove back our skirmishers rather quickly, and fired with their artillery, on the whole advance, to warn the fort of their approach. From a hill close to Castalliano, we were within 800 yards of their cavalry; and on the light guns from the 7th Division coming up, they did not long keep their ground. The cannonade to both sides was sharp, but from our holding the commanding ground they suffered much more than we did.

Their light infantry pushed close to the position, and had an affair with ours from the 1st Division. There was a considerable fire on both sides, but at so long a range that nothing of consequence was done by either party.

After gaining possession of Castalliano, the enemy, at dusk, pushed on to their left to Castalliano de Morisco, half a mile distant from the other.

The Light Brigade of British infantry was placed in Morisco, consisting of the 51st and 68th from the 7th Division. The enemy sent a considerable force against the place, which was well defended by our troops; and just after the firing began an order came to evacuate the village. Infantry piquets were placed along the line with one or two of cavalry.

The cavalry retired behind the infantry at night. Lord Wellington remained at Villares, and Sir Stapleton pitched his tent in rear of the right of the line.

An attack at daylight is expected, though from what force the enemy have shown this day I do not conceive it possible. We have only seen 18,000 infantry or thereabouts, and 2,500 cavalry. We have 35,000 infantry on the position, and 3,000 cavalry, though this includes 4,000 Spanish infantry, under Don Carlos de Espana.

The general officers of divisions were this evening summoned to Lord Wellington. Whilst standing receiving the orders, several round shot came amongst them, and one close to Lord Wellington, he having a map in his hand. Very little confusion was occasioned—his Lordship moved a few paces, and continued his directions. I was with Sir Stapleton, and close to Lord Wellington at the time.

The troops in position were posted as follows, from right to left, on the heights of Castalliano:—

7th Division.
1st Division.
4th Division.
Light Division.
3rd Division.
Pack's and Bradford's brigades.

5th Division in reserve, with one brigade from the 6th Division, one British brigade under General Bowes, with the Portuguese brigade, both from the 6th Division, were left to watch the fort, the operations against which were suspended.

Cavalry: Major-General Alten's Light Brigade on the right, supported by the two Heavy Brgades. Lieutenant-Colonel Ponsonby's on the left, near Christoval.

The position the enemy held close to us was one of considerable risk. We could have attacked them with our whole force in half an hour, and their only chance of getting away was by defending the villages; by sending a large force against one we might have expected success, and so on to the other.

Had they both been carried by us, they would then have had to cross the plain before a superior force. The opportunity for an attack was so favouable, we all agreed Lord Wellington had some unknown reasons for not availling himself of their situation. It was said the arrival of a force on the eastern coast of Spain was looked for, and that he delayed, expecting it to operate in his favour in following up any success.

June 21st. the troops were all under arms at daylight. The enemy made no movement in the night, and now, as before, occupy Castalliano and Morisco with strong piquets in front. They have a large force in each of the villages, which prevent our seeing what force they have up.

They have likewise a large bivouac between the two, and appear to place their safety, should we move down, in the two villages; and will possibly secure their retreat by defending them to the last. On the right of Morisco there is a small hill, which is on the same range with those occupied by us. This the enemy gained, and Marmont twice rode up to reconnoitre. He could only see the right, without forming any idea of our force. Before he came up a trifling skirmish took place with General Alten's brigade, and the enemy advancing to cover his reconnaissance. On his retiring they kept the hill.

We underrated the enemy at 18,000 infantry; his force is now 30,000 having this day received a reinforcement of 5,000. Two deserters say they are waiting for Bonnet's division of 8,000, when they mean to attack.

The army is badly off for wood and water. Not a tree on the position, and what little water there is, is bad and only fit for cooking. The weather is not hot, and the troops do not suffer from the sun. Many of the inhabitants are employed all day in bringing wood and water up from Salamanca. The demand much exceeds the supply.

The enemy has unroofed Castalliano and Morisco for firewood-nearly every house is destroyed.

In consequence of Marmont's having looked at our right Lord Wellington thought he might have some idea of attacking on that point, and, in case of success, push us from the left of Santa Marta. The 7th Division was thrown back on the right, and the Light moved next the 1st.

In Salamanca I became acquainted with a priest, who was much with Lord Wellington, and had sent him nearly all the information he received from Salamanca. He was a superior, quiet sort of person; and during the time the enemy occupied the place, was on such terms with them as not to be suspected

I think the open way in which he is received at headquarters, and the manner his connection with Lord Wellington is spoken of, may operate against him in the event of the enemy's return.

The Spaniards are very good in obtaining and forwarding information-as in the instance of this priest-he ascertains all the detatchments in the country, the strength of any large assemblage of troops, by either having persons to count them as they enter the towns, or from the returns made to the alcades for provisions. These, when obtained, are sent by a foot-messenger, who will march ten leagues a day, and, if requisite, they can be forwarded from place to place by priests or alcades, who can be trusted, finding messengers at each place. They go frequently night and day.

June 22nd. The enemy remain nearly the same as yesterday. Their right extends rather more towards San Christoval.

One of 60th Infantry deserted this morning before the whole army. He was hit before he made the enemy's posts, and had I been a little quicker, might have taken him-the only service I ever attempted for the credit of my regiment. My exchange back to the 16th was not effected, and I was at this time a Captain in the 60th foot.

During last night two small fleshes had been thrown up on the right for the artillery of the 1st and 7th Divisions, with six heavy iron howitzers, that moved up from the fort.

At 7 a.m. two companies from the Light Battalions, K.G.L,, in the 7th Division, moved in front towards the hill above Morisco, supported by General Alten's brigade, and began skirmishing with the enemy's light troops, on that point. Lord Wellington arrived at this moment, and directed Sir Thomas Graham, with the 7th Division, to carry the hill; and would, if necessary, support him with the 1st and Light Divisions. The 58th and 61st moved forward to attack the hill, and carried it in one instant We had a sharp skirmish, 60 men killed and wounded. The enemy's troops got under arms, conceiving we intended to attack. They had about 100 men on the point of the hill, and did not support them. We kept possession of the ground with infantry piquets.

Marmont twice, this day, rode round our right to the high ground above Aldea Rubia on the Tormes. We still hear that the enemy expect reinforcements.

The inhabitants in the villages round the ground the enemy occupy have all left them. Casteallino and Morisco are both nearly unroofed. The enemy has no other wood but that taken from the houses.

June 23rd. The enemy retired during last night to the heights above Aldea Rubia, on their left towards Babilafuente, two leagues from the position. Our cavalry moved after them into the plain-the infantry remained in position. Lord Wellington was aware of this, having last night ordered six howitzers back to the fort.

The 6th Division moved into Salamanca, and operations began against the fort.

General Alten's brigade occupied Morisco, and General Anson's Castalliano and San Christoval-their piquets were a league in advance. Castallinano had scarcely a house left with its roof on; Morisco not quite so bad. The walls afford shade for the men and horses, and there are wells in both.

Sir Stapleton, after going round the posts, returned to Calvarizos. Headquarters went to Salamanca.

Major-General Bock's Heavy Brigade crossed the Tormes to Calvarrasa de Abaxo, watching the fords of Hucrta and others in possession of the enemy. The 1st Hussars, from Major-General Alten's brigade, occupied Aldea Lengua, on the right bank of the

Tormes, and on the main road, from Aldea Rubia to Salamanca, running along the Tormes the whole way.

In the evening a report came in from Aldea Lengua that the enemy were crossing the Tormes at the Huerta ford. Lord Wellington and Sir Stapleton went to the hill above Aldea Lengua, and on their arrival found that the enemy had only crossed a small force, which returned again. They did not leave the hill till after dark. Lord Wellington fixed his headquarters at Cabrerizos.

Major-General Vandeleur's brigade, from the Light Division, occupied Aldea Lengua, and the other brigade the hills above it.

June 24th. Lord Wellington and Sir Stapleton were both on the Aldea Lengua hill this morning at two. I was sent down to Aldea Lengua to receive Colonel Arentschildt's report of the 1st Hussars. At daylight it was so foggy we could not see what the enemy were about; it was certain they has made some movement, and a patrole ascertained that some few had crossed the Tormes. With this report I returned to Sir Stapletom. In a short time we heard the Heavy Brigade on the left bank skirmishing, and saw from their fire that they were losing ground. On this the 1st and 7th Divisions were ordered to cross the Tormes, taking up a position to the right and in advance of Santa Marta. The fog cleared away, and we saw General Bock retiring in excellent order before a superior force with artillery, from which he rather suffered, and ought to have had some artillery with him. Two guns would have saved many men and horses. General le Marchant's brigade moved across the Tormes, ready to support the other. The 4th Division moved on the road to Aldea Lengua, ready to act on either bank. The 5th closed to the point above Aldea Lengua, where Lord Wellington remained the whole day. Sir Thomas Graham had the command over the Tormes of the island 7th Divisions. The enemy gained possession of Calvarrasa de Abaxo with cavalry and infantry; they passed 8,000 infantry, and fourteen squadrons of cavalry, and advanced as far as that village almost in line At 3 p.m. they began to withdraw, and recrossed the Tormes with their whole force before dark. Just before they began to retire I thought their advance looked serious.

Our position with 1st and 7th was good, and had they fought with what they crossed, our force would have been the greater.

Major-General Alten's brigade crossed the Tormes, relieving General Bock's, which encamped for the night close to Careizos. Major-General le Marchant's recrossed, taking up their ground close to the village of Cabrerizos. The 1st and 7th Divisions likewise recrossed, taking up their camping ground close to Santa Marta.

The operations since the enemy retired from their ground near Castalliano were continued against the Salamanca fort, and last night a breach was considered practicable in one of the outworks, commanding the brigade. 300 men from General Borne's brigade (6th Division) moved forward to attack, commanded by himself. The first attempt failed, and he was wounded. He got dressed, and again brought forward his men; the attack failed, and he was killed on the glacis. The numbers employed were inadequate to the attempt, and it is much questioned if the thing was practicable. The best spirit does not exist in the 6th Division, which, no doubt, from heading so small a number, he was well aware of. the enemy left his body, with those of several wounded, close to the fort, and would neither allow us to take it away, nor do so themselves.

June 25th. The enemy's troops remain as yesterday. Our operations against the fort continue.

June 26th. No alteration in either army, excepting a small detatchment sent to Alba de Tormes to bring off the small garison left there by the enemy. They plundered the town. Sir Stapleton rode into Salamanca this evening. We commenced firing red hot shot against the fort. The third set fire to the convent. The inhabitants say their powder is well secured, though it is supposed, from the size of the work, that it will be so hot when on fire that they cannot remain long in it.

Detachments were paraded to assault the out fort. They had much said to them on the failure of the 23rd, and after all returned to their quarters.

June 27th. Rode this morning with Sir Stapleton into Salamanca. The fort was to be attacked this morning, and at

11 a.m. the enemy hung out a flag, a detachment being ready to attack the outwork. Certain terms were proposed. Lord W. would hear of none excepting surrendering prisoners of war, and protection to private property. He waited ten minutes, when our guns opened and the detachment moved forward to attack. The outwork at the time we attacked had a flag up, and another was hoisted on the main work. Our troops carried the work, the enemy scarcely making any resistance; we had only 2 men killed and 4 wounded. The 6th Cacadores, from the 6th Division, moved on towards the fort, and claimed the credit of taking it by assault. The first person who entered was helped in by a French officer; 500 prisoners fell into our hands. The enemy lost 100 during the siege. The work, for a small one, was excellently constructed, and had the convent been bomb proof, I do not know how, with the means we had, the place could have been carried. As it was, it was doubted by some whether the governor was justified in surrendering, and certainly, had the troops in the outwork done their duty, it would not have fallen.

In the construction of such works the French excel, and knowing their talent for such things, I cannot but think the means we have with the army in heavy artillery inadequate to the undertaking.

June 28th. In consequence of the fort surrendering yesterday, the enemy began their march on Valladolid at one this morning. On riding out at daylight we found their rear moving off the ground they before held, and the rear of their column nearly out of sight.

Lord Wellington gave a dinner to the principal people in Salamanca, and in the evening the junta of the town returned it with a ball. I dined at headquarters with Sir Stapleton. Many people had been invited, but few came. At the ball they still kept in mind the chance of the return of the enemy, and many through fear, and some through inclination, did not treat us as I should have expected. We had heard much of Spanish beauty; Salamanca, I fancy, is an exception to the rest of Spain. The enemy, no doubt, have many friends among the upper classes, but none among the lower.

The majority of British officers say that all people in Spain like our army the least. What cause have they to hate us and like the enemy? They require rations for their men, payment for their army, transport of every kind without; payment and embargo all the horses for their cavalry, and many mules for artillery and baggage.

We draw nearly all our rations from the rear, and what we get from the country, we pay for in ready money or receipts are given. The whole of our transport is paid for, and we never require any contributions. Say we get half our rations from the inhabitants, and do not pay them, the diference in not taking any contribution must be a great relief. There is one point in which the French have a decided advantage, viz. religion, which they do not fail to impress upon them. Their officers mix more with the higher classes. Indeed, from the short time we remain, it is scarcely possible to associate much in the cathedral this morning; it was attended by Lord Wellington and most of the general officers.

The cathedral is a fine building, though much spoiled in its internal appearance by the orchestra being railed off from the body of the place, and fixed nearly in the centre. The outside is covered with fine masonry, and for so large a building I think has too much. The square in the centre of the town is the next thing to the cathedral; it is the finest I have seen in the peninsula, and had the gates into it been regularly placed, would be perfect Piazzas run all round, affording a cool walk.

We get ice in abundance, and in Salamanca it is excellent; it can be had in nearly every village in this part of Spain.

Sir Stapleton Cotton received the account of an affair in the mouth with the Heavy Brigade, under Major General Slade, and the French Brigade under General L'Allemand, the same we attacked at Llerena, consisting of the 17th and 29th Dragoons, and one Chasseur regiment. It took place near Maguilla, June 11th, 1812.

Major-General Slade had a squadron for some time past, encamped in rear of Llerena, which the enemy attempted to surprise, but failed. He then took the 1st (Royal) Dragoons and

3rd Dragoon Guards, in pursuit of the enemy, through Llerena on the Maguilla road, and in a short space fell in with the 17th and 29th French regiments, about the same force he had. These he charged and completely routed, taking 120 prisioners. He pursued with his whole force for nearly two leagues close up to Maguilla, in front of which there is a defile; and the enemy having the Chasseur regiment, here formed, charged our scattered troops, retook all we had gained, and turned the day completely against us. Our loss was great and the General's letter to Sir Stapleton with the account the best I ever saw. He made mention of his son having stained his maiden sword.

	Officers	Sergeants	Rank&File	Horses	
3rd Dragoon Guards		1	9	6	killed
			1	7	wounded
	1★	6	67	82	missing
1st (Royal) Dragoons		1	11	6	killed
			19	14	wounded
	1★	4	39	127	missing
Totals		2	20		killed
			20		wounded
	2	10	106		missing

June 29th. The whole army moved this day on Valladolid in three columns.

Advanced guard: General Alten's Cavalry. Light Division, Pack's Briagade Infantry.

Left column   *Centre column*   *Right column*

★Lt. Homewood, 3rd D.G
★Lt. Windsor, 1st Drag.

Gen. le Marchant's	1st Division	Gen. Bock's
Brig.Caval.	5th Division	Brigade of
Third Division	6th Division	Cavalry.
Bradford's Brigade	7th Division	4th Division
Spanish Infantry	Headquarters	
Don Julian's Cavalry		

Major-General Anson's brigade marched on the Toro road on the left of the whole.

The army marched four leagues from Salamanca.

Headquarters of the cavalry, Parada de Rubalis. We saw the enemy's rear moving off, a league from Parada.

June 30th. We saw the enemy's rear this day on the hills in front of Alaejos. It was Marmont's intention to make a stand on the right bank of the Guarena, and he had collected his force for that purpose. He moved off before the advanced guard came up. Headquarters of the army moved to Fuente la Pena, those of the cavalry to Tordesillas de la Orden. The enemy still occupied Alaejos with 5,000 infantry, and a considerable force of cavalry. In the evening they withdrew the force to Castrajon, a league from thence on the La Nava del Rey road. Major-General Alten's brigade occupied Tordesillas de la Orden, and had an alert when the enemy's troops moved from Alaejos. The 11th Light Dragoons lost two sergeants and open man, prisoners, this day. Sir Stapleton was much vexed at the manner they were lost, and said the 11th should leave the brigade. I do not know that he could say so with reason.

July 1st. The enemy last night left Castrejon on his route for Valladolid. Our advanced guard, with the addition of Major-General Anson's brigade, which this day joined from the left, occupied La Nava del rey, two leagues from Tordesillas. The enemy's piquets were a league from us, and Marmont only left the place this morning at 7 o'clock. Sir Stapleton went to La Nava. Headquarters of the army, Alaejos.

Major-General Anson joined his brigade this morning from England.

The army marched about three leagues this day, and

bivouacked On the Trabancos without a tree to shade them or wood to cook with nearer than a league from their camp. The inhabitants frequently use straw to cook with.

July 2nd. Major-General Bock's and Le Marchant's brigade joined the advance this morning, and the whole moved forward at daylight on Tordesillas, situated on the

Right bank of the Duero. We found the enemy's piquets on the heights about a league from La Nava del Rey, on the right bank of the rivulet Zapardiel, occupying the high ground near Torresilla. Lord Wellington, in his orders of last night, directed the advanced guard not to cross the rivulet, but to halt there for further orders. Major-General Alten's brigade gained the heights, and Sir Stapleton supported him with General Anson's brigade, halting the infantry at the bottom. The enemy occupied the plain leading to Tordesillas with their cavalry, and had a considerable force if infantry in Rueda.

The plain is covered with vineyards, the trees three feet from the ground, but no hindrance to cavalry acting.

Sir Stapleton advancing contrary to Lord W's orders will not be forgotten by him.

We halted close to their piquets with the two brigades, when Lord W. came up and ordered us to advance. Major-General Alten's brigade, with the horse artillery, drove their cavalry over the plain, supported by General Anson's. We left Rueda to our right, obliging their infantry to evacuate that place. Our guns did considerable execution, but the cavalry was not allowed to charge. A league from Tordesillas, the ground falls much and suddenly, and on our gaining this point, the guns were opening on their infantry, and had fired a few shots. We thought the opportunity a fair one, when the whole was ordered to halt.

Lord W. said that had he been aware of the ground, and had the infantry up, he might have attacked them with great advantage. He either thought there was some chance of success with their rear in passing the Duero, or that Marmont intended to fight on the Zapardiel. It was said the latter, as he ordered the advanced guard to halt before it crossed. The enemy withdrew their whole force over the Duero, occupying the town of Tordesillas in considerable force, and has barricaded the bridge. They are encamped in considerable force immediately behind the town, and have troops watching the ford of Pollos on the left.

Sir Stapleton Cotton, with Generals Anson's and Alten's brigades, and the Light Division, occupied Rueda for the night. Headquarters of the army came to Villa Verde. The place is famed for a light white wine. The men cannot be kept out of them.

July 3rd. The troops at Rueda were directed to show themselves on the high ground near, and on hearing any firing on the left were to move down into the plain, with the appearance of making an attack on Tordesillas. The left column was strengthened by the two Heavy Brigades of cavalry, and moved on Pollos, with the idea of attacking the ford at that place. We heard firing at 10a.m on the left, and moved agreeably to the orders.

The attack on Pollos was confined to a cannonade on the part of the enemy, and on ours to a skirmish of light troops, a few of which passed the river, and then retired again.

The troops at Rueda remained out till near dusk, and then occupied their former quarters.

All attempt to force the passage of the Duero was given up, and arrangements issued this evening for the halt and disposition of the army.

The enemy had broken open every cellar in Rueda; the men had got drunk and beaten their officers, and form the account of the inhabitants, had we attacked on our advance from La Nava, early in the morning, they would have suffered a good deal.

It seems to be Lord Wellington's intention to attack, the Duero, once Tordesillas and another the same time at Villa Nueva. They remained for about an hour, and retired.

They have thrown small breastworks up on the Adaja, and in some places on the Duero for the protection of their infantry piquets.

General Bonnet is said to have joined with 5,000 men from the north.

A squadron from the 11th Light Dragoons went to Medina del Campo on the right. The duties were changed. The 16th found a squadron at Serrada, the 12th at Ventosa, each to be relived every three days, and for the time they were out found all the duties. The centre squadron went on the 14th to Serrada.

July 15th. The enemy's force opposite Villa Nueva marched last night on Tordesillas, which was still occupied by the enemy, though not in such force. Their main body was assembled near Pollos, to which place the Light Division moved, and Headquarters left Rueda for La Nava del Rey. At 9p.m the brigade marched from La Seca to Rueda. The squadron of the 12th at Ventosa joined the brigade, and the one of the 16th retired to La Seca. Headquarters of the cavalry, Rueda. Lord Wellington moved to Alaejos. The enemy extended from Toro on the right to Pollos. They have 1,000 men in Tordesillas. There is a report that 9,000 men are moving from Madrid on Valladolid. We have Lieutenant Wheeler with three men stationed at Venosa, with orders to watch that road.

July 17th. The brigade moved last night from Rueda on Melina del Campo, and from thence to Castrejon, on the Trabancas. We received an order at daylight to leave La Seca for Castrejon. In marching through Rueda, the enemy had crossed at Tordesillas with some cavalry, and were driving out piquets back. We remained a short time on the high ground near that place. The enemy did not push us, and only came as far as Rueda, some time after we retired. We marched four leagues to Castrejon. A remount of ninety horses this day joined the 16th Light Dragoons from England, with four subalterns,- Lieutenants Lockhart, Lloyd Crichton, and Baker, junior. The enemy pushed on in the evening as far as La Nava del Rey in force, and sent a small party up to Alaejos, which was withdrawn towards La Nava. Lieutenant Baker did not long remain with the regiment.

The 4th and Light dragoons were encamped close to Castrejon, and General Cole, on riding out, fancied the enemy were coming to attack the two divisions with two squadrons. He rode back into the town, sent his baggage to the rear, and no doubt would have ordered the troops to turn out had he commanded.

July 18th. Sir Stapleton sent for me before daylight to proceed with a patrol in front of the piquets, with orders to see as many of the enemy's troops as could be overlooked by a patrol, and report immediately, as it was not known whether the enemy had crossed the Duero in any force. My patrol was of six men, and I was to accertain particularly if the enemy's infanty had come up to La Nava, and should there be nothing but cavalry we were to drive them back; and the Light division, with General Anson's and Alten's brigades were to march to Rueda, and the 4th Division to La Nava.

I had scarcely got beyond our piquets when I met a squadron of the enemy's cavalry. More were coming up, and in half an hour the piquets were driven back on Catrejon, and from the number of squadrons shown by the enemy, it was evident they were in force, and advancing. I joined one of the 11th, and with them retired on the brigade. We were a good deal pressed, and once obliged to turn round and charge. Captain Deakin, A.D.C to Sir Stapleton, with one man of the 11th, was wounded. The enemy's cavalry all appeared on the plain in front of Catrejon, and on seeing the brigade, halted their guns and ammunition and commenced a cannonade. Our squadrons were fortunately dispersed over the ground, and at first did not suffer much. Major Bull's and another troop came up and opened against the enemy. Captain Buchanan was absent, which gave me the centre squadron. I was sent with it to cover three guns of Major Bull's troop, and with my own troop moved forward and drove some of the enemy's skirmishers off a small hill, on which the guns were to act; leaving the other troops at the foot of the hill, covered from the enemy's fore. The enemy brought 16guns against us, which obliged our guns to retire. The guns being gone, they directed the whole of their fire against my troop, and before I could move off killed Corporal Hardiman and Dragoon Stone (the shot, round shot, hit him on the belly, and sent pieces of his insides all over the troop-a piece on Lieutenant Lloyd's shoulder, the first time he was ever in action-he lived an hour), wounding four others and five horses. It was the sharpest cannonade, for the time, we were, or I, was ever exposed to, and almost impossible to get the men away in complete order. Many shots went over us and struck the 11th Light Dragoons in the rear. On the left, two squadrons, one of the 11th and 12th, were supporting two guns from Major Ross's troop. The squadrons were supporting one another, and on the advance of some of the enemy's cavalry (inferior to the two squadrons), the one in front went about. Some of Marshal Beresford's staff seeing this, conceived the guns were in danger, rode up to the retiring squadron, calling "Threes about!" This of course put the other squadron about in the place of the fronting the one already retiring. One person gave one word, one another, and the enemy's cavalry came up to the guns. There was no harm done, and out dragoons (the 11th) immediately advanced and drove them back.

The cannonade on the Castrejon plain continued for two hours, during which time we kept our ground with little loss, considering the fire. The enemy's practice was bad.

During this a large column of French infantry had moved on Alaejos and gained that place. The two divisions retired on Toresilla de la Orden, covered by Major-General Anson's brigade, whilst Major-General Bock's and Le Marchant's were sent on our left towards Alaejos, and retired, under a considerable cannonade, on the Guarena. On our arrival in the valley of the Guarena, the Light and 4th Divisions were moving up the road to Canizal to their place in the position the army was now about to take upon the heights in front of Canizal. The enemy gained the heights commanding the road before our troops had got off. Their guns opened on the infantry, from which we (the infantry) suffered. During this the enemy passed the Guarena at Castrillo, with a view to gain the heights of the left. Major-General Alten's brigade, supported by the 3rd Dragoons, was engaged with the enemy in passing the village.

The enemy supported their cavalry with infantry, and pressed in until they got up to our line, when Major-General N. Ansons's brigade, from the 4th Division, supported by Colonel Stubbs' Portuguese, drove them back with the bayonet. The brigade of cavalry pursued immediately, and took General Carrier and 240 men. The attack here ceased, and the enemy employed the remainder of the day in closing up their troops, and at night their whole force was on the left bank of the Guarena. Our position is strong, extending from Castrillo on the left, to the right of Canizal. Headquarters of the army are at Canzal, to which place the brigade moved, leaving our squadron on piquet in front of the infantry on the Guarena. The weather is very hot and water very scarce.

The operations of the day were very interesting. We were covering the retreat of the army to the position on the Guarena, with a force very inferior to the advanced column of the enemy, and effected it with little loss; our brigade remained in the neighbourhood of Castrejon long after the enemy had approached by their movement on Alaejos nearer to the Guarena than the ground we occupied.

July 19th. The two armies remained quietly looking at each other the whole day till 2p.m, when the enemy's troops fell in and marched to their left by Tarragona.

Return of the 18th July, 1812

Majors	Captns.	Lieutenants	Staff	Ensigns	Sergants	Rank&File	Horses	
British								
-	-	-	1	-	3	56	59	killed
1	4	9	1	1	7	273	65	wounded
-	-	-	-	-	-	27	21	missing
Portuguese								
1	1	-	-	-	2	31		killed
2	2	2	2	-	3	16		wounded
-	-	-	-	-	-	27		missing

	Killed	TOTAL Wounded	Missing
British	61	297	27
Portuguese	34	96	27
	95	393	54

Total loss in men, 442; Horses, 145,

(Circumstance of Dragoon Whelan of my troop being on vidette when a flag of truce came in, and the manner he used his sword on the French trumpeter who would not halt when he was ordered by Whelan, but continued to advance, sounding as he moved forward.)

The allied army made a similar movement to its right, passed the Guarcna at Vallesa, assembling on the right of that place before the enemy could close up their main body. We joined the brigade on the plain, and found our guns engaged with the enemy's advance.

Our shells set fire to a considerable tract of corn, it burnt for above a mile in extent, as the little air there was carried the flame. I could not help thinking how dreadful it would be to be wounded, and to perceive it approaching without the power of getting away.

The brigade bivouacked in rear of the 6th Division. The infantry were in two lines in order of battle.

Captain McIntosh of the regiment on sick leave. This gave me the right squadron, changing my troop for his.

July 20th. The allied army was this morning drawn up in order of battle. The enemy at daylight began his march by his left on the chain of heights leading to Babila-fuente. He crossed the Guarena at Cantalapiedra, keeping the heights above the river, and at night encamped near Babila-fuente and Villoruela.

The allied army made a corresponding movement in column, each army moving the whole day within gun shot of each other.

The enemy from the heights frequently cannonaded our troops, but to little effect. Both armies made a long march, and fortunately the day was cloudy. We marched four, the enemy five leagues.

A squadron from each of the regiments of our brigade remained on piquet, mine was the one of the 16th. The 7th Division took the piquets at night. The 6th Division, with Major-General Alten's brigade, occupied Aldea Lengua, and the remainder of the army bivouacked at Cabeza Vellosa.

The two armies marching so near to each other that either might bring on a general action in half-an-hour, was a very singular sight. Lord Wellington perceived Marmont's object in a moment, and ordered a corresponding movement Marmont is a great manoeuvrer.

The following is the force of each Division taken at Cafrizal:—

1st Division		6,000
3rd "		4,500
4th "		3,200
5th "		5,700
6th "		4,500
7th "		4,500
Light "		4,000
Pack's Brigade		2,000
Bradford's Brigade		2,000
		36,400
Spaniards		3,600
	Infantry	40,000
Cavalry, British and German		3,200
Portuguese		800
		4,000
Don Julian's Spaniards		500
		4,500

July 21st. My squadron was relieved at daylight, and marched with the brigade to Castalliano and Merisco, the 11th and 16th occupying the latter. The brigade left a squadron from each regiment in piquet. The enemy closed his troops towards the Tormes, and was employed in passing the whole day by the ford at Huerta. The allied army did the same at the ford of Santa

Marta, and in the evening the whole was over the Tormes, with the exception of the 3rd Division and Portuguese cavalry left on the heights near Cabrerizos. General Anson's brigade bivouacked near Santa Marta. Dreadful thunder an hour after dark. The greastest number of the horses of the 5th Dragoon Guards ran away over the men sleeping at their heads, by which eighteen in the brigade were wounded, and thirty-one horses not found the following morning.

We saw the different columns very plainly, from the lightning being reflected on their muskets, which at that time of night was beautiful.

The loss was said to be accounted for on the 22nd, they returned those lost as horses lost in action on the 22nd. By each flash of lightening we saw the columns of infantry marching to their ground for the night.

Colonel and Mrs. Dalbiac, of the 4th Dragoons, were sitting down on the ground in front of the brigade; he had just time to carry her under a gun, which stopped the horses and saved them both.

July 22nd, 1812. The enemy during last night pushed their advance into Calvarassa de Arriba, and took possession of the height of Nuestra Señora de la Pena, our cavalry still occupying Calcarassa de Abaxo. The light troops from the 7th Division and General Pacs's brigade were engaged with the enemy on the height of La Pena, which we gained and kept throught he day.

The whole army assembled on one of the two heights called Los Arapiles, and the 3rd Division crossed the Tormes with the Portuguese cavalry, and marched on the right. About 12a.m the troops were ordered to attack, and the 1st Division moved forward to gain the other height of Arapiles which the enemy had taken.

The Division was countermanded and returned to the left, occupying the other of the Arapiles.

It was now said that we should retreat during the night, as the enemy's intention was to threaten our communication with Ciudad Rodrigo.

BATTLE OF SALAMANCA.

Between 3 and 4 p.m. Lord Wellington, with the 5th, 6th, and 7th Divisions, made a rapid movement at double quick time to the right; the 11th and 16th moved at the same time along the line to the right under a considerable cannonade, which did neither the infantry nor ourselves much injury. The 3rd Division just as we arrived on the right was in motion to attack the enemy's left, supported by Major-General Le Marchant's brigade, which the 11th and 16th followed in line; the 12th remained on the left.

The appearance of the 3rd Division on the right of the army when we thought that it was still on the other side of the Tormes, was a surprise to us.

The 3rd Division, commanded by General Pakenham in Picton's absence, attacked the enemy's left, whilst the 4th and 5th, supported by the 6th and 7th and Light, attacked the enemy in front, the cavalry supporting both. At 5 p.m., height after height was carried. The enemy's left rallied on their centre. Major-General Le Marchant's brigade broke the 6th Division of the enemy, making 2,000 prisoners: At the last height the enemy charged the 4th Division, which gave way; but the 6th Division supported, and this attack of the enemy, though well supported, failed. It was his last effort. General Pack, with his brigade, attacked Bonnet on the hill and was repulsed, but this drew fire from the 4th and 6th Divisions. The enemy did not follow up their success over General Pack by an attack on the 1st Division on our left, which seemed as peaceably inclined as the enemy's right. Cocks thought it lost an opportunity of turning that flank, and cutting off La Foy's Division. At 7 p.m. the enemy was in full retreat. Bonnet finding the hill turned by the 1st Division, abandoned it La Foy, with his division, retreated on Huerta, the remainder of the army on Alba de Tormes.

The cavalry during the attack on the last hill was ordered back to the point on the left, where we assembled before the attack, leaving the infantry to pursue without us. Had this not been done, though it might not have been prudent to pursue with both at night, yet, by being at hand, there was a greater chance of doing more. The order came from Sir Stapleton. The infantry moved in pursuit by moonlight.

The 6th Division, supported by the 3rd, moved on Alba de Tormes; the Light, supported by the 1st, on Huerta. This arrangement was unfortunate (as Lord Wellington afterwards said), for the Light fell in with nothing but stragglers; and the 6th were so tired, as not to be able to reach Alba de Tormes, where, we afterwards learnt, the enemy were employed from 8 p.m. to 4 a.m. in passing the river.

We made between 6,000 and 7,000 prisoners in the action, and took two eagles, and six stands of colours, with twenty-two guns. Marmont was badly wounded in the arm, but carried off; General Thomiere was wounded, and fell into our hands. The retreat of the enemy from the Arapile to Alba was made in the greatest confusion—cavalry, infantry, and baggage all mixed—and had we had two hours more daylight, their whole army would have been annihilated. Had the two armies changed situations we should have left our baggage on the right bank of the Tormes, which the French dare not do, on account of the guerrilla system. They must either have theirs close to them, or make a large detachment to guard it. The brigade, according to orders, which another brigade did not obey, returned to their former ground. Our squadron remained on piquet, and through Colonel Cummings went with one squadron of the 11th to Santa Marta.

(Circumstance that occurred with General Le Marchant previous to the attack of the enemy, and his feelings on the occasion.)

I heard from an officer in the 6th Division, that, although they had been marching all day, and were so tired when ordered to halt for the night that they could not possibly have marched much further, yet they sat up through the night talking over the action, each recalling to his comrade events that happened.

A soldier of the 3rd Division said he was after a French chap with his bayonet, who tried all he could to get out of his way; as a last resource he threw away his musket, and attempted to leap up one of the low oak trees on the field, when he ran his bayonet into him as he was getting up.

Mrs. Dalbiac, wife to Colonel Dalbiac of the 4th Dragoons, was close to the field of action—perhaps two miles from it. At nightfall she was anxious to ascertain the fate of her husband, and set out to seek him. She was accompanied by a dragoon of the 4th, and had the ill-luck to lose him. She wandered some time alone on the hill where the action had taken place, amongst the killed and wounded. I cannot conceive a more unpleasant situation for a woman to be in, particularly at night.

She always sleeps in her colonel's tent when the regiment is in bivouac. In 1811, she layout a couple of nights on the Guadiana, in incessant rain, with nothing but a blanket to cover her.

2,000 Spaniards were placed, before the action, in the castle of Alba de Tormes, and ordered out by Don Carlos de Espaila, without the knowledge of Lord Wellington. His lordship acted as if the place was occupied, and therefore directed the 1st and Light Divisions on Huerta, where he supposed the enemy could only cross; the castle at Alba de Tormes commanding the bridge.

Before the action Don Carlos asked if he should not take his troops out of Alba—after he; done it—hoping for an order. Lord Wellington said, "Certainly not"; and the Don was afraid to tell what he had done. Lord W. acted of course as if it was in our possession.

There was, I think, something singular in Lord Wellington ordering the 1st and Light Divisions to attack early in the day (about 12), and counter-ordering them after they had moved. Marshal Beresford, no doubt, was the cause of the alteration from what he urged. Yet, at the same time, Lord W. is so little influenced, or, indeed, allows any person to say a word, that his attending to the marshal was considered singular. From all I could collect and observe the peer was a little nervous. It was the first time he had ever attacked, and possibly his orders from England might be to avoid an action if not prudent. When he determined on the attack it was well done, and in the most decided manner. There was possibly some little trouble in arriving at that decision.

Major-General Le Marchant was killed at the head of his brigade; his conduct before he fell was much spoken of as particularly forward. Marshal Beresford was shot through the body, at the head of the Portuguese Brigade in the 6th Division. Generals Leith, Cole, and Alten were wounded. Sir Stapleton Cotton* was shot through the left arm by one of our own sentries after dark. This was a great loss to the cavalry, as no report was sent in to headquarters. Major-General Bock succeeded Sir Stapleton in the command of the cavalry.

RETURN OF THE ALLIED ARMY ON THE 22ND OF JULY, 1812, IN THE GENERAL ACTION OF SALAMANCA.

GenStaff	Lieuts.Cols	Majors	Captns.	Lieutenants	Ensigns	Sergants	Drummers	Rank&File	Horses	
British Loss										
1	1	1	11	10	4	24	1	335	96	killed
4	8	9	43	88	23,3 staff	136	18	2387	120	wounded
								74	37	missing
Portugese Loss										
			7	4	2	4		287	18	killed
			19	13	27, 3	42	6	1432	13	wounded
			1			1	1	179	7	missing
Spanish Loss										
								2		killed
								4		wounded

*He went in front of the piquets after dark, and being challenged by the sentry on his return did not answer. The two sentries fired; one hit Sir. S, and the other his orderly dragoons. Somewhat singular that both shots should take effect.

	Killed	Wounded	Missing
British Total	388	2,714	74
Portuguese	304	1,552	182
Spanish	2	4	–
	694	4,270	256

```
                                    4,270
                                      694
                                    -----
          Total Loss of the Army    5,220
```

Relating to 20th July, 1812. On the retreat from Rueda previous to the Battle of Salamanca, and near the height of Babila-fuente, the number of eagles and vultures was very great. They were brought together by the dead horses and men left from our position near Salamanca, and on the enemy's retreat to Rueda. They are always found to hover about an army, and I was frequently impressed with the horror of being wounded without the power to keep them off.

July 23rd. The 1st and Light Divisions, with Major-General Bock's and Anson's brigades, this morning crossed the Tormes in pursuit of the enemy. The two brigades of cavalry did not amount to 800, being so weakened by detatching squadrons during the night. The cavalry came up with their rear guard, consisting of both cavalry and infantry, near the village of La Serna. We charged the cavalry with two squadrons from the 11th and 16th, which fled, leaving the infantry to its fate. General Bock attacked the infantry with his brigade; rode completely through them in one of the best charges ever made. We took 2,000 prisoners, and followed their rear two leagies farther, when about 1,200 cavalry from the north joined their rear guard, and covered its retreat to Penaranda de Bracamonte. (Lord W. in his dispatch, names this as certain to happen from his information from the north previous to the action.)

The army bivouacked on the Almar.

The Heavy Germans in their charge lost thirty killed and from forty to fifty wounded.

The enemy on crossing the Tormes retreated in three columns; that to our right moved by Macotera, three leagues; Muxera de Abaxo, half league; Jurnalion, one league. The centre column by Garichermandez and Penaranda de Bracamonte. The left (la Foix), after crossing at Huera and Encina, moved on El Campo, two and a half, Zoritas and Cebolia, one league. All three were to unite at Flores de Avila.

Return of the affair this day :—

Killed, 51; wounded, 60; missing, 6.

We took eleven guns on the 22nd, and five ammunition tumbrils.

July 24th. General Anson's brigade, with Major Ross's and Bull's troop of artillery, this day marched on the Arevalo road. For five leagues we saw nothing of the enemy, and just before we came up with their rear the body of the brigade was halted, and a squadron from each of the three regiments sent forward. We came up with them at the village of-, and had the whole brigade been up we might have got into their camp before they turned out. They moved off without a shot being fired, excepting at their rear skirmishers, who remained long enough for two guns to come up. Had the whole brigade and twelve guns come, we might have stood a fair chance of taking 500. The greatest part of their infantry were without arms. Our advance got nearly as far as Aldea Seca. We marched seven leagues.

General Anson here missed a good opportunity of doing something with their rear. It is always the case. When we come near the enemy, the body of the brigade is halted, and three squadrons sent forward under the field officer of the day. The same in retiring, three squadrons are always left unsupported.

July 25th. The brigade this day halted. It does not look like a quick advance following up a great victory, and I think they will be let off too easily, The peasants represent them in a dreadful state. All their cavalry, excepting a few for their rear guard, is employed in carrying their sick.

Our baggage this day joined us.

Major-General Alten's brigade (now under Lieutenant-Colonel Arentschildt) moved this day into Arevalo. The beaten army has taken the route of Valladolid. King Joseph moved up part of the way from Madrid with 12,000 men, but has retraced his steps. His advance came close to Arevalo.

A commissary, with twenty-five Spanish* Chasseurs in the French service, was this day taken near Arevalo. It was a patrol from the advance of King Joseph's army.

July 26th. The brigade this morning moved at daylight three short leagues to Arevalo, which place they occupied.

July 27th. The brigade marched on the Valladoid road, occupying Almenara and adjacents. Colonel Arentschildt to Arevalo. The enemy nearly destroyed Almenara by fire; they leave many stragglers dead in the corn by the side of the road, and any person leaving their column is killed by the peasants.

July 28th. The brigade marched to Ornillios; the 11th and artillery occupied the remains of the small village; the 12th and 16th encamped.

Headquarters came to Olmedo, a league in our rear.

July 29th. The brigade crossed the Eresma and Ceja, marching through Mojados, and on the heights near Pedreja and Cardiel saw the enemy's rear in front of Aldeamayor.

There we remained for some time, and on sending on a squadron from each of our regiments, and Colonel Arentschild appearing at the same time with his brigade, the enemy withdrew close to the Duero. We bivouacked near Pedraja, which place was occupied by the Light Division. Headquarters came to Mojados. The whole army is closing up; the heavy cavalry are encamped close to us. If they attempt to defend the passage of the Duero, we shall attack; but they are well beat and well frightened from the manner they have got out of our way. They must have marched the whole of two nights following the 22nd.

July 30th. The two Light Brigades assembled this morning before daylight on the Duero, near Boccillo. The enemy had marched in the night on Valladolid. We passed the Duero at a ford below where we assembled and marched through La Cisterniga, a small place half a league from Valladolid, and from thence down

---

The enemy have taken some Spainards into their service; they however, keep them near the capital, and where they are tolerably strong, for fear of their deserting. They

the main road, halting on some rising ground close to the town which the enemy had abandoned.

Lord Wellington went into the place, and was received with *vivas* and rejoicings. We all went in; it is a much better town than Salamanca, though it has nothing equal to the square and cathedral at the latter place. The brigade returned for the night to La Cisterniga. Headquarters came to Boccillo. One of the enemy's columns has retired along the Duero to Aranda, and another taken the route of the Esquieva.

July 31st. The army halted this day.

August 1st. We marched before daylight to Villavanez on the right, leaving a squadrom of the 11th Light Dragoons on duty with the Light Division at Tudela. We sent a captain's patrol of fifty men to follow the enemy towards the river Esquieva. The enemy retreated on Valtanas. Our patrol went up to Castroverde, and then returned.

The brigade occupied Villavanez.

The enemy destroyed the bridge over the Duero at Tudela. The people there say that Marmont died at Tudela, and to conceal his death from the soldiers his body was carried in the litter. (A country town report.)

Here the advance ended, and I think has not been made the most of. We certainly might have presses them harder, though, as it is, I conceive that the French army will not be fit for the field again for some time.

Lord Wellington has moved his headquarters to Cuellar, six leagues on the Madrid road. On the 3rd the Light Division marched from Tudela on Cuellar.

August 5th. Received instructions this day from General Anson to proceed with a party of observation towards Burgos, and by finding out where the party of guerrillas were, to produce what information I could. I marched to Villa Fuerte, three long leagues from Villa Vanez. My party consisted of a corporal and six men.

August 6th. Marched this morning through Bertavillo and

are not very numerous, badly mounted, and not well equipped. It is not a service they enter with much zeal, and consequently not much reliance can be placed on them.

from thence on to Valtanas, two short leagues further, where I found Don Julian with his corps of guerrillas near Palenruda, on the Alanza. Their troops that were in Aranda and Lerma have moved on the Alanza. Their parties came close to Vallanas.

August 7th. Two divisions of infantry with cavalry of the enemy's marched to Torquermada; they sent a few men towards Palencia, which is occupied by Marquenez with his guerrillas.

August 8th. The enemy's patrols this day came so close to us that Don Julian marched to Bertavillio, leaving fifty men in the Valtanas. I moved with him.

Mendizabal, with a Spanish force from the north, is said to be in Formista, and that the enemy's force in Torquemada has left it for Astudillio.

August 9th. Don Julian last night received an order to join the army which is moving on Madrid. I, in consequence, marched to Castroverde, supposing the brigade had moved with the army. I there learnt they were still in their former quarters, and therefore marched to Villavanez, where I found the 16th and brigade headquarters.

Santicildes, with 3,000 of the Gallician army, has been since the 6th in Valladolid. He left it the other day to join the remainder of his force now besieging Astorga.

The 11th Light Dragoons marched this day to Penafiel on the Duero, four leagues from Villavanez. A squadron from the 12th occupied Olmon, and the right squadron, 16th, Villavaquerin.

Headquarters of the army have left Cuellar, and with the army have moved on Madrid, leaving Major-General Clinton with 10,000 infantry at Cuellar, and Major-General Anson's brigade on the Duero.

August 13th. The enemy are making a show of coming on from the north; their advanced guard came as far as Zevico de la Torre.

Lord Wellington yesterday entered Madrid, and this evening the Retiro surrendered with the honours of war. We made 2,506 prisoners. General Maitland, with 7,000 Spaniards and 5,000 British, landed 18th of last month at Alicant.

August 14th. The brigade marched this morning to Tudela,

leaving the centre squadron, 16th, and one from the 12th on duty, the former at Villavanez, the latter on our left at Renedo.

The enemy came on at daylight, marching on the line of the Pisuagre on Valladolid; they halted in the heat of the day, and in the evening pushed on to that place with their advanced guard, sending a strong patrol as far as Simancas. The Spanish troops retired on Astorga.

The 12th and 16th both retired to Tudela; the 11th closed in to Quintanillia Abaxo.

August 15th. I left the brigade this morning with a detatchment of a corporal and six men for the Puente de Duero to observe if the enemy pushed on that way. I remained near it all day, and retired at dusk a long league to Valdestillia. The enemy remained as last night, their advance occupying La Astrniga.

The 11th Light Dragoon's joined the brigade from the right, and Captain Buchanan's squadron (centre), 16th, came to Boccillo on the banks of the Duero, a league to the left of Tudela.

August 16th. Six thousand men this day marched into Valladolid. Before this force arrived the enemy had about 5,000; Clausel commands. General Foy, with 5,000 infantry and 800 cavalry, this day marched on Torrelobaton, on his route to relieve the garrison of Astorga. I retired this evening to Boccillo.

August 18th. The enemy, finding we has nothing but cavalry in Tudela, this morning moved from 3,000 to 4,000 infantry and 800 cavalry with six guns on the place. The brigade on their approach crossed the river at the ford close to the town. The bridge was destroyed, but the Light Division had rendered it passable for infantry. Their work was not destroyed, and the enemy pushed a company over the water.

Lieutenant Lindsell, of the 11th Light Dragoons, was killed in the act of charging them back. The brigade dismounted every other man, placed them in some old houses and ruined walls. There was a sharp fore kept up for some time, and at night the enemy kept possession of the town. Our artillery set fire, by its shells, to one or two houses, the enemy to many more, and, between the two, the town was nearly burnt down. The artillery was a good deal engaged, and lost seven men wounded. The 16th had one man killed and seven wounded. He was killed by one of the enemy; being sent on patrol from Boccillo after dark, he did not know that the French piquet was on this side the water, and rode up to their sentry, taking him to be Portugese, as there was a report that a battalion of Cacadores from Cuellas had arrived. They came as far as Monte Mayor, and had they proceeded on, would have been of great use, and might, if necessary, have kept Tudela-no place being so capable of defence with a small force, having only one entrance from the Valladolid side. In the evening the brigade retired to the following places-

Monte Mayor (headquarters); 2 squadrons 12th Light Dragoons, 2 16th Light Dragoons.

Parilla: 2 squadrons 11th Light Dragoons.

Valdestillias; 1 squadron 11th.

Boccillo: 1 squadron 16th Light Dragoons.

The brigade found one squadron for duty near Tudela.

(Circumstance of the dragoons, when defending the bridge from behind a wall, dressing up a figure of straw, and holding it up for the enemy to fire at.)

August 19th. Marched this day to Monte Mayor by order of General Anason, to be detatched with a corps of guerrillas placed under his command.

August 20th. I, this day, with one dragoon, marched to Santovanez, where I joined Colonel Sorniel, a guerrilla chief, commanding about 600 mounted peasants.

El Principe Bourbon, the other attatched to the brigade, was in Quintanilla de Abaxo. His party (of a little better description than Sorniel's) consists of 180.

My orders were to send into General Anson all the information I could gain, and see they went nowhere without his orders.

The enemy, this day, evacuated Tudela. The two parties were ordered to cross the Duero. We moved so late that we encamped (or rather bivouacked, never having and tents) on the banks of the river without crossing.

August 21st. Sorniel, this morning, occupied Villavaquerin.

Principe moved last night to Castrillo de Texoriego, and this day to Pena, on the Esqueva.

At the time the enemy entered Valladolid, at the commencement of the revolution, Sorniel was in prison, and released by them, and has ever since been organizing this corps.

They are complete banditti, two-thirds clothed in things taken from the enemy. The only pay they receive is from plunder; each horse belonging to the rider. The country provides them with regular rations.

This evening I left Sorniel and joined El Principe at Pena, a long league in advance.

August 22nd. A requisition made by the commanding officer of the French, at Duenas, on the adjacent villages.

The original was brought in to El Principe.

Requisition:-
Wheat	2,000 Fenegas
Barley	2,000
Rye	2,000
Meat	28,4000 pounds.

The enemy's parties were in the villages in the valley de Cerrato this day. In the evening we marched to Pollacion, where they had been three hours before we marched in. their parties at night all withdrew to Duenas or Cabezon de Camps.

Some infantry, either four or five, were taken by the guerrillas the other day, having stayed at a fountain to drink; they were not a quarter of a mile from their detatchment. The French call them brigands; they are troublesome ones.

August 23rd. As El Principe's object was to protect the rich country round Duenas, we, this day, moved a league to Valoria la Buena, where the enemy had sent a party of 100 infantry. They moved away on our advance. We remained all day in the place, and returned at night to Poblarion.

A change took place this day in the quarters of the brigade. Its headquarters moved to Peobraja.

I got the following state of the enemy's force from a Spanish officer come from the north:-

Valladolid	4,000 infantry
Palencia	3,500 "
Duenas	1,500 "
Cabezon de Campos	1,000 "
Detatchment made from Valladolid to Astorga	10,000 "
	20,000
Total Cavalry	1,800
Total force	21,800

The greater part of their cavalry is gone north, and the remainder is opposite the brigade on the Duero. We do not see a man on this side.

August 25th. In the evening the party marched to Zevico de la Torre. These parties cannot remain long in one place, as the village they occupy always supplies them. To remain for any time in one place would ruin the inhabitants. We occupied the town the first night; and the second bivouacked in its rear. He (El Principe) depends entirely on peasants for information of the enemy, and has only one piquet on the main road.

August 27th. A detatchment of 1,300 infantry, 50 cavalry, and 2 guns, escourting 4,000 reals, marched yesterday from Burgon, arriving this day at Duens, a distance of sixteen leagues. Eight stragglers were taken by a party of El Principe's. They say 2,000 men remain in Burgos; that Marmont in there, and has not lost his arm.

August 28th. We marched from our bivouac this morning to Valoria la Buena, two short leagues, and there saw the enemy's detatchment, that arrived yesterday at Duenas, proceed on its route for Valladolid.

About 200 infantry afterwards marched to Duenas from Vallodolid. This was a dispatch sent from Clusel to Burgos; he could not trust it with a smaller secourt.

El Principe, for some days back, had been in communication with Spaniards in the French service at Valladolid. There were only a few, and the officer commanding them was formerly in his corps. They, this day, came from Valladolid and joined his party, amounting to one captain, one lieutenant, and eighteen rank and file. They belonged to the Chasseurs, and were all the enemy had of that kind of troop with the army. There were miserably mounted, and brought with them an officer from the Etat major in the French service, who was going to Duenas to see the regiment he belonged to; he had placed himself under their protection. When he came up to us, he took our party for Spainiards in the enemy's service, and was not a little astonished when I asked him if he was a deserter like the others. We retired in the evening to Pollacion. The poor fellow was in the greatest distress. The French consider these parties quite as banditti; and I am not quite clear what my fate would be if taken prisoner with them. They certainly would use me very harshly.

August 29th. Marched this day to Pena

August 30th. This day went to see the brigade. Found its headquarters in Pedraja, with the 16th in Valdestillas.

The enemy's detatchment to the north this day returned, part to Valladolid with 5,000 infantry, and some cavalry to Tordesillas.

They had brought with them the garrisons of Zamora and Zera. That of Astorga surrendered in the evening of the 18th; and General Foy arrived the following day. It consisted of 1,200 men, who surrendered on the promise of being marched to the first French post. They left Astorga for that pupose under a Spanish escort, whioch, finding the enemy advancing changed their minds and marched the whole of the prisoners to Corunna.

I returned on the 1st to El Principe at Pena; and, having explained to him General Anson's orders, rejoined my regiment the following day. The brigade was cantoned as follows:-

Headquarters, 2 squadrons 12th Light Dragoons; Pedraja.

Two squadrons 11th, one 12th Light Dragoons; Aldea Mayor.

One squadron 11th Light Dragoons; Boccillo

Three troops 16th, headquarters: Serrada

Three troops 16th Light Dragoons: Valdestillas.

The centre squadron, 16th, is the one divided; my troop is at Valdestillas.

The enemy occupies Tordesillas in force; and has 1,000 infantry in Simancas, the bridge at which place is ready for explosion.

Sept 4th. We, this day, heard of the army's moving up from Madrid. Lord Wellington arrived at Olmedo.

We see peasants who came from Valladolid; they say the enemy has all his baggage, etc., ready to move, but have not heard any hints that he knows of our army being so near. Captain Murray has had the direction of the piquets from Valdestillas, on the right of Tordesillas. He has placed three men on duty where one would have done. The officers come on piquet once in three days, and the men can scarcely find a relief. The enemy have little or no cavalry near us; and his (Captain Murray's piquets are much stronger than when the enemy had the whole of their army on the Duero, before the battle of Salamanca.

The troops are out every morning before daylight; and the officer's baggage at Serrada is likewise ordered out. General Anson found out how he was going on, and ordered the troops not to turn out at daylight.

Sept 5th. Lord Wellington this day rode through Valdesillas to look at the fords on the Duero. The army came up, encamping on the Ceja, a league in rear of Valdestillas.

Sept 6th. The army assembled on the Duero, at Boccillo

CAVALRY:-
Major-General Bock's Heavy brigade.
Colonel Ponsonby's Heavy Brigade, late Le Marchant's.
Major-General Anson's Light Brigade.

INFANTRY:-
1st Division
5th
6th
7th

Brigadier-General Pack's and Bradford's brigades of Portugeses infantry.

Remained in the neighbourhood of Madrid:-

Major_General Alten's Brigade of Cavalry
Major-General Slade's and Major-General Long's brigades of cavalry

3rd Division Infantry ⎫
4th   "   " ⎬ Lieutenant-General
Light   "   " ⎪ Sir Rowland Hill,
2nd   "   " ⎭ commanded.

We passed the Duero by different fords-the main body by Herrera de Duero. The advance of the brigade, consisting of a squadron of the 11th Light Dragoons, took a few stragglers. We halted within a mile of La Cisterniga, on the heights near which the enemy showed about 3,000 men.

The day was employed in passing the troops over the Duero. The centre squadron remained on piquet; the army bivouacked on the river after crossing it. Headquarters at Boccillo.

Sept 7th. The army retired in the right from La Cisterniga; and at daylight we advanced with the squadron close to Valladolid, which the enemy occupied in force, but withdrew all their infantry into the town with the expectation of a small piquet.

The detatchment from Simancas did not join their main army before this morning; and had we moved on yesterday, they must habe left this behind them;

About 12a.m they blew up the bridge over the Pisuagre close to Valladolid, and marched on Duenas witht heir whole force. We moved parallel with them on the opposite bank of the river, and in the evening encamped in the rear of Santa Obenia, which was occupied by the 12th, and headquarters of the brigade.

Headquarters came to Vallodolid.

Before the bridge was blown up, Lord Wellington wished to save it by Lieutenant-Colonel Ponsonby's charging over with a squadron of the 12th Light Dragoons, and ordered the remainder of the brigade close to the bridge.

Sept 8th. The 16th moved this day into Caberon de Campon, two leagues from Vallasolis. The army halted. I rode into Valladolid to hear the Constitution proclaimed. This was done from the Town Hall in the square; few people of any respectability attended. The town was illuminated in the evening.

Sept 9th. The 6th Division, with General Pack's and Bradford's brigade, this day moved through Calezon, crossed the Pisuagre at that place, and emcamped on its right bank, two miles in advance.

The brigade moved a league in their front. We found a squadron from each regiment for duty. The enemy occupies Deuenas in force.

Sept 10th. The 6th Divisions, with the two brigades that crossed the Pisuagre yesterday, this day moved up to the ground close to our brigade.

The whole of the army moved from Valladolid, headquarters leaving that place for Cabezon.

The enemy's force had been marching the whole day to the rear; and in the evening their rear left Duenas; and our piquets were placed in advance of that place.

Sept 11th. The army marched two leagues, encamping on the Carrion and Pisuagre. Headquarters advanced to Duenas. The 11th and 16th occupied Banos, the 17th encamped on the Carrio. I rode two leagues to see Palencis, a small but good town, and not in the least destroyed by the army.

Lord Wellington was in at the same time, and received in the usual flattering manner, as in other places, a thing he does not object to, thought he affects to despise such things. (Circumstance of the guerrilla going on before him to apprize them in Palencia of his approach.)

Sept 12th. Headquarters moved to Magaz, two leagues from Duenas. The army encamped in front of that village.

The brigade moved to the heights close to Torquemada; our squadron, with one of the 11th, was on duty. The brigade only found two squadrons with a field officer.

We remained watching the enemy until 12a.m when their infantry marched over the bridge on the Pisuagre for Burgos, leaving six squadrons of cavalry on this side the water, in front on the town. The brigade was a mile in the rear, and when too late General Anson sent for one gun; two were brought, but before these arrived the enemy had passed, and we could only come within range of their rear.

It was the most evident thing before it happened that could be, and we lost a chance that may never again occur.

The two squadrons on duty followed their rear close to Quintana, on the Arlanzon, and the enemy at dark, finding we had only so small a force up, attempted to drive us back. The road up as far as this is the finest I ever saw, and from Torquemada to Quintana raised two feet above the level of the ground. The country is covered with vineyards, and intersected with ditches. Cavalry can only act on the road, which made our small numbers equal to theirs. They came down the road at a trot, trumpeting to charge. We stood still, and they halted within thirty yards, firing volleys at us. When we moved forward they retired, and we kept our ground till dark. Colonel Ponsonby spoke highly of our squadron, and we can with equal justice bear testimony to his conduct. The enemy's rear occupied Quintana; the two squadrons bivouacked a league in front of Torquermada, which place was occupied by the brigade. It rained the whole night.

Sept 13th. The enemy during the night marched three leagues. We crossed the Arlanzon at Quintana, and marched through the defiles on its bank without seeing the enemy. The two squadrons relieving us occupied Villaverde. The enemy's headquarters were this day at Pamphiya. General Anson, with the two squadrons coming off duty, occupied Villajera, a little to the left of the main road, to which place he ordered the brigade; but this was not allowed by Colonel Gordon, the new quartermaster-general, just come from England. (He will not stay long with the army) It, in consequence, remained at Quintana. Headquarters came up to Torquemada.

Sept 14th. The brigade came up to Villajera. The army moved close to Quintana. Headquarters to Cordevilla.

Sept 15th. Headquarters came to Villajera-the army encamped in front of Villaverde. The enemy were a long league from the Venta de Posta, where the brigade remained till dark, and the enemy retiring we occupied Los Valbases, to the left of the road.

We are the only part of the army that is under cover. It rained considerably during the night.

The Gallician army is said to be in Palencia, and that we are waiting for them. As yet we have not advanced above two leagues each day.

Sept 16th. The enemy withdrew within a league in front of Calada, which place they occupied in force. Our squadron, with one of the 12th, under Major Lord Waldegrave, of the latter regiment, was on duty. About 12 we drove in their piquets with some skirmishing, in which I lost a horse from my troop. Our vedettes were close to the enemy's; we had a good deal of conversation with them during the day, and at dark two officers from the 22nd Chasseurs rode up to us. Since Salamanca their tone is a good deal altered, they talk of nothing but joining the grand army in the north, and say the Emperor is at St.Petersburg.

The Spaniards this day joined the army, and were in orders this night to advance with us. It rained nearly the whole night. Headquarters came up to Pamphiya. The 5th Divisions, with Major-General Bradford's brigade, encamped close to Pamphiya. Bivouacked.

Sept 17th. Lord Wellington thought the enemy might have kept the position they yesterday held near Celada, and the 6th Division, with General Pack's brigade, and one squadron from General Anson's, was to march on the left of the road, whilst General Bradford's brigade advanced on the left bank of the Arlanzon, with one squadron from General Anson's brigade, and the main body at the same time moving on the main road. The enemy at daylight left Celada, which the squadrons on the duty occupied, and there waited for the infantry and remainder of the brigade.

The 5th Divison came up, and sent their light companies on, with two squadrons in advance of the brigade. The enemy occupied some strong gound half a league from Celada, on the Hormaza, but which they abandoned, being turned by the 6th Division. We then followed them for nearly two leagues, and cannonaded their rear until they crossed the Arlanzon at Villa Bumiel, keeping the bridge over that river, and heights near it.

The road is planted on each side with popular trees. The 16th lost two men killed by cannon shot from advancing too close to the brigade. The 6th Division again turned them, and the enemy retired close to Burgos. The army encamped in front of Villa Bumiel, and the left column near Tardajos, on the other side the Arlanzon.

Headquarters came to Tardajos.

The high road runs through Villa Bumiel, though in the maps it is placed opposite side the river.

Sept 18th. The army assembled close to Burgos, encamping half a league from the town. Two squadrons from the brigade moved in front of Burgos. The enemy evacuated the town this morning, leaving considerable garrison in the castle close to it. I went in to see the town, but could not go all over it; many streets were close to the castle; and wherever the enemy could they fired at us.

Sept 19th. The 1st Division, with General Pack's brigade, this morning assembled at Villa Toro, and invested the castle. The 5th Division moved to some ground a league in front of Burgos, and General Anson's brigade a league in their front. Headquarters of the army were placed at Villa Toro. The brigade occupied the following villages:-

Headquarters Artillery and 12th: Bellema
11th: Villa Fria
16th: Villamoro.

The enemy's piquets are in Quintanapallia, a league from Vitta Fria; their main body has gone back as far as Briviesca.

The Light Companies from the Highland Brigade in the 1st Division, this morning drove in the enemy's piquets in front of the horn work to the north of the castle. Major Cocks commanded them, and remained watching the work the whole day.

In the evening the following orders came out:-

Brigadier-General Pack volunteered the duty of attacking the horn work, and was directed with his brigade to escalade the front of the work, whilst Major Cocks moved in the rear of the work to prevent any reinforcement coming from the castle, and make a false attack on the gorge, which, should circumstances admit, he might convert into a real one; eight o'clock was the time fixed for the troops to move.

At eight the attack was made, and that of General Pack's failed. Cocks never thought of the false attack, and moved with the intention of a real one. The castle opened a heavy fire on him as he advanced. He ran up a slope of fourteen feet, at the top of which palisades of seven feet were to be passed. These he got over without the help of ladders, and under a heavy fire from the troops stationed to protect the gorge, gaining the body of the work with about 140 men. Those troops of the enemy's employed in repulsing the attack made by General Pack were all in the ditch, and Cocks, by gaining the work, drove the remainder of the garrison to them.

With his 140 he took possession of the right demi-bastion, as the most commanding point he could find, and from it kept up a heavy fire on the ditch. He had so few men that he could not square sufficient numbers to guard the sally-port into the ditch, and he could not go there with his whole force, not knowing how many passages they might have out of the ditch; and had there been another and they had come into the work, be being at that point all would have again been lost.

The people in the ditch found their case desperate, made a rush at the enterance, drove back the men there placed, and gained the body of the place. They had no sooner entered than he charged them, drove them out at the gorge, bayoneting fifty, and making as many more prisoners, leaving him, with his handful of men, in possession of the place. The affair was as well done as it possibly could be, and I think Cocks will obtain his Lieutenant-Colonelcy for the business. (This he did, but never lived to know it.) Lord Wellington told him he carried the fort, and that the affair was all his own. It was much spoken of at headquarters.

Cocks took great pains to get the men their dinner before he attacked, which not many officers would have considered in the way he did. It was cooked in bivouac with the 79th, and brought up to their post near the work about dark.

Sept 22nd. The brigade marched two leagues in advance of Burgos, occupying the following places:-
11th and 12th Light Dragoos: Monestario.
Headquarters Brigade Artillery, 16th: Frenso de Rodillio.
The 5th and 7th Divisions occupied ground in the rear of Quintinapallia, where it is said we shall fight if the enemy attempts to relieve Burgos.

The troops at Monestario do the duty, our piquets are in Castil de Peones, five miles in front of Monestario. The enemy's headquarters are in Pancerbo, with their advanced guard at Breviesca. I went to see Cocks, and visited the trenches with him-our progress against the castle is not much; only three guns, 18-pounders, are employed.

Sept 27th. I was this day detatched to the right, with six men, and halted in Villa Franca, three leagues from Fresno. The enemy occupy the whole of the Rioja, on the banks of the Ebro; their left extends as far as Santa Dorningo de la Calzada. The guerrillas are on their left, but do not appear very active. The enemy sent 600 infantry and 11 cavalry on the 28th to Pedroso; expecting this no change took place in their cantonments. I returned the same evening to Fresno.

October 1st. Lieutenant-General Sir S. Cotton this day joined the army from the rear, fixing his headquarters at Bellema. Lord Wellington invested him with the Order of the Bath, given for his services as second in command to the army during the battle of Salamanca.

The village of Monestario was on the side of a hill, which was so steep that you entered the upper story of the houses from the ground. The horses were put in the upper stories as well as below, and looked very absured with their heads out of the windows above stairs.

October 3rd. The 11th and 12th Light Dragoons having had the whole of the duty since we occupied these cantonments, a change this day took place in the quarters of the brigade.

Right and left squadron 16th, one 11th; Monestario.
12th Light Dragoons, centre squadron 16th: Fresno.
Two squadrons, 11th and Horse Artillery: Quintanapallia.

As we were turning out at Fresno a report came in that the enemy was advancing, which caused us to move as quick as we could to the main road in rear of Monestario.

They had come on at daylight, and driven in our advanced piquet from Castel Peones, and the support being placed off the main road, nearly gained the point where they joined before they had time to make it. It fortunately happened that as the troops were that morning to be relieved, the squadron of the 11th remaining at Monestario, was turned out to relieve the one of the 12th on duty, and on hearing the fire moved down the road and came up in time to charge at the bridge over the small river half a league in front of Monestario, over which the 12th had retired in no small confusion.

Their advanced piquet was so surprised under Lieutenant Fulton, of the 12th, that he had scarcely time to mount his men, and the whole squadron came from St. Clalla in such confussion as to make no stand, and at the time the 11th came up the whole was retiring on Monestario.

The 11th charged them at the bridge drove them back; the enemy turned again, and so advanced a second time. The enemy's intention was to surprise the advanced squadron, in which they failed, and retired again to their former posts. Had not it so happened that the 11th were turned out to relieve them, I have little doubt they would have taken the greater number of the 12th, and gained Monestario before the troops there could have turned out. The two squadrons took from the enemy one captain and twelve men, and lost one corporal and one man from the 11th, with eleven privates from the 12th.

We took up our quarters agreeably to the arrangement General Souham has joined the enemy from the north, and now commands.

October 4th. One battalion from the 7th Division this day came into Monestario. It is the Brunswick Infantry, and I fear many will desert to the enemy. They find fifty men for piquet at the bridge, with an inlying piquet of fifty more; one subaltern of cavalry with eighteen men as an outlying piquet with one troop inlying.

October 7th. I went to Burgos this day to see how the operations were going on against the castle. The mine under the outer wall had succeeded, and our troops were in possession of the outer wall, and had made some approaches close to the castle. There were two breaches in the outer wall, which had been carried by the 24th Regiment in the morning. Major Cocks was this day field officer of the trenches. I did not see him.

October 8th. I dined yesterday with Sir Stapleton, and returned early this morning to Monestario.

Little did I expect to return so soon again to Burgos, and still less the mournful event that called me back. A letter from Colonel Ponsonby, 12th Light Dragoons, came to me at 4p.m to inform me of the death of Major Cocks, who was killed that morning between 3 and 4a.m. I went as far as Quintanapallia, and there remained till the following morning.

October 9th. I this day proceeded to the camp ground of the 79th. He fell by a ball which entered between the forth and fifth rib on the right side, passing through the main artery immediately above the heart, and so out at the left side, breaking his arm: the man was close to him. In Cocks the army has lost one of its best officers, society a worthy member, and I a sincere friend.

He had always been so lucky in the heat of fire that I fancied he would be preserved to the army. He was killed in the act of rallying his men to regain the outer wall, which the enemy had carried, and was at the top of the breach when he fell. The man that did the fatal deed could not have been more than five yards from him. We buried him in the camp ground of the 79th, close to Bellima. Lord Wellington, Sir Stapleton Cotton, Generals Pack and Anson, with the whole of their staff, and the officers of the 16th Light Dragoons and 70th Regiment, attended him to his grave. He is regretted by the whole army, and in those regiments in which he has been not a man can lament a brother more than they do him. I took upon myself the arrangement of his affairs, and disposed of what I though should be sold the day after his funeral.

It is usual on these occasions to sell all appointments, etc. In this instance I took upon myself to give most of them to his friends. The sword he had in his hand when he fell I keep myself. He had used it for a log time when in the 16th, and I intend to keep it whilst I am able to carry one. From my first joining the 16th as a boy (in Kent) he took me by the hand. He applied for and kept me in his troop through the whole of his service in the 16th, and was of the greatest service to me. We always lived together, and had I left it to him, I should not have paid one-third of my share. He always put off the day of settling, saying we would arrange it at the end of the campaign. The men in his troop in the 16th were very fond of him, and would hollo, when in a charge, "Follow the captain, stick close to the captain!" The men called his squadron the fighting squadron.

(Circumstance of dispute we had at Woodbridge, in Suffolk, respecting £2 10s. he won from me at cards, and his invariable kindness from the time.)*

He was very fond of hunting and shooting, and all out-of-door amusements. His education had been private, but very good; he worked hard and in a useful manner after he entered the army. It was his object from a boy; yet on being in it a few years, he was near leaving to devote himself to parliament, at his brother's suggestion-this was before the breaking out of the Spanish war.

Extract from a dispatch of the Marquis Wellington to Lord Bathurst, dated Villa Toro, October 11th, 1812:-

> My Lord,- The enemy have made two sorties on the head on the sup, between the exterior and interior lines of the Castle of Burgos, in both of which they materially injured our works, and we suffered some loss.
>
> In the last, at three in the morning of the 8th, we had the misfortune to lose the Honourable Major Cocks, of the 79th, who was field officer of the trenches, and was killed in the act of rallying the troops, who had been driven back. I have frequently had occasion to draw your Lordship's attention to the conduct of Major Cocks, and in one instance very recently, in the attack of the horn work of the Castle of Burgos; and I consider his loss as one of the greatest importance of this army, and to his Majesty's service, etc., etc.

Nothing can show more the estimation in which he was held than his flattering dispatch, considering Lord Wellington speaks rarely of any officer, excepting the common mention made of general officers at the heads of divisions and departments. He was really sorry for his loss, and after the unfortunate termination of the siege, he said he should not have considered it but for the loss of Cocks. Major Cocks was unknown and unconnected with Lord Wellington or any of his staff, and made his acquaintance at the headquarters through his zeal and exertions. On the day he mounted guard in the trenches he went himself round to every sentry, to see that they understood their orders. This is generally left to a sergeant; it is a rare thing for a subaltern with twenty men to explain and make the sentries know their orders. He, the field officer, went to every subaltern's piquet, and to the sentries of those piquets. He was indefatigable.

The following letter, published in pamphlet form, may not be deemed out of place here, as a tribute to the memory of one of the most distinguished officers of the time.

HERMITAGE, OPORTO, 6TH JUNE, 1855.

MY DEAR SIR JOHN RENNIE,-

During our conversation of last night I observed that you took an extraordinary in the anecdotes I related respecting my former brother Officer and companion in the Peninsular War, Major the Honourable Charles Somers Cocks, of the 16th Light Dragoons. I did not then enlarge on the subject, fearful of falling into the error (so frequent among veterans) of becoming garrulous; however, as you afterwards expressed a wish to know more of that Officer's military career, I now address you.

In 1808, as Lieutenant it that Regiment, and in Captain Cocks' troops, I was quartered at Woodbridge Barrack. He was then a member of Parliament; consequently, whenever he wished to go to London or elsewhere, according to the regulations of the army of that period, he had merely to wait on the Commanding Officer, Colonel (the late Sir George) Anson, and report that he should be absent on Parliamentary business. This he did very

---

It need hardly he said that the dispute arose through Cock's unwillingness to receive the money in question.

frequently, and therefore he paid little attention to the common rountine of Regimental duties.

As we were all at the mess-table one evening, a dispatch was delivered to Colonel Anson, as coming from Sir Stapleton Cotton, the General commanding our bridge of the 14th and 16th Dragoons, with a troop of Horse Artillery. Having read it, he said: "Gentlemen, I congratulate you: here is an order to prepare for foreign sevice." There was a general exclamation of delight: but Captain Cocks immediately filled his glass, and jumping on the table, he demanded that we should give three times to our speedy embarkation.

From that hour he became a new man: he appeared to have been electrified. He began by performing all the duties of the youngest subaltern; he was constant in his attendance at every parade of instruction, from the drill of the recruits to the field of regimental manoeuvre: a sergeant attended him daily in his room to teach him the sword exercise, and he soon became an expert swordsman; he was equally assiduous in his pistol practice on horseback and on foot. When Sir Stapleton Cotton exercised the Regiment and the Horse Artillery in out-post duties, he always took the advance guard; that, as "Eclaireur," he might himself learn, and teach us, according to "the King of Prussia's instructions." In this way did he spend his hours by day; but at night nothing could seduce him from the study of military works hastily sent for from London. He so devoured the elements of the Spanish language, that is a very short space of time he spoke it fluently: his lighter reading was a translation of Caesar's Commentaries.

The no ardently desired order for marching at length arrived; the route was for Falmouth, where we were to embark, to land at Corunna, and so join Sir John Moore's army. On arriving at Honiton we met Lord Paget (late Marguis of Anglesey) and General Stewart (late Marquis of Londonderry), they were posting to town, and they gave us the news of their disastorous retreat to Corunna, the annihilation of the Hussar Brigade, and of our hopes of embarking for foreign service.

After some delay an order arrived for the embarkation at Falmouth of the 14th Light Dragoons only. Captain Cocks immediately exerted the influence of his family, and his own as Member of Parliament, and obtained leave to attend (I think)

Sir Stapleton Cotton; and therefore, leaving his own regiment in Devonshire, he sailed for Lisbon with the 14th Light Dragoons, to form part of the army then under Sir John Craddock, but which was afterwards to be commanded by Sir A Wellesley.

Captain Cocks, finding the British army in a state of lazy repose at Lisbon, and that Sir A. Wellesley was not immediately expected, obtained leave from Sir S. Cotton to join the Spaniards in the South of Spain; and carrying letters of introduction to the Duque d'Albuquerque, he volunteered his services in outpost duties. But so soon as he heard of the arrival of the 16th Light Dragoons in Portugal, followed by that of Sir A. Wellesley, and forseeing that the British army would meet the enemy then in Oporto, he hastened to join us, and we marched to Coimbra, where the troops were collecting. His ardent mind, however, could not brook the tedious delays of marching five leagues a day; he left us again, and rode post to headquarters. Having there ascertained that Colonel Trant (the late Sir Nicholas) was, with a few Portuguese troops, watching the enemy on the Vouga, he joined him; and there we found him on the 9th of May, 1809, when we advanced with the army, under the command of Sir A. Wellesley, to the attack of Oproto.

By the time Captain Cocks had obtained the most ample and correct information of the force and positions of Soult's advanced guard under the command of General Francesca (I think). He immediately waited on Sir Stapleton Cotton; and accompanying him in his reconnaissances, a plan was formed by that General, and submitted to Sir A. Wellesley, for cutting off the whole of the enemy's cavalry, which would assuredly have been performed had not the Portuuese guide lost his presence of mind through fear (and consequently misled us) as we advanced during the night's march to surprise them. We found ourselves in the front and not in the rear of their outposts.

The Oporto Campaign having ended, our brigade retired to the banks of the Tagus, and Captain Cocks again left us, and joined sometimes the Spaniards, sometimes Sir Robert Wilson's detached corps, whichever might happen to be more immediately in the presence of the enemy. On one of those occasions he was with the Duque d'Albuquerque in his retreat to Cadiz, and there and then Captain Cocks gained golden opinions for the remarkable zeal and intelligence with which he fulfilled the outpost duties, as a volunteer with the rear guards.

Our advance on Talavera brought Captain Cocks again to his Regiment; for, having been employed to obtain and forward the most ample information of the enemy's movements to Sir A. Wellesley, he foresaw that this march, threatening Madrid, would assuredly bring on a general engagement,-he resolved on that occasion to have no Staff appointment, but to fight with his regiment.

During the battle of Talavera Sir John Sherbrooke ordered Sir Stapleton Cotton to "advance with the brigade to a rising ground, and draw off the attention of the enemy's guns whilst the infantry formed." The enemy's artillery, considering this movement as preparatory to a charge, soon got our range. The Captain of our squadron, having been thrown by the violence of his horse as a shell burst under him, Captain Cocks sprung forward to take his place. Never shall I forget the proud look and tone of voice with which he turned round: "Steady men!"-he seemed to grow in this saddle-he had obtained the dearest wish of his heart-a command on the field of battle.

After this battle of Talavera, Captain Cocks took no rest until he had personally attended the few wounded men of the brigade as they were carried into the town; and during the four days we remained in position, twice a day did I see him. Like a second Telemachus, visiting and consoling them. Lieutenant William Tomkinson, of Dorfold Hall, near Nantwich, if alive, can bear witness to this and many other facts of the same kind; for, as his favourite companion, he had accomainied him.

We retreated to Oropeza, leaving our sick and wounded in the hands of the enemy; and there we learned that Soult had interrupted our retreat to Pincentia. The army was discouraged: some of the officers of all ranks murmured; nothing was talked of but "Verdun" and a French prison. We were then young soldiers in the art of War! One young subaltern of cavalry (a would-be De Siethen or Blucher) actually wrote on that occasion to his friends in England:-"Sir Srthur Wellesley, there is no doubt, can fight, but he can't manaeuvour;"-his only excuse must be that others, of much superior rank and wiser heads, expressed the same opinions at the moment, though they would not so frankly confess it now. How different was Captain Cocks! He at the same time turned round to the famous Colonel Ponsonby, his confidential friend;-"I'll bet any man here one hundred pounds and a hogshead of claret, that I shall yet be one of a victorious column of this army that will enter Madrid:"-and he would have won his bet, for he did so enter Madrid:-such was his confidence in Sir Arthur Wellesley. On that same day the British army crossed the Tagus at the bridge of Arnobispo, and thus was the first step taken for the fulfillment of his well-founded expectations, for by that manouvere the plans of the wily Soult were defeated.

In the evening of that day, either from over-excitement and fatigue, or from contagion while visiting the sick and wounded at Talavera, or (as I am more inclined to believe) from having drank water from a well in which several dead bodies had been thrown, Captain Cocks was seized with malignant typhus fever. He was placed in a covered cart, to follow with the baggage. In the same cart lay a sick or wounded man (for he never spoke), who, next morning, when visited by a comrade, was found to be dead; therefore his body was laid in a ditch, and Captain Cocks had the cart to himself. His only attendant was his servant: became one of the regimental surgeons having been left with the wounded in Talavera, the other could not remain so far in the rear to give him medical assistance. After four days or more of severe sufferings, he suddenly found that the cart had halted in a rivulet which crossed the road. It struck him that cold immersion might be a remedy for his fever; therefore, sternly resisting his servant's remmonstrances, he was lifted into this cold bath; and being afterwards rubbed dry, and wrapped in blankets, he slept. On awaking, a change had taken place; and by the time our painful retreat was over, on his arrival at Badajos, he was again fit for duty as actively as ever.

At eight o'clock of the evening of the battle of Talavera, a large body of Spanish troops, cavalry, infantry, and artillery (formed in position of half-moon in front of the town), supposing that the few carbine shots (it was getting dusk) fired by the enemy on the skirmishers of the 16th Light Dragoons, that I then commanded, as they retired within the lines was a regular attack, were struck with panic; they fired one general volley, and as instantly all went to "the right about," and precipitately retreated on the road to Oropeza, carrying with them in the vortex all our bat-horses and baggage,-for this reason we had nothing the days of the battle, and afterwards for twenty-four hours, but beef and ration biscuit, and without any untensil to cook the meat. Captain Cocks said: "Come, Owen, you are a handy fellow; there is a French brass drum; cut out a piece with your sword, turn up the edges of it, and let us have a frying-pan." No sooner said than done, and we all gaily satisfied our hunger.

Lord Wellington having now become acquainted with the superior talents of Captain Cocks asan out-post officer, he employed him especially, confidentially, and constantly, in gaining intelligence of the enemy; for which purpose he frequently remained out days together at the head of thirty dragoons, working on their flanks and rear. To point his adventurous daring, and his escapes on those hazardous duties, would take up too much time at this moment: besides, as about this time I was attached to the Portuguese cavalry under Lord Beresford, I lost sight of him in some degree. However, it will suffice to say, that when the great struggle for the invasion and defence of Portugal had approached, Captain Cocks had earned the highest reputation as a soldier in every trench of the service. This activity had brought him in contact with the 1st German Hussars, commanded by Colonel Arestchild, and he formed the closest military connection with a Captain Krauchenbergh of that regiment. And here I beg frankly to say, that the German Hussars in the Peninsula army were our first masters in outpost duties.

During the retreat of the British army to the lines of Torres Vedras, Captain Cocks and Captain Krauchenbergh, each with a squadron of cavalry, frequently formed the rear-guard. In the early part of this retreat they received orders from Sir Stapleton Cotton to make no great resistance when the enemy might make their usual evening's attack on the outlying pickets for the purpose of obtaining the already collected forage. This apparent want of hardihood on the part of our cavalry encouraged the enemy's advanced guards, and gave great discontent to our Officers who were so engaged, and gave rise to animadversion from others. They represented their griefs to Sir Stapleton Cotton, who answered: "They are Lord Wellington's orders, and you must obey them." Here I will presume to suppose that Lord Wellington, having formed his plan of drawing the enemy to the lines of Torres Vedras, where he would have every advantage in his favour, was fearful that the invading army might half on the line of the Douro, or of the Vouga, and winter in the north of Portugal. Such an event, by lengthening the campaign, would have discouraged the Portuguese army and the emigrated population: would have entailed on the British Government a still more enormous expense by so long a detention of the fleets in the Tarus: thus rendering the people of England discontented, and increasing the influence of those who openly disapproved of and opposed the defence of the country. The ministry would have been overthrown, and that would have led to the recall of the army. But when Lord Wellington saw that Massena advanced with confidence, persuaded that he was "driving us into the sea," he gave leave to the rear Guards to show their courage. Captain Cocks and Krauchenbergh received the intimation with delight. They chose their ground with care, and at night seven times did they charge the confident enemy sword in hand before they could persuade them that they were soldiers, and worthy of the title.

When Lord Wellington took up the position of Busaco, my Portuguese regiment of cavalry, under the orders of the Honourable Sir Henry Fane, had the outpost duty on the river Ava, in front of the right flank. I was surprised by the arrival of Captain Cocks at the head of thirty dragoons in out bivouac. "Owen, I am going to work on the enemy's flank for the purpose of abtainmgin information: as I passed through Sir Henry Fane's quarters I obtained his leave to take you and your little troop with me; therefore report that to your Commanding Officer, and while your men turn out we will breakfast under these trees." We ere all mounted and ready to march, when a dragoon rode up to us, and delivered a note to Captain Cocks. "God, Owen, I am sorry our fun is spoiled; read that." It was the following note written in pencil:

"MY DEAR COCKS:-
"I have reason to believe that the enemy are making important movements on my left flank, and as I wish to employ your valuable services in that direction, return to Head Quarters as soon as possible. "

Yours
"WELLINGTON"

This not only shows Lord Wellington customary confidence in Captain Cocks, but also proves that Lord Wellington's was not taken by surprise in the flank movement made by Massena after the battle of Busaco, which has been so frequently asserted! Should there be cavilers on this point, I appeal to Lieutenant Tomkinson (now Major), who was the favourite subaltern that he had chosen to accompany him in this, as in many other enterprises of the same nature.

Now let me hasten to the close of the brilliant military career of this splendid soldier. Anxious to improve himself in other branches of his profession, particularly in everything relating to sieges, he exerted himself to obtain a Major of Infantry. I cannot follow Captain Cocks' services after leaving the cavalry; but while I was Aide-de-camp to Sir Benjamin d'Urban, he informed me, that at the siege of Burgos Captain Cocks rendered himself conspicuously known to the enemy by his gallantry (always wearing the kilt of his highland uniform); that in a very severe affair he fell; that his body was brought in with a flag of truce, "to be buried with military honours, in compliment to his distinguished bravery!" that Lord Wellington attended his funeral, when the painful expression of his countenance was so marked, that no one, excepting himself, presumed to approach him. After a considerable time passed in silence, he said: "D'Urban, had Cocks outlived the campaigns, which from the way in which he exposed himself was morally impossible, he would have become one of the first Generals of England."

There are no bivouac tales; therefore, when, in Colonel Napier's History of the Peninsular War, I read the beautiful language, the eloquent and heartfelt praise, as a tribute to the worth and memory of Frere, Lloyd, and Colquhoun Grant, I clapped my hands with delight; but when I turned to the page which records the death of Cocks, I closed the book in bitter disappointment.

"He was of modest demeanour, brave, thoughtful, and enterprising: he lived and died a good soldier."

It is just; it is a high eulogium; but where gallant deeds and gallant men are so frequently mentioned, it is only a character that hundreds of British officers have most richly deserved; while I will be bold to say, that Major Charles Semors Cocks was more than that, for he was more than his followers: and in a work which will go down to prosterity, as his extraordinary services must have been known to, and noticed by, the military historian (for they were noted by everyman who actively served in the Peninsula), I confidently expected a more detailed statement of his unequalled energy of mind, activity of body, and zeal for the service; his unwaried search after a scientific knowledge of his profession, and his distinguished bravery on all occasions. I hoped to have seen it recorded in the history of the Peninsular was that Major the Honourable Charles Somers Cocks was not only the never-tiring, confidential outpost officer of Wellington, but that he was, both in cavalry and in infantry, the pattern soldier of the British Army.

This is not the language of flattery to him, for he is gone,-nor to his family, for I know them not.

I remain,
>My dear Sir John Rennie,
>>Yours very truly
>>HUGH OWEN
>>Late Major 18th and 7th Hussars
>>Lieut-Col. and Col. h.p. Portuguese Army.

October 18th. I was this day so ill, and the enemy making a show of an advance, that I left Fresno for Quintanapallia. I caught cold in attending Cock's funeral, and neglected myself.

October 19th. Marched this morning to headquarters of the cavalry, they having moved from Bellima to a small village ont he right of the road. The sick of the cavalry remained at Bellima, to which place I moved the following day. Lieutenant-Genral Sir Edward Paget has joined the army as second in command.

October 21st. Headquarters of the army moved this day to Villa Fria, and the army closed to the position in rear of Quintanapallia, leaving one brigade to watch the castle. From despatches received from General Hill (from Madrid), the baggage was ordered to the rear, and the whole to retreat at night. I think Lord Wellington was aware the army must retire before he moved up to Villa Fria, and by that advance conceived the troops would be more easily got off over the Arlanzon. It so proved, for at the time we retired the enemy did the same. I marched nearly the whole night, and could not get on my horse without assistance. At daylight I halted near Villa Burniel.

October 22nd. Marched four leagues, halting in the evening at Pamphiya. Headquarters of the army were at Celada, with the infantry encamped close to the village. The peasants had a report that the enemy were coming round the hills on our right, and that they were close to Pamphiya, which obliged me to march again at night to a small village, two leagues to the rear.

October 23rd. Marched this day to Torquemada, four leagues. The 1st and 6th Divisions were encamped close to the town. I was quite delirious for an hour or two together frquently whilst going along the road, and was kept quiet with difficulty.

October 24th. Lieutenant Lockhart, of the 16th, this day came wounded into Torqumada; he is shot through the body, and I fear there is little chance of his recovery. Lieutenant-Colonel Pelly, just joined from England, is made prisoner, and Lieutenant Baker taken at the same time. Had I fixed on two people to be spared to the regiment, I should have chosen out of the three the two subalterns. The army retired fast, which obliged me to march four leagues to Duenas and two on to Cabazon, where I halted for the night.

October 25th. Marched this day to a Quinta on the other side Valladolid, where I halted, not being able to remain in the town, the sick being ordered to the rear. I was so ill I could not get on my horse without assistance, was without medicine or attendance, and owe thanks to a good consitution and change of air for not ending my days when I left Burgos. Had I remained in the miserable village of Bellima I know not what would have happened. Several officers had their notions fixed on England, and one of the 16th, Captain Mackingtosh (raised from the ranks), went before a medical board and got sick leave to England. He was much better than myself after he had passed the board. I should never have shown my face again with the regiment had I applied for such leave.

October 26th. Crossed the Duero and Adaja, this day, halting at Villa Nueva. The bridges over the two had been constructed since we advanced-the rivers were not fordable.

Lieutenant Lockhart is here, and from what Assistant-Surgeon Evans, 16th, tells me, I have some hope, thought another medical man declared there was none. This was the first time since I left the 16th that I could procure any medicine, and had only once seen a surgeon. All they think of is to get will to the rear and procure a good billet for themselves. Their sick is quite another duty. A church they consider excellent, and frequently allow them to sleep in the cars.

On the 27th I moved to Medina del Campo, and by marching about four leagues a day arrived at Salamanca. I was so reduced as scarcely to be able to get my billet. The sick, both officers and men, are numerous, and most of the quarters taken up. there are 5,000 sick, and 3,000 on the road.

Lord Wellington has taken up the line of the Duero. Headquarters are at Rueda. Soult has moved on Madrid. Hill is retiring on Arevalo.

LA SECA, NOVEMBER 1ST 1812

MY DEAR SIR,-

You have probably heard from your son since his illness, I have not been able to see him in consequence of our retreat from Burgos, at the commencement of which the sick and wounded of the army were of course sent to the rear. I am happy to inform you that he is better and likely soon to return to his regiment. I shall request he will come to my quarters and remain till his health is thoroughly restablished. I beg my best respects to Mrs. Tomkinson and all your family.

I am, my dear sir,
Yours very faithfully,
STAPLETON COTTON.

November 7th. Lord Wellington is within five leagues of this place, and General Hill has retired as far as Peneranda de Bracamente. The sick are ordered to the rear.

November 8th. I left Salamanca, with Captain Jackson of the 3rd Dragoons, and marched four leagues to Mattilha.

(Circumstances of a row with some Spanish soldiers, and our threatening to kill the Alcalde.)

November 9th. Iomames, four leagues.

November 10th. Marched to Tenebron, three leagues.

November 11th. Marched to Elbodon, five leagues (two beyond Ciudad Rodrigo), not being able to produce a billet in the latter place.

The two armies on both sides have united, Soult with the army of the north, Lord W. with General Hill. Lord W. has taken up the position of St.Christoval and that of Alba de Towmes. The enemy crossed at the latter, and the 2nd Division moved to attack. They were too strong for us, and we contended ourselves with a cannonade. The whole then united in the left bank of the Tormes, and began the retreat into Portugal. From Salamanca nothing could equal the irregularity of the troops, as well as the bad arrangement of Colonel Gordon, the quatermaster-general. The cavalry all retired by one road, and allowed that of the enemy to follow our infantry. The troops subsisted by shooting pigs, discipline was lost, and men did (in the infantry) what they pleased, unreproved by their officers.

The enemy took Sir Edward Paget with 3,000 stragglers, and had they at all pressed would have taken many more. From Salamanca they never advanced with their main force, and the few that followed the army did not press them.

November 17th. The sick this day left Rodrigo for the rear, and headquarters expected in there to-morrow.

November 18th. I, this day, with Captain Jacson, left ELboden for Celorico, where I arrived on the 21st, and that night put up in Casas de Rio, on the Mondego, not being able to produce quarters in Celorico. We moved the following day to Frasches, six miles from Celorico. The whole army has crossed the Agueda, and headquarters established at Freynada. Sick in great numbers are coming into Celorico.

December 1st. The 16th arrived this day in Frasches on their route for the banks of the Mondego. Considering the work they have done, both men and horses are by no means in bad order. The regiment on the retreat lost about fifty horses. We here received our new clothing.

December 2nd. Marched to Fornos, four leagues, the right squadron under Captain Murray. F and B troops went to Covos, half a league in advance.

December 3rd. Marched to Villa Nova and adjacents.

December 4th. We, this day, took up the following cantonments:-

Madoens: Headquarters brigade and artillery.
Travanca Boadilla:11th Light Dragoons.
Olivera de Conde:12th Light Dragoons.
Olivera de Hospital and adjacents: 16th Light Dragoons.

December 5th. F, K and B troops were in Olivera de Hospital, the other three, with headquarters of the regiment, were at Ligares. We were rather crowded at Olivera, for which reason I this day moved with my troop to Esquivenias de Alaxo, a mile from Olivera.

In consequence of Major-General Ponsonby's Heavy Brigade being ordered into Ligares the following arrangement took place:-

Headquarters of the regiment went to Olivera de Hospital with G and D troops, E and L.

I to Oliverinha, and B and K to Covos.

We have made a change for the better, and have forage in abundance. Headquarters of the cavalry are at Travanca, a league from Covos.

Copy of a letter sent to Generals of Brigade and Division throughout the army.

FRENEDA, NOVEMBER 28TH 1812

SIR,-

I have ordered the Army into Cantonments, in which I hope that circumstances will enable me to keep them for some time, during which the Troops will receive their Clothing, Necessaries, etc., which are already in progress by different lines of communication to the several Regiments of Brigades.

But besides these objects I must draw your attention in a very particular manner to the state of discipline of the Troops. The discipline of every army after a long and active campaign becomes in some degree relaxed, and requires the utmost attention on the part of the General and other Officers to bring it back to the state in which it ought to be for service. But I am concerned to have to observe that the Army under my command has fallen off in this respect in the late campaign to a greater degree than any Army with which I have ever served or of which I have ever read. Yet this Army has met with no disasters, it has suffered no privations which but trifling attention on the part of the Officers could have prevented, and for which there existed no reason whatever in the nature of the service; nor has it suffered any hardship excepting those resulting from the necessity of being exposed to the inclemency of the weather at the moment when it was most severe.*

It must be obvious however to every officer, that from the moment the Troops commenced their retreat from the neighbourhood of Burgos on the one hand and from Madrid on the other, the Officers lost all command over their men. Irregularities and outrages of all descriptions were committed with impunity, and losses have been sustained which ought never to have occurred.

Yet the necessity of retreat existing, none was ever made in which the Troops made such short marches, none in which they made such long and repeated halts, and none in which the retreating armies were so little pressed in their rear by the Enemy. We must look therefore for the existing evils and for the situation in which we now find the Army to some cause besides those resulting from the operations in which we have been engaged.

I have no hesitation in attributing these evils to the habitual intention of the Officers of the Regiments to their duty as prescribed by the regulations of the service and by the orders of the Army.

I am far from questioning the zeal, still less the gallantry and spirit of the Officers of the Army, and I am quite certain that if their minds can be convinced of the necessity of minute and constant attention, to understand, recollect and carry into execution, the orders which have been issued for the performance of their duty, and that the strict performance of this duty is necessary to enable the Army to serve the country as it ought to be served, they will in future give their attention to these points. Unfortunately the inexperience of the Officers of the Army has induced many to consider that the period during which an Army is on service is one of relaxation from all rule, instead of being, as it is, the period during which, of all others, every rule for the regulation and control of the conduct of the soldiers, for the inspection of their Arms, Ammunition, Appointments, Necessaries and Field Equipments, and his Horse and Horse Appointments, for the receipt and issue and care of his provisions, and the regulation for all that belongs to his food, and the forage for his horse, must be most strictly attended to by the Officers of his Troop of Company, if it is intended an Army, a British Army in particular, shall be brought into the Field of Battle in a state of efficiency to meet the enemy on the day of trial.

These are the points then to which I most earnestly entreat you to turn your attention, and the attention of the Officers of the Regiments under your command, Portuguese as well as English, during the period in which it may be in my power to leave the Troops in cantonments.

The commanding Officers of Regiments must enforce the orders if the Army regarding the constant inspection and superintendence if the Officers over the conduct of the men of their Companies in their cantonments; and they must endeavour to inspire the Non-commissioned Officers with a sense of their situation and authority: and the Non-commissioned Officers must be forced to do their duty by being constantly under the view and superintendence of the Officers; by these means the frequent and discreditable recourse to the authority of the Provost and to Punishments by the sentence of Court-Martials will be prevented, and the soldiers will not dare to commit offences and outrages of which there are too many complaints, when they know that their Officers and Non-commissioned Officers have their eyes and attention turned towards them.

The commanding Officers must likewise enforce the Orders of the Army regarding the constant inspection of the Soldiers' Arms, Ammunition, Accoutrements and necessaries, in order to prevent at all times the shameful waste of Ammunition and the sale of that article, and the soldiers' necessaries-with this view both should be inspected daily.

With regard to the food of the soldiers I have frequently observed and lamented, in the late campaign, the facility and celerity with which the French soldiers cooked in comparison with those of our Army.*

The cause of this disadvantage is the same as that of every other description, the want of attention of the Officers tot he Orders of the Army and to the conduct of their men, and their want of authority over their conduct.

Certain men of each Company should be appointed to cut and

bring in wood, others to fetch water, and others to get the meat, etc., to be cooked, and it would soon be found, if this practice was daily renforced and a particualr hour for seeing the Dinners and the men dining names, as it ought to be equally as for the Parade, the Cooking would no longer require the inconvenient length of time which it has been lately found to do, and that the soldiers would not be exposed to the deprivation of their food at the moment in which the Army may be engaged in operations with the Enemy.

You will of course give your attention to the Field Exercise and Discipline of the Troops.

It is very desirable that the soldiers should not lose the habits of Marching, and the Division should march ten or twelve miles twice in the course of the week, if the weather should permit, and the roads in the neighbourhood of the Cantonments of the Division should dry. But I repeat that the great object of the General and field Officers must be, to get the Captains and Subalterns of the Regiments to understand and perform the duties required from them, as the only mode by which the discipline and efficiency of the Army can be restored and maintained during the next Campaign.

I have the honour to be, sir,
Your most obedient servant
(Signed) WELLINGTON

To Major-General ANSON, or Officer commanding the Brigade of Cavalry, consisting of 11th, 12th, and 16th Light Dragoons.

N.-This letter was confidentially addressed to the Generals, and never intended to be published: in the place of which it was inserted in the regimental books, and from thence found its way into the London papers. It was not intended for colonels of regiments to see it, and when first it came out it was with much difficulty Colonel Ponsonby, of the 12th, read it at headquarters.

The one to Major-General Anson was inserted in the orderly books and no further notice taken of it. Colonel Ponsonby stated that it was not intended to have been made public. This he said as wishing to make the best of an imprudent letter. It was regretted by Lord Wellington, being written in a hasty moment when vexed with the result of the Campaign.

December 26th. The forage became scarce, and 11th and 16th marched this day to the Mondego to the following places:-

Santa Cambadao: Headquarters brigade and 16th, with G troop 16th Light Dragoons.
Coila de Menalario: B and F troops, 16th.
Evoa: K troop
Argarita: E troop.
Reguna: D troop.

The 11th Light Dragoons occupied Trashada and adjacents.

On the 28th, I moved with my troop to Evoa, and K went to Santa Cambado.

I am now in the same quarters I found Captain Cocks in on my return from England.

December 31st. I this day set off with Captain Weyland to Oporto. We went seven leagues, halting at Agueda. The 1st January we went eight, and halted at some farmhouses near the convent of Grijo. The following day we arrived in Oporto, passing over the ground where I was wounded on May 11th, 1809. I recognised the spot, and remembered the whole of the affair.

The Prince of Orange was in Oporto, which made the place very gay. We remained there nearly a fortnight and returned tot he 16th on the 15th January, after three days' march.

We here saw the 29th Bulletin from the Army under Napoleon, giving an account of the retreat from Moscow. The expression was that the horses of the French army did not die by hundreds but by thousands.

January 31st, 1813. Forage becoming scarce, and the whole brigade being about to move to the banks of the Vouga, my troop, with E from Argarita, this day marched over the Oris to Matagua.

February 8th. The whole brigade this day moved from their

cantonments, occupying, after two days' march, the following cantonments:-

Agueda: Headquarters brigade, 11th Light Dragoons.
San Pedrodosal: 12th Light Dragoons.
Esquiera: 16th Light dragoons.

The 16th occupied the folowing villages:-
Esquiera: E and G. Headquarters.
Cisco: I,K.
Olivamtria: D.
Requeixo: B, my troop.

I at first was ordered to Osdo Ribiera, but only remained there three nights, and then occupied Requino. The least rain would have made the river Osdo Ribiera not fordable.

The whole regiment, with the exception of (original illegiable), is quartered on the Agueda.

General Anson remained a fortnight at Agueda, and then moved to Aviero.

Major Hay got the lieutenant-Colonelcy, and Captain Murray the majority. Lieutenant King, from the 11th, succeeded to the troop.

The 4th Dragoon Guards, 9th and 11th Light Dragoons, are ordered to England, their horses to be given to the different regiments.

April 3rd. The 11th Light Dragoons this day left the brigade on their route for England. Their horses were given up near Coimbra. We received 72.

I think there are other regiments not so efficient as the 11th, but the man at their head(Colonel Cumming) is and old officer, and in the way of others more deserving to command brigades.

April 7th. The 12th Light Dragoons this day came into Agueda from their former quarters.

April 28th. The brigade marched this day by a route from headquarters. The 12th moved to Olivera, and the 16th were

---

*The constant exposure to rain, night and day, without tents, is some hardsheip, and the supple was more deficient than is allowed in this letter.

ordered into Agueda, but in consequence of the German brigade moving in, were obliged to occupy the villages on the Vouga. Headquarters to Arrancada. My squadron, B and D troops, crossed the Vouga to Albergaria Velha.

April 29th. Marched with the Headquarters to Olivera. My squadron, Arrifana and St. Antonia di Arrifana four leagues.

April 30th. The whole regiment to Villa Nova, on the Douro, close to Oporto, 5 leagues.

May 1st. Marched 5 leagues to St. Turso, my squadron a league in advance, to Villa Nova. We scarcely got in before dark, through the badness of the road.

During our long halt in these quarters, the regiment received regular rations of corn from Coimbra, and was tolerably well supplied with straw or Indian corn straw. The latter is not so good, and a large bulk affords but little nutriment. We were within four leagues of excellent wine, equal I think to Lamego (best port wine). We got it at two or three wintines a quartillia. A vintine is three half-pence, and two quartillias more than a quart bottle. Three will nearly fill two bottles. I was in a very good house, and the other officers of my troop were in good billets. We got fish in abundance from Aviero, which the padre procured for us. I saved a field of his green barley from being cut,-the only one left in the neighbourhood when we moved. This I afterwards regretted, as from the price of fish in other places I found he had cheated us quite considerably. If ere we are again in the neighbourhood, I will accommodate him with half a dozen quiet dragoons.

May 2nd. The whole regiment this day marched and occupied Braya, three leagues from Villa Nova. Brigadier-General Ponsonby's Heavy Brigade marched in our advance, and occupies Gimaraens and adjacents.

The Heavy German brigade is moving in our rear.

The object appears to be, from moving us in this route, to form a column of the infantry and cavalry, now on the Douro, to enter Spain by the Braganza route, moving on the right bank of the river the whole way. The infantry have not moved, and a brigade of Guards remains still at Oporto, where they have been sent for recovery of health.

Lord W. gives it out to be his object, in moving us up here, that officers commanding regiments may have no excuse for the bad condition of their regiments. We heard in Oporto that Madrid had been given up to plunder for three days. King Joseph has established himself in Valladolid.

May 6th. The right and centre squadrons moved this morning from Bruya, occupying the following places:-

I and K troops, Light Squadron: Conselio de Amars.
D troop: Pica de Regulados.
B troop: Coito de Tabiens.

My troop was so widely cantoned that I left the convent of Tabiens on the 8th, and occupied a farmhouse about two miles from Coito de Tabiens, called Panoyos. I was well supplied with green forage (young wheat and barley), which hereabouts is just coming in. The country is not so forward by two months as that about Aviero.

Whilst in the convent the monks elected a general of their order. They were Benedictines, the most numerous order in Portugal. there were deputies assembled from all the other convents of the same order. Seventy monks were collected, scarcely one under 16 stone. The appointment continues for three years.

The move from Braya was in consequence of Major Fraser's (late Bull's) troop of artillery being ordered in. The roads were so bad that they did not come so far, and halted in Santa Tyrso.

The 12th occupied Bucellas and adjacents.

May 12th. The following route this day arrived:-

May 13th	Perdeciras
" 14th	Ruivaes
" 15th	Alturas
" 16th	Boticas
" 17th	Chaves
" 18th	Halt

*If we were allowed to take doors, etc., in every village, as the enemy do, without having to go two or three miles for wood, we could cook in as short time.

"	19th	Monforte
"	20th	Val de Arnuiro
"	21st	Vinhaes
"	22nd	Braganza
"	23rd	Halt

We marched about three leagues each day. The villages named in the route were so bad that one squadron with the staff of the regiment could only remain in them, the other two went to adjacents, which were equally miserable. The roads were dreadful in many places-much easier to march up and English staircase than to ascend them. The troops suffered very little, and the horses were not much reduced by the work.

The 12th moved the whole way, a day's march in our rear, and the artillery followed us as far as Chaves, where finding the roads so bad, they took another route more on our right. At Braganza we moved to three villages, each holding one squadron a league in advance. The following Divisions of the Army are on their route for this point, and will be up on the 23rd and 24th. Lieutenant-General Sir T. Graham is to have the command of this column:-

1st Division
3rd
5th } The 4th Division and the English Hussar brigade have crossed the Duero and joined this column
6th
7th

Major-General Anson's and Brigadier-General Ponsonby's brigades of cavalry with Major General Bock's.

Brigadier-General Pack's and Bradford's brigades of Portuguese infantry.

The Portuguese brigade of cavary has been cantoned in this neighbourhood since last campaign, and is the same that entered by this route last year; as before, they are now under Brigadier-General D'Urban, and have moved three leagues on the route for Zamora. They are 700 strong.

The enemy have withdrawn their force over the Esla.

There is a bridge at Benevente and no other. The river is not fordable.

It proved to be passable for cavalry, but with difficulty.

Lord Wellington, with the Light Divisions, Major-General Alten's brigade, the Horse Guards and Hussars, moves on Salamanca. We hear nothing of Sir Rowland Hill. (Sir Rowland Hill moved on Salamanca at the same time from the Alenjeto.)

Sir John Murray has had an action with Suchet, near Valencia, and has completely beaten him. We have not heard the particulars.

Reports say King Joseph has left Valladolid for Palentia, and is expected to move on to Burgos. The troops of the Army of the centre, that were at Segovia, have moved to the right bank of the Duero.

On the 18th the enemy had troops in both Madrid and Toledo.

The route arrived for us to move on the 25th, on our march for Tabura, by the route of Santa Crux. A new arrangement took place, which kept us a day longer in these cantonments.

May 26th. The order came yesterday for us to march to Nices, in Spain, four leagues from Braganza. Nices was occupied by Brigadier-General Ponsonby's Heavy Brigade, which caused us to move to Trabazos, half a league to the right, which put the whole regiment under cover for the night.

We crossed the Manzanas, dividing the two kingdoms at a ford near La Quinta, to which place the infantry of this column came.

The troops north of the Duero move in three columns.

1st Division. Pack's brigade of Portuguese infantry, General Anson's brigade of cavalry, with Brigadier-General Ponsonby's from the left column, and march on Tabara.

2nd Division. 5th Division, Major-General Bock's brigade of cavalry the centre, and move on.

4th division. 6th and 7th Divisions, with Colonel Grant's brigade (hussars), the right, and move on Carvajales.

May 27th. Marched five leagues this day, encamping neat the village of Sensnande.

May 28th. Marched one long league, encamping in a wood two miles in advance of Tabara. Brigadier-General Ponsonby's brigade came into the same bivouac.

The enemy have left Benevente, four leagues from this withdrawing over the Esla. They occasionally patrol into that place, and have come a league in its advance.

It rained very much the whole night of the 20th. The following day it cleared, and became very hot.

On the 29th the infantry of the left column came and encamped in rear of Tabara.

Sir Rowland Hill is moving on Salamanca with Lord Wellington, who was to enter that place on the 27th. From all we hear the enemy are not prepared for us, and think that the force north of the Duero is only a demonstration, and that they have nothing to fear from this point.

We are bringing with the army six eighteen-pounders.

Pontoons are moving north of the Duero, and will, I conceive, be employed in the passage of the Esla.

The enemy occupy Zamora with 3000 men, but are moving men from Toro and adjacent to Valladolid.

From the number of sick last campaign, the infantry are all under canvas, carrying three tents to each company on the horse that was allowed for the camp kettles. The iron camp kettles are exchanged for tin ones, which are light, and in the proportion of one to six men. They are carried on the top of the knapsack alternately by the men in the mess. The arrangement is excellent. The cavalry have no tents; we shall get the oftener into villages.

The Heavy Germans and Portuguese crossed at Monte Martha. The remainder of the army at Monzanos.

Major-General Slade is at length gone to England, and is succeeded by Major-General Fane. The change I consider a good one, and so do most others.

May 31st. Orders came out for the left wing of the army to move at 1a.m this morning, and march three leagues to the ford of (sic). On our arrival within a league of the Esla the ford was found to be impractical, and we were on our return to Tabara, when we were again ordered up to the ford, two leagues from the place where we received the first order. On our arrival, the Heavy German brigade and Portuguese cavalry had got over, losing seven or eight horses and three or four men drowned.

The ford was as bad as possible, and we were ordered two leagues lower down the river. A pontoon bridge was thrown over, by which the infantry were passing. General Anson's and Ponsonby's brigade passed by a ford a mile below, and marched a league in advance of the Esla, halting at 8p.m at Andivias. We were on horseback nearly twenty hours. Colonel Grant's brigade (10th, 15th, 18th Hussars) passed the ford early this day and took the enemy's piquet of thirty-two men and an officer.

Lord Wellington joined this wing of the army yesterday and is this day at Carvajales.

The pontoon brigade was thrown across in two hours and a half, and the greater part of the army has passed this day.

The advance of the Salamanca column had an affair with the enemy on their leaving that place, and made 150 prisoners. 3000 infantry remained in the town, and were completely surrounded by our cavalry, and the guns going to fire grape into them, when all was ordered to retire, and the enemy escaped.

Lord Wellington said, had he known the situation of the enemy he would have taken them all.

Why did he not?

June 1st. The brigade marched two short leagues to Torres. The 4th, 5th, Pack's and Bradford's brigade encamped on our right, a league on the Valderadery river. I marched my squadron about 2p.m to Ceruenon, a short league to the right.

The cause for sending out a squadron on piquet was, that the enemy in the morning occupied Belver and the adjacent country, but had retired a long way during the day. All was quiet.

Headquarters of the army this day moved to Zamora.

June 2nd. The brigade marched four leagues to Vinmarbres. Sir Thomas Graham came there likewise.

Headquarters of the army this day at Toro.

Vindemarbren is a good town of 500 houses. The enemy have taken in money (besides wheat, cattle, etc), 80,000 reals, £1,000.

June 3rd. We moved this morning under the idea that the heavy Germans were engaged in our front. We saw nothing of the enemy, and moved to our cantonments.

General Anson's, with Captain Ramsay's troop of artillery and the 16th, occupied Villavalid, a league from Voydo Marban. The 12th, Almuray, half a league in advance.

(Circumstances of a general officer in the street at Villavalid during an alert.)

At 8p.m a report came in that the enemy's cavalry were in Almaray, had taken all the 12th, and were expected every instant to enter the village we were in. In a quarter of an hour the whole regiment was out, and in a short time it was ascertained to be Spanish cavalry, and that the report had been spread by the muleteers attatched to the 12th, who had been out in front for corn. Had it stopped with us, there would have been no harm done, but unfortunately Brigadier-Major Baertling sent off instantly to the infantry and cavalry in our rear, and turned them out.

It was the most ridiculous alert I ever heard of. The 12th literally thought they were in the village; at the time no enemy was within six leagues.

June 4th. Marched three leagues and, with the Heavy Germans and artillery, occupied Villa Garcia. The 12th, half a league in our front, to Tordchumos.

The enemy's infantry yesterday left Valladolid, retiring on Burgos. Sir Rowland Hill crossed the Duero at Toro.

Headquarters left Toro for La Mota del Marquis. Our force, British and Portuguese, is rated at 75,000, six of which I calculate to be cavalry.

About 10,000 men of the enemy's are retiring before us on Palentia. Their outposts are this day in rear of Madina de Rio Seca, four leagues from us.

We find one squadron from the brigade for duty each day.

June 5th. Marched five leagues to Palacios, a league in advance of Rio Seca. The 16th and artillery occupied the village, the 12th a small village to the left.

Sir Thomas Graham came, this day, to Medina de Rio Seca.

Headquarters of the army moved to Castre Monte. The enemy's rear is in Palentia, they tell the peasants that they are moving direct on Burgos, and shall not attempt to stand before they reach that place.

June 6th. The brigade moved three leagues to Padraza, which the enemy passed yesterday. Their piquets were qithin two leagues, and two squadrons from the brigade were ordered on duty, under Lieutenant-Colonel Ponsonby, to Villa Martin, in front of which the enemy had their piquets half a league. The squadrons of the 12th went up to Nortillio on the right, mine of the 16th remained in Villa Martin.

On the right, the 12th drove the enemy's videttes in from the high ground overlooking Palentia, and we saw a review of the enemy's troops on the other side of the town.

(The review of the troops was King Josef looking at the part of the army that had been on the Esla. He came from Magaz for that purpose, and returned as soon as it was over.)

We kept the heights for an hour, and were driven back. At night all their piquets withdrew on the other side the canal, a mile in front of Palentia.

We retired for the night a league in rear (with both squadrons) of Villa Martin. It rained considerably the whole night.

The enemy's infantry marched seven leagues.

June 7th. The enemy's troops moved from Palentia during the night, and the piquets this morning entered at daylight, the enemy's retiring as we pushed on.

Colonel Grant's brigade, Brigadier-General Ponsonby's, and the Light Division, moved in advance of the town on the Torquemada road.

Major-General Anson's and Bock's brigade moved to the left to Husillos came to Palentia. Sir Thomas Graham, with the infantry of the left column, to Grixota.

The appearance of Colonel Grant's brigade (Hussars) just come from England, with the Heavy Brigade and Light Division, all passing Palentia amidst the *vivas* of the people, was very interesting.

I never saw the army in such order, and since the march the sick have decreased.

Sir Rowland Hill is near Duinass, having left Valladolid to the right.

June 8th. General Bock's and Anson's brigade marched three long leagues to Pena de Campos. The day was as cold as I ever felt at this season of the year, with considerable rain.

Headquarters moved to Amusea, and a considerable column on our right to Tamara.

Sir Thomas Graham still continues with the left column, composed of 1st, 5th Divisions, Park's and Bradford's brigade with Bock's and Anson's brigades of cavalry.

June 9th. We expected Lord Wellington would have reviewed is, but we were ordered to march four leagues to Osorno. We got under the walls of the village, the day being as unfavourable as yesterday.

Headquarters halted.

From the time of our crossing the Esla up to this period, we have been marching through one continued corn-field. The villages are but thinly scattered over the country, so that it appears a difficulty to find hands to cultivate the crops. The land is of the richest quality, and produces the finest crops with the least labour possible. It is generally wheat, with a fair proportion of barley, and now then a crop of vetches or clover. The horses fed on green barley nearly the whole march, and got fat. The army has trampled down twenty yards of corn on each side the road (forty in all) by which the several columns have passed. In many places much more, from the baggage going on the side of the columns, and so spreading further into the wheat.

But they must not mind their corn if we get the enemy out of the country.

June 10th. From our route since we left Palentia I thought we were marching on Aguilas, so turning the Ebro by its source. We, this day, turned to our right, passing the Pisuagre at Zarzosa, encamping a league in advance at Barrio de San Filezes.

The infantry came to Zarzosa.

The enemy do not appear to be aware of our move on this point. We see nothing of them, and hear reports of their dismantling the castle of Burgos.

June 11th. The 16th marched two long leagues, and occupied Vellasto; the 12th, with Major-General Anson, two villages to our right. The infantry of the left columns are encamped two miles in our rear.

June 12th. The whole army halts this day. All commissaries are ordered to have four days' bread in hand by 7a.m on the 13th. From the rapid advance of the army, no supplies can come from the rear. The country gives bread and corn, as hitherto these have not failed, and this is a country that has been plundered and destroyed by the enemy for the last five years. It was said before our march, that until the harvest came in not a pound of bread, by was of supplies to the army, could be procured.

Lord Wellington this day (12th) made a reconnaissance with the right wing of the army under Sir Rowland Hill, consisting of the 2nd and Light Divisions, Conde d'Amarantes' (Silviera) Portuguese Division, and a division of Spanish infantry under Brigadier-General Murillo, with Alten's, Ponsonby's and Grant's brigades of cavalry. General Reille, commanding the army of Portugal, had the direction of the troops occupying the heights above the Hormaza, and their left in front of Estepar. Their right was turned by the Hussar Brigade (Grant's), supported by General Ponsonby's and the Light Division, whilst General Alten's brigade, supported by the first brigade of the 2nd Division, under Colonel O'Callagham, moved on Hormaza, and the remainder of the division threatened the heights of Estepar.

The enemy, seeing himself turned, moved off at double quick time, and allowed a squadron from the 14th to charge and take a gun, which was firing on the road covered by a few infantry. Lord W. says a squadron took it, though it was about twenty men, under Lieutenant Southell, of the 14th. The Horse Artillery, under Major Gardner (his own troop), fired at the enemy's colums, and, at the time, it was said their loss was great, though they did not leave many on the field. This is no certain way of ascertaining their loss, as in nine cases out of ten they carry off their wounded and dead.

The enemy employed the whole night in getting all clear of Burgos, and immediately after the affair took up a position on the left of the Arlanzon.

On the morning of the 13th, at 4a.m, the castle was blown

up, and everything as far destroyed as time could allow. Since our retreat, much labour and expense had been employed in strengthening the works, and the horn work on the hill, taken by Cocks, had received its share. From what we could learn from the peasants, the enemy had been employed the whole winter.

June 13th. The left column moved three leagues on La Piedra, where the infantry encamped with the two brigades of cavalry in their front. Major-General Anson's went to Quintana, sending my squadron a short league in advance to Monterio. I occupied the village, all the enemy's force having retired from this neighbourhood on Burgos.

The peasants say it was blown up this morning at 4 o'clock.

Headquarters came to Villadiego.

June 14th. Burgos, as the peasants told us, was certainly blown up yesterday at 4a.m. The enemy are on their march for Vittoria by the main road at Miranda de Ebro.

I received an order, about 9, to march on San Martin on the Ebro. On arriving there, I found the whole of the left column had crossed, and encamped on the right bank. The column marched four leagues, and over bad roads.

The enemy cannot be aware of our movement, as a division might have stopped the whole column at the bridge of San Martin, as well as at the other of Bocamonde, where some of the column likewise crossed.

Lord W. this day looked at the brigade, and was much pleased with its appearance.

He is in high spirits, and says to-morrow the whole of the army shall be across the Ebro. They must either fight or retire out of Spain.

Remembering the disasters of Burgos last year, we were all delighted to hear of its fate. What a thing it would have been had it never been attempted! The army would probably have wintered near Salamanca, and Cocks would now have been with us, half mad with delight at our rapid and successful advance.

June 15th. The left wing marched four leagues to Villareayo, encamping close to the town. We did not get in through the badness of the road, till evening, and the infantry not before the middle of the night. The whole of the army is across the Ebro, having passed by the brigades we came over, and the one of Puente Avenas.

June 16th. Marched three leagues to La Cerca, encamping in front of the town. Headquarters came to Medina.

June 17th. The left wing marched to San Martin de Cora. The enemy have shown nothing in our front, and have troops considerably to our rear of the Ebro, on the Burgos road. Our crossing on the left has been quite unexpected by them. We hear it was their intention to fight on the main road, near Breviesia, and they have kept a division at Frias for the purpose of observing our movements on the left bank of the Ebro.

June 18th. On the 16th and 17th the enemy assembled a considerable force near Espejo, which moved this day on Osma, where it was met by the left column. The 1st Division came up, and sent forward the light battalions of K.G.I. to the heights on the right of that village, on which was placed Captain Ramsay's troop of horse artillery, covered by two squadrons from the brigade (mine of the 16th). The enemy showed about six thousand infantry, with six squadrons of cavalry, and on seeing we had troops up, halted a mile in rear of the village. The 1st and 5th Divisions, with Pack's and Bradford's brigades, formed in our rear of Osma, about two miles. Osma lies in a plain, surrounded on all sides with steep hills, the enemy occupying the foot of them on the Vittoria road, whilst we held those to the right on the Bibroa road, and the valley in the bottom to the opposite range. This range is very steep, and commands the villages as well as the position the enemy took up, and over which the light companies from the 1st Division were detached.

This movement, with the 4th Division coming up on the hills to our right, caused them to move, after a little skirmishing from the detatchment made to the left, and a considerable cannonade from those on the right, as well as from our guns.

As the enemy was moving off, the 5th Division was passed from the valley along the range of hills to the right, and came up with the enemy's rear with their light troops. There was a considerable fire on both sides, but little done.

The Light Division came up, near St. Millan, with the division of the enemy that had been at Frias. It was commanded by Moncane, and suffered considerably, losing 300 prisoners and a considerable quantity of baggage. The brigade encamped close to Osma, with the greater part of the army near that village.

June 19th. The left column again moved from the army. We assembled on the Bilboa road, a league in rear of Osma, before daylight, and were then pushed half a league towards Orduna, by mistake. We marched to Jocano, and although only two leagues from Osma, did not arrive before 6 p.m. It rained the whole day, which rendered the roads-always bad-almost impassable.

With the body of the army Lord Wellington marched straight on Vittoria, and found the enmy's rear-guard in a position on the left of the Bayas. They were turned on their position by the Light Division, whilst the 4th attacked them in front, and drove them back on their main body, which was on its march from Panarbo to Vittoria, having only left the latter place last night. (This, and the way the enemy approached Osma yesterday, convinves me they did not know of the movement over the Ebro to their right.)

Headquarters of the army were this night at Sabijana, on the left bank of the Bayas.

Return of casualties from the 12th to the 16th, inclusive:-

Majors	Captns.	Staff	Lieuts.	Ensigns	Sergts	Drumrs	Rank &File	
1	2	-	3	-	5	-	78	wounded
-	-	-	-	-	2	-	12	killed
-	-	-	-	-	-	-	6	missing

9 horses killed   13 wounded   1 missing

June 20th. The left column marched three leagues on the banks of the Bayas to Marginia. The brigade was pushed a league on the main road, and occupied for the night Olano, and adjacents. The Spanish infantry, under Longa, are a league in out front, and one league only from Vittoria. The enemy made a reconnaissance on them this evening, in which they kept their ground, and a battalion of Cacaored was ordered up close to us in consequence of the firing. I think we are pushed too far, as the enemy may be aware of our advance on this road, which is the main one from Billble to vittoria, and I fear have seen the officers who went to look at the affair. The main body of the army closed up this day, and Lord W. reconnoitred the enemy's position.

If the enemy are aware of this column being in the situation it is, I conceive they make arrangements to defeat our object in turning their position, and if so, the mere curiosity of some may have brought it about. The want of common prudence in those employed with an army frequently defeats the best arrangements.

Nearly all the towns from Vittoria to the frontier, and down to Burgos, have been fortified in some degree by the enemy. They make wooden gates for the entrances, and loop-hole the houses on the outside, connecting those which do not join by a wall, which is loop-holes in the same manner. In many instances they pull down the houses on the outside for the sake of the outer wall, which they leave standing. Tolosa was done so, and every town on this route where they had any garrison.

They were obliged to keep a garrison in these places constantly, which were in a state of alarm from the guerrillas, and not an officer dared to ride out for any distance without a strong escort. Their dispatches were sent by detatchments of from 200 to 300 men. They always halted at night in one of these towns, and on their march were obliged to keep together and proceed with caution. The number of them employed in keeping up on the communication and carrying dispatches were very great, and the system so harassing and disorganizing to an army, that is only to be wondered at where men could be found in sufficient numbers and with patience to endure such a proceeding for any length of time.

Where they had been established for any length of time they occasionally pain peasants to take their letters; these frequently fell into the hands of the guerrillas, and no communication could be depended on but under a strong escort. The want of information as to the movement of different columns must have been a great inconvenience.

June 21st. BATTLE OF VITTORIA.-The enemy have at length collected their army and taken up a position in front of Vittoria. King Joseph nominally commands, with Marshal Jourdan as chief of his Etat-Major.

The left column moved at 8a.m, assembling on the main road to Vittoria, a league from that place.

We were joined by 4,000 Spanish infantry, under the guerrilla chief Longa. In our front the enemy have from 4,000 to 5,000 infantry, and about six squadrons of cavalry, occupying strong hills to the left of the road, and with reserves in the villages of Gamarra Mayor, and Abechuco, covering the passes over the Zadorra river, which, for the security of their right and their main road to retreat by on Tolosa, it is necessary for them to retain.

A squadron from the 16th, with two guns, were sent down the road a short distance, covering the formation of the troops to its left. The 5th Division, and Major-General Pack's brigade of Portuguese infantry, with a squadron from the 12th Light Dragoons, the whole under Major-General Osqald of the 5th Divison, were detached to attack the enemy on the right by Lord Wellington, regulating our movements by what might there happen. The enemy's position on their left rested on the heights of Puebla de Arlanzon, in front of Ariniz. The right of their centre occupied a height commanding the valley. Their right was thrown back to the other side of Vittoria, occupying the line of the Zaborra and the heights in front of our left column. In fact, quite a separate position from the other.

They had a reserve in rear of their left at Gomecha. Lord Wellington, with the 2nd, 4th, and Light Divisions, all the cavalry (excepting the two brigades with the left column), and the divisions of Portuguese infantry, under the Conde de Amarante (Silviera), with General Morillio's Spanish corps Burgos to Vittoria, whilst the 3rd and 7th Divisions, under Earl Dalhousie, moved on Mondossa.

The day commenced by an attack on the enemy's left by

the 71st Regiment and the light battalion from Major-General Walker's brigade in the 2nd Division, with on brigade from General Morillo's Spaniards, carrying the heights of La Puebla, the importance of which the enemy were aware of, and which they attempted to tetake, but always without success. In the attack, and afterwards in the defence of the heights, the 71st suffered considerably, and Colonel Cadogan died of wounds there received.

(Lord Wellington) mentioned him in his dispatch in the handsomest manner, as follows:-"I am concerned to have to report that the Honble Lieut.-Colonel Cadogan has died of wounds which he received. In him his Majesty has last on officer of great zeal and tried gallantry, who had already acquired the respect and regard of the whole profession, and of whom it might be expected that if he had lived he would have rendered the most important services to his country.")

(The 6th Division was left at Medina de Pomul to cover the march of the supplies, etc, from the rear, and was not in the action.)

The possession of this point enabled Sir Rowland Hill to pass the Zadorra at La Puebla with the 2nd and Portuguese Division, and the Paish corps under Morillio, and to attack and gain possession of Sabijana de Alava, a village immediately in front of the enemy's line, which was strongly contested, and on being occupied by us, the enemy made repeated attempts to retake, but were invariably repulsed. Our loss here was severe.

The 4th Division then crossed the Zadorra at the Bridge of Nanclares, the Light at the one of Tres Puentes, whilst the 3rd and 7th, having arrived at their appointed ground, crossed the Zadorra a little higher up, and these four divisions, forming the centre of the army, were destined to attack the height commanding the valley of the Zadorra, occupied by the right of the enemy's centre.

(The operation of the day were a little delayed from it being impossible for the commander of the forces to know of the arrival of the 3rd and 7th Divisions at their appointed place.)

The enemy perceiving our intention to be on this point,

retired from his position, marching on Vittoria in good order. The attack on their left, and our possession of Sabijana de Alava, caused them to weaken their centre to regain what they had there lost, and they were by this means turned out of their position.

Our troops suffered considerably in their attacks on the heights of La Puebla, and afterwards on Sabijana de Alava; and from the commanding position the enemy occupied, their artillery was particularly destructive. The whole of this was seen by us from a hill near where we had assembled.

The enemy retired on Vittoria from the attack on the right in tolerable order, and had there been nothing done on the left, would probably have kept Vittoria through the night, and employed it in moving off their artillery, etc, to the rear. The left column was not in the main attack, but was, in my opinion, the cause of the very hasty retreat of the enemy, the loss of their baggage and artillery, and made the battle a decisive one. Nothing could be more fortunate than the Spaniards showing themselves last night, and the enemy in the reconnaissance they made yesterday on them not seeing our column. The force they had placed on Gamarra Mayor, and Abechuco, and on the heights to our left, was thought quite sufficient to retain them against the Spaniards. When they found the heights carried, the villages, and bridges over the Zadorra in our possession, I have no doubt the troops were ordered to the rear with least possible delay, and all idea of saving their guns, probably from that moment abandoned. No army is so soon put in a panic from any operations on their flank as the French; a much less serious on that this general suffices.

In the meantime, the attack made on the hills to our left by Major-General Pack's brigade, supported by the 5th Division and the Spaniards under Colonel Longa, had succeeded, the 4th Regiment of Caladorres belonging to General Pack's brigade having distinguished itself, charging the enemy from the heights with the bayonet.

There was some little anxiety shown by Lord Wellington on the right, not hearing the attack commenced so soon as he expected from the left column. Sir T. Graham looked to the right the whole day with the greatest anxiety, to time his attack. That by General Pack was made on the hills immediately, and the enemy being repulsed with one brigade, it did not appear probably to be so general as Lord W. Expected. Had Sir T. Graham attacked sooner, the enemy might have reinforced their troops before him to that extent as to render his success doubtful. I think he conducted the thing well, and so did Lord Wellington, I fancy, when in was over. His anxiety on such an occasion was natural and excusable.

The possession of these heights placed us within a mile of the Zandorra, and gave us the command of the plain from there to the river. A squadron from the 12th Light Dragoons had been detatched with the troops making the attack on the heights, and the enemy showing two or three of theirs at the foot of the hills, mine of the 16th was ordered to that point. I had to go a league at a trot, and before I could get there their cavalry had retired to the rear of their infantry.

(All marches are made at a walk, and cavalry should never go faster excepting before an enemy. It is impossible where you have daily a change of forage, and some days none, to keep the horses efficient if you move faster.)

I joined the squadron of the 12th Light Dragoons, and remained in rear of Gamarra Mayor, whilst the 5th Division, under Major-General Oswald, attacked and carried the village at the point of the bayonet. The leading Brigade was the 2nd Brigade, under Major-General Robertson, consisting of the 4th, 47th and 59th, and were moving in an echelon of regiments from the left. (The brigade would run from the right 4th, 59th, 47th left, consequently the 4th was the last.) there was either some shyness in the two leading regiments, or some misunderstanding of orders; but Colonel Brooke perceiving it called, "Come on, Grenadiers 4th!" passed the other two with his battalion, and carried the place, taking 2,000 prisoners and three guns.

(This account I has from Colonel Brooke, and therefore some allowance must be made for his won statement of the fact. He' however, is quite a person to do as stated, and, in corroboration, the 4th suffered considerably.)

During this, the 1st Division and Major-General Bradford's Portuguese brigade moved on the high road to Vittoria, Colonel Halkett's brigade of Light German infantry, supported by Major-General Bradford's brigade, and covered by Captain Duberdin's brigade and Captain Ramsay's troop of artillery, attacked and carried the village of Abechuco, so giving is possession of both the passes over the Zadorra. The light battalions charged the enemy on the brigade, and drove them away, taking a howitzer and three guns.

The possession of these points completely turned the enemy off the main road from Vittoria to Bayonne, which passes Mondragon and Tolosa, and so on to Yrun, obliging them to take that of Pampeluna, which so completely put them in confusion, that by 4p.m their whole force had passed Vittoria, making off how they could, leaving in the rear of the town all their artillery, ammunition, wagons, money, and baggage, only taking their arms and the men's kits on their backs.

The enemy so little expected a general action, that they probably had not made the preparations they should for a retreat, if necessary. The holding the villages in front of the left column evidently implied that it was their intention to keep open the road to Tolosa, and we may therefore conclude that our depriving them of it caused some confusion.

Had all the cavalry been brought forward to have acted the instant the enemy passed Vittoria, I think there was a fine chance of taking a great many prisoners; but as is always the case the cavalry was not up, and two squadrons from the 15th Hussars, and two from the 18th, were brought forward to annihilate the French army. The two of the 15th charged about 2,000 of the enemy's cavalry, got into a scrape; and the two of the 18th, it was said, did not do all they should have done to bring them out of it. The enemy's cavalry was mixed with their infantry, the latter, in almost double quick time, making for a wood on the Pampeluna road, almost half a league from Vittoria. On perceiving this, Major-General Anson's brigade was ordered to pass the Zadorra at the village of Gamarra Mayor, where there is a brigade, and where the Spanish Division, under Colonel Longa, had moved to, on Gamarra Mayor being carried by the 5th Division. We saw them from near Gamarra Mayor, where we were, running in the greatest haste and confusion. From where we stood it appeared to be only necessary to come up with them to secure half the army. Had cavalry been up to have charged in amongst them, and some to have moved with a view of cutting them off, the greatest success would have attended it.

The two squadrons which had been detached with the 5th Divison being on that road, we formed the advance of the brigade, preceding the brigade about a mile. On passing the river we turned to the right, on the road to Vittoria, a mile from which place we came up with the enemy's scattered infantry pursued by Major-General Pack's brigade, and made a few prisioners. We were now at the edge of the wood, and being a little puzzled by a deep impassable drain, it was necessary to ascertain how far the enemy had gone and what there was in the wood. This gave time for the brigade to come up, together with the Heavy Germans, under Major-General Bock, and in ten minutes we were in march through the wood, which is for the most part open, through the trees are so close and low that infantry cannot be attacked with cavalry. Major-General Pack's brigade moved on with us and a few of Colonel Lonega's Spaniards.

The enemy collected in the wood a rear-guard of six squadrons and a regiment of infantry, with others scattered as light troops in all directions. With this force they occupied a plain about half a mile across, surrounded with wool and ending in a defile, thus keeping the head of the lane, along which we could alone get at them. The Spanish infantry got into a field of corn and down the lane, and on firing a few shots the enemy moved off, and we pushed on after them. My squadron was in advance, and on arriving on the plain formed immediately and advanced to the charge. All was confusion, all calling "go on" before then men had time to get in their places. We got half across before I was able to place them in any form, and had we been allowed one minute more in forming, our advance might have been quicker, and made with much more regularity.

The enemy had about six squadrons in line, with one a little in advance, consisting of their Elite companies. This I charged, broke, and drove on their line, which, advancing, I was obliged to retire, having had a good deal of sabring with those I charged and with their support. A squadron of the 12th was in my rear, and in the place of coming up on my flank, followed me, so that they only added to the confusion of retiring by mixing with my men. Captain Wrexon's squadron of the 16th then came to the charge. We were so mixed that I could not get my men out of his way, was obliged to front and make a rally back, and the enemy, seeing the remainder of the brigade coming up, retired through the defile with their cavalry, leaving a square of grenadiers in its mouth. We came close upon them without perceiving they were there, and on our going about they fired a running volley, which did considerable execution, and then they made off through the defile. (We followed them about a mile, when, night coming on, the persuit ceased, and we bivouacked on the ground we halted on.) I rode up within a yard of the enemy's infantry; they had their arms on the port, and were as steady as possible, not a man of them attempting to fire till we began to retire. They certainly might have reached myself and many other with their bayonets had they been allowed. I never saw men more steady and exact to the word of command.

I lost in my squadron Lieutenant the Hon. Geo Thelluson,* of the 11th Light Dragoons, who had been attatched to the 16th. It was the first time he had ever been engaged, and he was so anxious to distinguish himself that he rode direct into the enemy's ranks. When his regiment went to England he wished to remain on service; he was annoyed at the opposition made by his friends to his marrying Miss H-, of Dorchester. He sacrificed himself, never desiring to return to England, leaving a will by which he gave her all his fortune-from £10,000 to £12,000. She has since married.

Corporal Hollinsworth and Foxall of my troop are killed; Waterman and Hollinsworth mortally wounded; Barns and McKewin have lost each an arm; Mendham, McKee, and Crabtree,

*Second son of the first Lord Rendlesham

severely wounded. We always loose the best. The whole, with the exception of the last are the best men in the troop; I may say, the two killed the best in the regiment. I am minus nine men and nine horses. The other troop of the squadron lost one man killed and two wounded. They were not so much exposed to the infantry fire. The army encamped in front of Vittoria, with headquarters in the town.

The 18th Hussars got into a great scrape in plundering. They were detected doing so when, I believe, they ought to have been moving forwards. Lord Wellington was so much enraged that he would not recommend any of their subalterns for two troops which were vacant by two captains killed, a thing very unusual. One was given to Lieutenant Owen,* 16th Light Dragoons, the other to Lieutenant Luard,* 4th Dragoons. One reason I heard, was that a carriage belonging to the Etat-Major of the French was ordered to be guarded by a sergant and some men of the 18th; it contained papers of the consequence, which Lord Wellington wished to keep. The sergeant left the carriage, and the papers were lost. This, with their plundering, exasperated him. There might be other reasons.

We have taken about 200 pieces of cannon, many heavy pieces collected from their different forts near Vittoria, and nearly 500 ammunition wagons. 151 of the former and 415 of the latter was hthe number stated by Lord Wellington; but many were afterwards discovered. The Eagles of the 100th Regiment of French infantry were taken, with Marshal Jourdan's Baton Staff of a Marshal of France. The Eagles were claimed by the 87th Regiment. Carriages, wagons, miles, monkeys, parrots, were all left in rear of the town. Everything useful to an army we have taken, and the whole of this, I conceive, was secured previous to a shot being fired; for from the dispositions prior to the battle, it was impossible the enemy could get clear away; and when Marshall Jourdan was told the English were attacking his right, he said it was but the Spainiards under Longa. The Paymaster-General, with all the military chest, fell into our hands. None of

*The writer of the pamphlet on Major Cocks
*In the 16th Light Dragoons at Waterloo

it was saved for the public service; the soldiers took the greater part.

Sergeant Blood of my troop, with six men, secured a car load of dollars, and kept them till night, when the infantry came and plundered his wagon. He brought 6,000 to the regiment.

Mr. Dallas, commissary to the 16th Light Dragoons, got 150 doubloons as his share with five others. A doubloon is worth £4, making his share £600.

Had it not been for the wood our brigade was engaged in, many more prisoners would have been made, and before they could have reached it, had the cavalry been up on a body, all their stragglers would have been taken; indeed, from the confusion they were in, we might have got into their infantry. Every advantage cannot be taken, and considering what we have this day gained, our exertions have been fully repaid. I think, however, we are rather deficient in the pursuit of a beaten enemy. Lord Wellington may not like to entrust officers with detatchments to act according to circumstances, and I am not quite clear if he approves of much success, excepting under his own immediate eye.

Madame Gazan, wife to the General, was taken, with all the women of the army; she and another were sent, on the following day, to the enemy.

The inhabitants of Vittoria had not done plundering the day after, and many have amply repaid themselves for the sums taked from them in contributions. In the army six and eight dollars were offered for a guines, it being impossible to carry dollars. Mules, worth 250 dollars, were sold for three guineas. Guineas had been struck in England, and sent out for the payment of the army. They were ordered to be taken by a decree from the Regency in Portugal, and passing there they went current through the whole of the Peninsula. They were not the same die as the old guinea, and lighter. It was a great saving, instead of giving 6s. for dollars which were paid to the troops at 4s. 6d. All the Portuguese boys belonging to some of the divisions are dressed in the uniforms of French officers, many generals. The camp of the infantry near Vittoria was turned into a fair-it was lighted-the cars, etc., made into stands, where the things taken were exposed for sale, and many of the soldiers, by way of adding to the absurdity of the scene, dressed themselves up in the uniforms found in the chests. The king's baggage fell into our hands; he passed through Vittoria at half-past 4p.m-our advance entered a little before 5. Amongst the papers found was a copy of a letter from Jourdan to the Minister of War at Paris, stating that his plans had not been so much attended to as he could have wished, and that he thought it the intentions of the English to pass the Ebro where they did and manoeuvre on their (the French) right flank. The enemy in the morning conceived it only a skirmish, as Gazan wrote from the field to his wife not to be in a hurry, but to get her dinner and go off with the baggage in the evening. The Paris cipher which they constantly vary, and as in a letter the least deviation from the preceding one will make the greatest difference, there arises considerable difficulty in arriving at the meaning. I do not believe we were ever deceived in these letters, and Colonel Schovel (Commandant of the Corps of Guides attached to headquarters) was the person who made them out. There was, however, one letter that never could be deciphered.

Vittoria was not injured by the action. The enemy's loss was great in men, yet probably not much exceeding our own.

Return of Casualties in the Action of Vittoria, June 21st, 1813

British loss

GenStaff	Lieuts. Cols	Majors	Captns.	Lieutenants	Ensigns	Staff	Sergants	Drummers	Rank&File	Horses	
-	1	-	6	10	4	1	15	4	460	92	killed
1	7	5	40	87	22	5	123	13	2,504	68	wounded

British Total
501 killed
2,807 wounded
3,308

Portuguese Loss

GenStaff	Lieuts. Cols	Majors	Captns.	Lieutenants	Ensigns	Staff	Sergants	Drummers	Rank&File	Horses	
-	1	4	16	10	19	6	35	1	811	-	wounded
-	-	-	3	1	3	-	4	1	138	1	killed

Portuguese Total
130 killed
1,003 wounded
1,153

Spanish Loss

GenStaff	Lieuts. Cols	Majors	Captns.	Lieutenants	Ensigns	Staff	Sergants	Drummers	Rank&File	Horses	
-	1	4	16	10	19	6	35	1	811	-	wounded
-	-	-	3	1	3	-	4	1	138	1	killed

Spanish Total
89 Killed
464 wounded
553

Grand Total Loss of the Army

GenStaff	Lieuts. Cols	Majors	Captns.	Lieutenants	Ensigns	Staff	Sergants	Drummers	Rank&File	Horses	
-	1	-	10	14	7	1	19	5	683	93	killed
2	9	9	59	103	41	7	138	14	3,768	68	wounded

Total Loss on the 21st June, 1813

740 killed
6,170 wounded
4,910

OBSERVATION ON THE BATTLE OF VITTORIA

The enemy had one division absent, under Clauset, another to the north of Tolosa, both which had orders to join the army, and would have done so had the battle been delayed a couple of days.

Nothing can speak more for the judgment displayed in pushing on our advance, and the excellent arrangement is making the columns move to those points where they were required to attack. Had the left column moved with the remainder of the army, to the point on the main road before the enemy's position, and then been detached to its appointed place, two days, or one at least, would have been lost, and the divisions of the enemy in question might have joined. Most generals would, I think, have reconnoitred the enemy's position, having their whole force collected, and then have detached to the left. I took upon it as the best thing we have done connected with the whole advance. We marched on the 28th April, and arrived at Ernani, close to the frontier, on the 30th June, being a march of sixty-three days. We halted a few days at Braga; from leaving which, May 13th to June 30th, is forty-eight days. Lord W. kept out of the way of the infantry columns for some days when up near Burgos, thinking he should see the men so footsore and straggling the he must, contrary to his desire, half them a day or two. He saw a couple of the columns pass him one day on the march, and kept saying, as they passed him, that they got on better than when they first moved, asking those near him if they were not of the same opinion. As if they could differ from him! Men will do anything on an advance. The common talk of the infantry on coming up with the enemy is, that they will pay them for making them march so far.

June 22nd. The whole army moved this day at 10a.m in pursuit od the enemy's flying troops. The infantry moved on Salcatierra, to which place headquarters likewise came. The brigade moved by a route to the left of the main road,a nd encamped for the night two short leagues in advance of Salvatierra. Major-General Altern't brigade came up with the enemy's rear, retiring on Pampeluna, which moved off after exchanging a few shots.

June 23rd. There was no small confusion with the generals moving without orders. General Pack moved into our village by way of getting on; we futher to another, and the artillery was ordered still further, which vexed Lord W. so much that he vented his rage by placing Captain Ramsay under arrest, and would not hear a word (Ramsay was hardly used, as he moved by his general's orders). The 5th Division, under Major-General Osborne, fell into the same error.

We were left without orders till late, and in consequence of the whole army moving, general Anson conceived we were to do the same, and advanced us on the main road, when Lord Wellington turned us back, and directed us to Sir T Graham for orders. It appeared that the 1st Division, with Pack's and Bradford's brigades of Portuguese infantry, and Major-General Anson's of cavalry, were directed to cross the mountains to Villa Franca, and from thence to move in the Bayonne road in pursuit of the enemy's convoy, which had left Vittoria on that route for France.

Sir Thomas, with the Light infantry, got as far as Segura, the 16th halted at Cigama. The 1st Division and 12th Light Dragoons bivouacked in the mountains.

We marched four leagues in incessant rain, which made the mountains so slippery that many horses came down, and it almost prevented the infantry moving at all.

(The road in one place was conducted through the mountain for twenty yards, under a height of 200feet.)

I was sent with my troop to Segura at 10p.m to find patrols on the Villa Franca road. The enemy are still passing, and I think there is some chance of our coming up with them.

We are now in the province of Gulpuzcoa, where the people do not speak a word of Spanish. It is a language not unlike the Highland, not one word of which can we understand. All the upper classes speak Spanish, the lower not a word. In Cigama very few spoke the two languages.

June 24th. The 1st Division, with the exception of one brigade, this day assembled at Segura. The 12th and 16th came in soon after daylight and remained three hours before we moved on. Sir Thomas Graham then, with the Light Companies K.G.L., and Pack's and Bradford's Portuguese brigades of infantry, pushed on towards the main road leading from Vittoria to Bayonne. The enemy's rear was just at this moment passing the junction, and they occupied in some force very stron ground on the right of the main road, and to the right of the river Oria, in front of the small village of Olaverria, a mile and a half in front of Villa Franca.

Our advance was in Villa Franca, the 16th occupied Lazcano, the 12th Ataun. Sir Thomas Graham's quarters were in Villa Franca.

The attack began by Bradford's brigade on the right near Olaverria, and his advance, consisting of a battalion of Cacadores, got rather into a scrape, having pushed on too quickly, and came on the enemy so suddenly that they were not prepared to receive the fire and attack that came against them. The enemy conceiving our intention to be to turn their rightm attempted to reinforce it, which gave the troops on the main road an opportunity of advancing. The Light Brigade K.G.L., under Colonel Halkett, attacked and carried the village of Veasaya, supported in their attack by nine companies of General Pack's brigade. This placed us within a mile of Villa Franca, though they still kept the strong hills on each side of the orad. These positions were about to be turned by the different troops, but before all could be arranged, the enemy moved off, allowing us to take possession of Villa Franca. The road the whole way is carried at the bottom of the valley the hills rising right and left close to its sides, and yet in riding twenty leagues there is scarcely an ascent of 100 yards. It is quite a pattern for carrying roads through hilly countries, and the road is excellent, very wide, and raised two feet above the level on which it is constructed.

June 25th. The whole moved forward, assembling at Algeria. The enemy held a position in front of Tolosa, about half a mile. Their right rested on a high mountain, their front was covered by an inaccessible hill; the ground on their left was a sstrong as possible. This it was impossible to attack, and the guerrillas, under Colonel Longa, being sent to turn the enemy's left, whilst some other Spanish troops acted on their right, coming from Aspeytia, the whole waited the time necessary for their arrival at their appointed places. The Line Brigade of three battalions K.G.L., with Brigadier-General Bradford's Portuguese brigade, and a detatchmnet from General Pack's, were detatched to the right, and the one battalion from General Pack's brigade, under Colonel Williams, of the Cacadores, attacked and carried an important height occupied by the enemy between the road we were on and the one leading from Tolosa to Pampeluna. This enabled us to act on the latter road, so attacking the place at its two principal entrances. It was long ere the Spaniards arrived at their destinations, and not before 6p.m could an attack with a view to carry the place be attempted. The troops on the right attacked on the Pampeluna road, and came most gallantly up to the town, in which they rather suffered. The Light German battalions, with the remainder of General Pack's brigade, supported by the Guards, attacked on the road we were on, covered by two guns from Captain Ramsey's troop, and two nine-pounders from Captain Dubordien's brigade: these were escorted by the right division of my squadron. The Spanish troops (about a regiment) moved to the left, attempting to get between the hills and the town.

Tolosa, like all other places, is completely enclosed, the walls loop-holed, and strong gates at all the entrances. The troops, under a considerable fore, gained the outer walls, and from them kept up a heavy fore against the enemy, in which, from being exposed, we were the greatest suffierers. The Spaniards, under Longa, showing on the hills to the right of the town, the enemy abandoned it retiring on Ernani, leaving Tolosa, half and hour after dark, when we entered and took possession of the town amidst the vivas of the inhabitants, they having made up their minds to be well plundered that night had we not succeeded. It is an important point giving is a direct communication with the high road to Pampeluna. Sir Thomas was hit directing the troops in the attack on the Vittoria gate, and on his going to the rear some confusion took place. The Guards was near faring on Colonel Halkett's people stationed at the edge of the town. I was standing close to him. I was the first with my squadron to enter after the enemy had left, and ordered all the people to shut their doors, fearing some parties away from their regiments might await themselves of the confusion, and plunder.

June 26th. Brigadier-General Bradford's brigade moved a league on the Pampeluna road. The German Legion from the 1st Division advanced in front a league on the Bayonne road. Sir T. Graham remained in Tolosa with the Guards, and my squadron, from having been on duty, was directed to remain in some houses outside the town, on the Pampeluna road. The brigade occupied Alegria. Our halt here was occasioned by Sir Thomas's ignorance of Lord Wellington's advance; he waited here till he ascertained his movements.

Sir Stapleton Cotton had joined the army from England, having missed the glorious affair of Vittoria.

The Spanish army, under Heron, is moving through Tolosa on towards Bayonne. They are about 20,000 men, well clothed and appointed.

June 29th. Sir Thomas Graham, with the column, moved up four leagues and accupied Ernane. The brigade moved to Lasarte and Zubieta, the 16th to the former, 12th to Zubieta.

June 30th. The whole assembled at Ernane this morning and after remaining there for some hours, the brigade returned to its former quarters.

The Spanish army is close up with the enemy, and General Heron is very anxious to attack. The country is too stoney, and I think the enemy will withdraw over the Bidassi without being forced.

July 1st. the enemy withdrew into France, and our advance was on the Bidassi. San Sebastian (of which the Engineers think nothing, through it appears to me strong, and the castle commanding the town very hard to approach) has a garrison of near 2,000-the 500 that were in Guetaria left in boats this morning and joined the garrison of San Sebastian. The fort of Guetaria was blown up at 2p.m, by which fifty poepole lost their lives. As it was the enmy's intention to blow it up, a match of two hours would have allowed them time to get away.

Heavy Artillery is landing at Deba, and the 5th Division is moving there from Vittoria with Major-General Bock's Heavy German brigade.

150 of the enemy's infantry left in Los Passages this day surrendered to the Spanish General Longa.

Lord Wellington, with the 3rd and 4th Light Divisions, and Major-General Ponsonby and Grant's brigades of cavalry, has been in pursuit of Clausel, who made his appearance within a few leagues of Vittoria on the 22nd ult., moving at the same time the 5th and 6th Divisions, with the house hold brigades and Colonel D'Urban's of Portuguese cavalry, that had been left at Vittoria, to Logronio. Clausel, with his division, was aware of his situation, and made some extra-ordinary forced marches. He crossed the Ebro at Tudela where he arrived on the 27th June, and moved on the road Lord Wellington was on, and would have met him. The alcalde informed him of this, when he recrossed the Ebro, and made his retreat good to Zaragossa, followed by Mina, with his guerrillas, leaving in Logronio four pieces of cannon, which fell into our hands.

There was something very singular in the manner the enemy's parties were marching all about the country in apparent ignorance of the army's advance. Their information must have been bad, or our advance quicker than they thought possible.

June 7th. Sir Thomas Graham this day directed the convent in front of San Sebastian to be attacked. The orders came out at nine, for it to be acted against at eleven. The Spaniards on their first investing the place, got possession of it, but were driven out, and now the enemy have got a gun in it loop-holed the walls, and on its left flank thrown up a trench on the hill, where we must place our batteries, and I believe the only point from which the town is to be breached.

A brigade of Portuguese nine-pounders were sent up to fire red hot shot against it, whilst the two brigades of Germans from the 1st Division moved up as a support to the Spaniards. Not a shot was fired before 2p.m and then they began with cold shot; this was done to ascertain the range, but unfortunately commenced long before the hot shot was ready. Nothing was done, nor could it be expected, no arrangement having previously been made.

The Spaniards knew nothing of it when it was time to begin. The direction of the affairs was entrusted to Major Smith, of the Engineers, who could not order things when senior officers were on the ground.

It will give the enemy confidence, make them value and strengthen the convent, and consequently give us much more trouble and cost more lives when really attacked.

Major-General Vandeleur, from the Light Division, this day joined and took the command of the brigade, Major-General Anson being placed on the Home Staff in England.

Sir John Murray, with the Alicante army, has embarked and relanded at Taeeagona, which place he has attacked. Various reports have told us it has surrendered. We now hear the unfortunate intelligence of his having in a hurry embarked the whole of his army, leaving behind his battering train, amounting to 27 pieces of artillery, and this at a time the enemy had not above 6,000 men up, when a little delay might have brought all off. Lord W. Bentinck has taken the command of that army.

The 700 men left in the castle of Pan Calo, on the main road from Burgos to Vittoria, have surrendered to the Spanish army under the Conde de Abispal. The lower part of the town was carried by the Spaniards, when want of water obliged them to surrender on retiring to the castle.

July 8th. The 1st division left Ernani for ground in the rear of Yrun, to cover the siege of San Sebastian, and the 5th came up from Vittoria tot ake the siege, encamping on the road to San Sebastian from Ernani.

Major-General Anson left for England, and is to go in a vessel now lying off Los Passages. The Heavy Artillery, which was coming round by way of Debu, is re-embarked, and is coming to Los Passages, a league and a half from Ernani.

We met on our march near Tolosa the six heavy eighteen-pounders, with the pontoons, which have come by land the whole way from Lisbon, and nearly kept pace with the army through the whole advance.

July 9th. The forage became so scarce that the brigade moved this day to Tolosa for cantonments near Villa Franca. We might have remained in and near Ernani cutting the wheat which is now so ripe, but it is bad forage, and destruction to the inhabitants. The 12th Light Dragoons have used nothing else since they have occupied these cantonments; the 16th, only the first day they came in, and one or two before leaving, when there was no grass left.

Tolosa was occupied by Spaniards, and the 16th remained for the night near Algeria in the scattered houses on the left of the road, and the 12th in those to the right, nearer Tolosa.

July 10th. The 16th occupied Atun and Idiazasat, 12th and headquarters brigade, Lazcano.

July 12th. The 12th Light Dragoons this day moved from Lazcano to some straggling villages to the right of Algeria.

July 16th. The two squadrons at Ataun left for Segura, a league lower down.

At Ataun we had green oats in great abundance and not far to go for them; they are here scarce and a long way off.

The chief reason for leaving Ataun was, that our Colonel had a bad house, which with him is the first consideration and his regiment the last.

We hear reports of moving, and on the 24th officers were sent from the 16th to examine some villages to the left of Tolosa.

A better appointed Spanish force than I have yet seen of that nation has joined the army. They are well clothed and appointed. British muskets, with a commissariat which affords them a regular supple. Their camp kettle is similar to the one used in the British army, and I saw a mess of men eating their dinner out of it. It was placed in the road, the men stood round it, each with a spoon, and each taking his regular turn to dip in the kettle. There were, I think twelve men, so that there were eleven spoonfuls taken out before the first could apply for a second dip, which being done with the gravity and slowness of Spaniards, made it ridiculous, and more tantalizing to a hungry man than calculated to satisfy him, particularly as it was the only meal they had in each day; but they are the most abstemious people in the world.

It was said a regular inspection of each spoon took place previous to the meal, that no one might have one larger than his neighbour.

July 24th. A route for the brigade to move up to Ernani arrived this day at 12a.m. We marched to Algeria, the 12th to Villa Bona, in advance of Tolosa.

July 25th. Marched this morning to our cantonments, the 12th Light Dragoons with General Vaneleur to Renteria, the 16th to Astigarraga. We were scattered all around the farm-houses. The people have cut their wheat, which gives is abundance of straw. From want of other forage the troops up here have been obliged to eat the standing corn, which has induced the inhabitants to reap before it is quite ready.

July 29th. The enemy made some demonstrations to the right of our line, which brought us up to this morning to Renteria, the 12th moving some ground in front of our position at Oyarrun. Two squadrons occupied Renteria, the right went to Lozo, half a league nearer the sea.

The household brigade had been quartered near Logronio, and on the enemy making some demonstration of advancing. General O'Laughlen, who commanded it, was ordered, under a discretionary route, to march to the front. From the nature of the country, cavalry could be of little service, and it was expected he would arrive in the course of three of four days. We marched nearly night and day, and in the last twenty-four hours had accomplished nearly 80 miles. His brigade consisted of 1st and 2nd Life Guards and Blues.

Lord Wellington was perfectly astonished at seeing them up so soon, saying he did not know how his regiment (the Blues) could fight, not having tried them, but he was sure they could march. The general was much blamed, and his brigade ordered into cantonments, not being required for some time. The very sending of a discretionary route implied a desire that the brigade might come up quickly.

July 30th. We were ordered to our former quarters at Astigarraga, but obtained leave to go to Lasarte. On entering Lasarte we were ordered back to Renteria, and returned there at sunset after a march of five leagues for no one pupose.

July 31st. Relieved the 12th in front of Oyarzun, encamping half a mile in front of the position. One squadron is sent on duty into the mountains to the right, where twenty men would do everything.

The 12th returned to Renteria.

Aug 2nd. As officer and twenty men from the 12th relieved the whole 16th, and we marched with the two squadrons to Lozo, leaving the right on duty where it was first sent.

From the defeat of the enemy on the right, there is a strong report of the army moving into France, and it is said that Sir Thomas has been out to fix the spot where the pontoons over the Bidassoa are to be placed. We may go far enough to drive the enemy from the strong position he holds in our front, but not much in advance of that.

Soult collected a considerable force, and moved to attack Lord Wellington on the right*. He moved his whole force near to one point, and from the different roads Lord W. had to watch, it was impossible to be prepared at all. The troops were much pressed, and but for the conduct of the 4th Division, which withstood five times its numbers, the enemy would have succeeded un relieving Pampeluna. The conduct of this division was much

---

**the Actions in the Pyresses*

spoken of, and Lord W. in his despatch mentioned it as being enthusiastic. His expression was "the enthusiastic conduct of the 4th Division". They were afterwards called "The Enthusiastics."

Aug 8th. The brigade moved to the rear, having no forage without cutting the Indian corn; headquarters of the brigade to Ibzarbille. The 16th to Zubietta, Belmonte, and all the straggling farmhouses in the neightbourhood. The 12th extended to the sea, occupying Ria at the mouth of the river we are on. The artillery and Major Webber Smith's troops occupied Lasarte. The left squadron was at Zubietta, the headquarters of the regiment.

Sir Stapleton Cotton has placed his headquarters at Renteria. Those of the army are at Lasaco.

Aug 12th. Our squadron moved this day from Zubietta to Aya, two leagues over the mountains towards the sea in the direction of Guitaria.

We hear strong reports of peace; they come from France.

When at Aya we attended a ball at Marshall Beresford's quarters at Zarauz. The people there were those who had left San Sebastian, and though the siege was going on, and their houses probably injured daily, no feelings as to what their town was suffering had any influence on their spirits. The people of Guipiozcoa are a fine race; on the whole, I think, the finest we have met with. The upper classes have profited by their long privilege of a free trade, or at least an exemption from many duties paid by the other provinces. During the wars with England, they were allowed to eat meat the whole of Lent, owing to the difficulty of procuring salt fish, a privilege they still claim.

The lower classes are tall, extremely well made, and good looking.

Aug 13th. Our squadron moved this day from Zubietta to Aya, two leagues over the mountains towards the sea, in the direction of Guitaria.

Aug 14th. The two squadrons in and near Uzurbille this day left it, marching to Cestona and adjacents, two leagues to the left of Aya on the sea. We remained quiet.

The regiment was cantoned as follows:-
D troop   Arrona
F   "   Oguina
G   "   Azzarnavel
K   "   Headquarters, Cestona.

The regiment left Aya and their quarters that place for Lasarte and adjacents, where they halted two hours, and then marched on to Renteria, where they halted at midnight.

Sept 3rd. The brigade this day moved to the rear, the 16th marching to Tolosa, three leagues on the main road.

One squadron of the 12th remained up at Renteria, the other two retiring to Zubietta and Uzurbille. Sir Thomas Graham thinks cavalry of use, in case the enemy makes an attack, though I cannot see ground to form a squadron on. The one left will be quite sufficient to find all piquets orderlies, and detatched parties, and will save the march up of the brigade on every trivial occasion.

Sept 4th. The 16th marched nearly four leagues, occupying Azpeytia and Azcoeta, two good villages, the right squadron with headquarters the former, and the other the latter. They are the best quarters we have been in for some time; each would hold a regiment. Sir Stapleton Cotton is expected at Azpeytia.

Went to Durango, six leagues on the Bilboa road. I here met the 16th remount from England. The horses in bad order, having been five weeks on board. The 7th Hussars are landed at Bilboa. I marched the following day four leagues to Bilboa, and having remained two there, returned with Captain Penrice, 16th, to the regiment, in the same quarters where I had left them.

Siege of San Sebastian

Since the arrival of the army on the 1st July San Sebastian had been blockaded. The garrison, at the time we got possession of Tolosa, was very weak (150 I believe), and all the inhabitants around this were of the opinion that had we pushed on the 26th, we might have got possession of it. This might be so, though it would have been prudent to have advanced from Tolosa ignorant of Lord W.'s progress on the right. As we missed the opportunity we might have availed ourselves of, it is to be regretted.

On the 13th the 5th Division, Major-General Pack's and Bradford's brigades commenced operations against the town. The advanced convent of San Bartolomew was breached, attacked and carried by the 9th Regiment and a Poruguese brigade, on the night of the 17th, with little difficulty. Twenty 24-pounders, four eight-inch howitzers, four ten-inch mortars, four 68-pound carronades were employed.

After the capture of the convent, the approaches continued against the town, and on the 20th the batteries opened. On the 21st Sit T. Graham sent a flag of truce, which the governor would not receive-it was to summon him to surrender. A breach was considered practicable on the 23rd, and the troops were to attack it at daylight, the tide being them out. It could only be acted against at low water, as, excepting at that time, the sea covered the space betwixt our approaches and the breach. The assault was ordered to take place on the morning of the 24th; but in consequence of some houses being on fire near the breach, the attack was countermanded. On the 25th, at daylight, 2,000 men were ordered to assault the breach. The distance from our approaches to the breach was 300 yards, over very difficult ground, covered with sea-weeds and many pools of water. The fire from the place was not destructive. The breach was also flanked by the fire of a couple of bastions, which were not abandoned by the enemy, though considerably injured by our fire. A mine had been formed at the end of a drain which was discovered in digging our approaches, and ran up to the ditch of the town. This was charged, and its explosion agreed upon as the signal for the troops to move. At 5a.m it was blown up, and the surprise of the enemy was such that they, for an instant, abandoned the works near the breach. The advanced guard (forlorn hope) ascended the breach, on gaining which most of them fell over the other side into the town, down a perpendicular wall, the space at the bottom of which was enclosed by another wall, which was loop-holed. The latter was erected by the enemy on finding the spot we intended to breach. The fire from the place was great, and the shells thrown on the breach so numerous that the troops could not succeed, and in a short time returned to the trenches with the loss of about 100 killed and 400 wounded. The enemy made a successful sortie on the 27th, and took nearly 200 men prisoners. In consequence of the advance of Marshal Soult against Lord W., Sir T. Graham embarked all the Heavy Artillery on the 29th at Los Passages, and sent the transports to sea.

In consequence of Lord Wellington's success, the guns were re-landed at Los Passages on the 6th August. On the 18th additional artillery and ammunition arrived from England, and on the 24th the siege recommenced. The enemy on the same night made a sortie, but were checked by a guard in the trenches. They, however, took twelve prisoners. On the 26th the batteries opened. On the night of the 27th the enemy made another sortie; but from a different and better arrangement of the sentries, the men had notice, stood to their arms, and the enemy were driven back without effecting the least mischief. By the fire from our batteries, the breach had been much enlarged, and on the 30th volunteers for attack marched into the camp of the 5th Division from the other divisions of the army. These detachments were, 150 Light Division, under Lieutenant-Colonel Hunt, 52nd Regiment; 400 from the 1st Division, 200 of which consisted of men from the Guards, 100 from the light battalion, K.G.L., 100 from the line battalions K.G.L., the whole under the command of Lieutenant-Colonel Cooke. The Germans were, I fancy, under Major Robertson, with the above detachments, formed the advanced column.

The assault took place at 11a.m. We all saw the forlorn hope fall in, as also its support. The men had a glass of wine each, which they drank to the officers' health and success. There was a considerable degree of spirit in the troops; the detachments from the Light and 4th Divisions saying they would show them the way up the breach as at Rodrigo and Badajos. The troops moved into the trenches, and we, spectators, all went to the convent of San Bartolomew to witness the assult. The enemy in the town were perfectly aware of what was about to happen, and we heard their drum beat to arms. There were a good many collected in the convent which was open in many places, the walls having been battered in. The enemy, seeing us, fired at the place, and we were obliged to conceal ourselves and select places where we could observe the attack without being seen by them. At 11 the troops moved from the trenches; the enemy opened a tremendous fire, the effect of which we perceived from the number they left on the ground they passed. Two mines of the enemy were blown up; the troops were not very near them, and did not suffer a great deal. The fire on the breach was so great, being flanked by the horn work on the left, and also from the castle, that our troops contested for the breach for above an hour, without getting possession, exposed to a most destructive fire. The troops were ordered to make a lodgment on the breach, but could not, owing to the fire kept up. The main curtain of the town was strongly occupied by the enemy close up to the breach; they had breastworks of barrels filled with samd to cover them, from behind which they kept up a tremendous fire. The left flank also of the horn-work was well manned, and protected with barrels as the curtain. The troops that had gained the breach had a little cover, from its being steep and rough, from whence they kept up a fire against the enemy. This was a dreadful suspense; we scarcely knew whether to wish for perseverance under such loss, or for the troops to retire and prevent any further destruction. In these doubts we saw our batteries open against the curtain of the place, which was so high above the horn-work that the guns acted without a fear of injuring our men; indeed, they were quite out of their range, being on the right of where they directed their fire, and I am not quite clear if the attack in the first instance ought not to have benn assisted with this diversion. At this time a Potuguese brigade of infantry was seen advancing along the sands on the right hand of the river Urumea, with a view to ford the river and assult the breach. They suffered from the fire in the castle, and we saw men fall on the ground they passed. They passed the river in the most gallant style, and proceeded to assist in the assault of the breach. Reinforcements of a brigade of the 5th Divisions were ordered to advance out of the trenches, under Colonel Greville. The 3rd battalion, 1st Regiment, supported by the 38th, moved to the assault, and at the moment some combustibles of the enemy's were set fire to by one of our shells. It was a considerable explosion, and I saw some of the enemy leaping from the curtain into the ditch. The moment was a fortunate one; the attack was renewed, and the breach carried, the enemy retiring into the town. The artillery in its fire on the curtain, was beautifully directed. We looked at the point they were firing on, and we saw shot after shot strike in the right place. The breach being carried, the troops descended into the town, driving the enemy from all their breastworks, etc., into the castle. Immediately after the attack I went to the breach, and the only thing I was struck with was wonder how, in daylight, it could be carried. The slaughter was very great–500 killed in the attack, 1,500 wounded. The surgeons attended in the trenches, and cut off one man's arm before he came to his camp. Sir Jas. Leith has his arm broken, and also a blow on the breast. General Robinson was wounded, having much distinguished himself. Lieutenant-Colonel Fletcher, of the Engineers, was killed by a musket shot when in the trenches; Lieutenant Le Blaine, 4th Foot, who led the Light Infantry company immediately after the Forlorn Hope, was the only officer who escaped, accompanying the advance.

The approaches were pushed on against the castle. The town caught fire soon after our success in carrying it, and by the 4th was nearly consumed. I fear there was not much trouble taken to extinguish the fire. On the 8th September, the batteries were ready, and at 10a.m they opened their fire. We had thirty-three pieces playing against it. The enemy were concealed along some narrow trenches they had thrown up; but from the small space they occupied, and the number of guns brought to bear on them, it was impossible they could long hold out. At 12 they hoisted a white flag, and surrendered prisoners of war.

They had 3,000 at the commencement of the siege at least–I believe more–and were reduced to eighty officers, 1,256 men, twenty-three officers, 512 men out of which number were in hospital. We expended above 70,000 shot and shells.

We lost during the siege:-

Officers	Men	
53	808	Killed
250	2,340	wounded
7	332	missing

Total 3,780 men lost

Sept 22nd. Persse and Penrice having joined with the remount, I this day left the 16th for Engald, there being seven captains, with myself, present, and marched four leagues to Zarauz. I found Hall very ill, having been left there since we moved up from Aya. He has been worse, and, I think, will recover. Dr. Evans is, however, of a different opinion. (He died shortly afterwards)

Sept 23rd. Marched three leagues to San Sebastian, and got room in Mac Nab's house, the former commissary to the 16th. There are not above ten or twelve houses left, the breach very little repaired, and only the guerrillas to garrison it-about 1,500.

Sept 28th. Embarked at Los Passages on board the Jubilee transport at daylight this morning, having got my horse on board yesterday. She is a victualler, but, from knowing one of the agents, I have had a stall made. Colonel Brooke, of the 4th Foot, was my companion on board. He was proceeding to England in consequence of ill-health, having suffered at the siege of San Sebastian.

Oct 5th. We this morning, after a favourable passage, made Spithead, and, after being on shore two hours, were obliged to go on board again to perform quarantine, the vessel having been six months in Gibraltar.

Oct 11th. The product to release us came down last night, and I this day landed.

Oct 13th. The vessel came into harbour yesterday. I landed my horse* and this day set off for London with Colonel Brooke.

*Here the military life of "Bob" came to an end. After five campaigns and an absence of four years and a half, he returned safe and sound to his old house, the servant reporting that he knew his way back to his stables at Durford perfectly. He lived for many years to carry his master with the pack of harriers kept by him

Chapter Four
The Waterloo Campaign

1815. The 16th Light Dragoons had been quartered, since November, 1814, at Hounslow and Hampton Court, and at the latter end of March, 1815, were called up to the neighbourhood of Westminster Brigade for the purpose of being in readiness for the riots occasioned by the passing of the Corn Laws. During our stay here, Napoleon entered France from Elba, and placed himself again on the throne. Immediately on this account arriving in London, all disturbance about the Corn Laws ceased, and the 16th returned to Hounslow to prepare for embarkation for the Netherlands.

We left Hounslow the first week in April, and embarked in two divisions on the 11th April at Ramsgate and Dover. Lieutenant-Colonel Hay commanded the 16th.

The regiment was composed of the following troops of 55 horses each-in all six, amounting to 350 horses.

Brevet-Major Belli's troop
Captains-   Sweetenham
Weyland
Buchanan
Tomkinson

Captain Weyland's troop, Buchanan's and mine embarked at Ramsgate, with the headquarters of the regiment. Brevet-Major Belli's troop, Captain Swetenham's and King's at Dover. AT 9a.m, the 11th, the troops at Ramsgate were on board, and at eleven the first vessel got to sea.

The vessels we embarked in were small coillers, holding from ten to thirty-five horses each. The horses were put loose in the hold, and it being fine weather we did not lose and from there being no bails. Larger vessels could not have passed the bar at Ostend, and to have fitted them up regularly for cavalry would have required so many, and caused so much delay, that the passage of any considerable body of cavalry would have been much retarded.

April 12th. The vessel I went in with some of the others arrived at Ostend about 9 this morning, and at 11a.m we began to disembark. We landed the horses on the sands, and at 6p.m we marched to Ghristiles, a small village six miles from Ostend. Lieutenant Luard came with me in the same vessel.

Lieutenant Beauchamp had been sent forward to Ghristiles, and on our arrival billets were ready for us. The men found forage in every stable they went into, and the officers supped at a small inn in the village. Our quarters were inhabited by respectable people, and we found beds on going to them for the night, and consequently we could not avoid contrasting the Pays Bas with Spain and Portugal, not at all regretting the change.

April 13th. That part of the regiment which came last night to Ghristiles marched fifteen miles to Bruges. We were put up for the night in the chateaux round the town, with part in an old barrack in the town. My troop went about three miles out; my own quarter was in an excellent chateau.

I went to dine with the other officers in Bruges; came to my quarter and went to bed without the people in the house being aware of it. They waited supper for me till near midnight, when a servant came into my room, and to his astonishment found me in bed. I marched early the next morning without seeing them, and they expressed their regret to my servant at my going to bed without supping with them. Whether they expected I should have exacted dinner from them, as any officer of their own, or any foreign army would have done, and therefore did not offer too much; and on finding that not to be the system of the British army, felt ashamed of allowing me to go to the town for one dinner, I do not know. Not that I should have troubled them, for we were all delighted at once more getting on service, and were so charmed with the abundance of the country, facility of march and transport of baggage, that we had a merry meeting after each day's march at some auberge, where dinner was ordered for all the officers. Champagne, too, at 4s per bottle, was a new thing.

The part of the regiment which had embarked at Dover marched to Bruges without halting, and arrived at 2a.m

April 14th. The whole of the regiment marched twelve miles to Ecloo. The men cannot stand the good treatment they receive from the persons on whom they are billeted, and some instances of drunkenness have occurred. The old Peninsular men know their best chance of good treatment is being civil (which at least they attempt in the first instance), and the inhabitants finding them not inclined to give trouble, generally repay them by something to drink, which, being spirits, sometimes overcomes them in a morning.

April 15th. The whole of the regiment marched this day to Ghent, and was cantoned outside the town in small villages and detached houses on the road to Brussels. Louis XVIII is here, and if what his staff state is to be relied upon, the accounts from France are very favourable to his cause. Marmont and Victor are with him, and if their old master Napoleon is successful, will rather sigh after the share they might have had in his glory.

The Duke of Wellington came to Ghent on the 16th, and inspected the works round the town. There has been a considerable sum expended since last year in repairing the walls, but much more is required before the place can be considered secure from the enemy. The Duke is making the tour of all the fortresses on this frontier, yet he will not, I conceive, lose many British soliers in occupying them. The garrisons must be found from their own army, as the system of war is too much altered to allow them to be of the consequence which, in Marlborough's time, was attached to them. Many are in a very ruinous state.

April 17th. We marched this day to Oudenarde, seventeen miles from Ghent, and were cantoned in the villages a league from the town. The headquarters of the regiment were at Pontigem. My troop at Oyke, one league from Oudenarde, on the Bruges road. The men are better off than I ever remember. They receive a pound of meat a day, a pound of bread, and a pint of gin to six. In general, they give their rations to the person they are billeted on, and he finds them in what they require. They are scattered about in farm houses, where hay is in such abundance that many of them do not bring their rations from Oudenarde, where they go every third day to receive them.

The 11th and 12th Light Dragoons are in the neighbourhood of Oudenarde on his way round the fortresses, and saw the brigade out near the town. He expressed himself pleased with its appearance, and the men on hearing what he said, expressed their satisfaction by cheering at again finding themselves under their old commander.

My farmhouse and the village of Oyke is situated on the position the French held at the Battle of Oudenarde, when attacked by Marlborough in 1709. Part of his troops passed the Scheldt below the town. Seven battalions of the enemy were taken in the village of Eyne. Marshal Vendome commanded the French under the yound Duke of Burgundy. Vendome made one disposition of the army which the Duke altered just before the attack. Oudenmarde was in possession of Marlborough. When Marlborough was advancing to attack the French, they moved forward from the position they had taken up and attacked him on his left. Marlborough directed the movements on the left, placing two-thirds of his army with all the British on the right, under Prince Eugene; his success was in the end complete. He estimated the enemy's loss at 20,000 men.

The country is very rich, and almost entirely arable. From the abundance we find in every place an army must be able, with management, to submit for a length of time in one place without magazines. In any movement for a short space of time I am convinced it might march to any point, entirely depending on the resources of the country.

We hear very little information to be relied on from France, and the present disposition of the troops appears more like a distribution for winter quarters than of an approaching campaign. It is generally supported we shall wait the arrival of the Russians and Austrians, and then commence a forward movement. The Prussians are closing up on our left, and will have their outposts in the neighbourhood of Charleroi, on the Meuse.

May 8th. An order came this day for the brigade to march. We moved about 12, and passed the Grammont in the evening, not arriving at our quarters at Denderwinche until midnight. From receiving the order to march immediately, we fancied it was some movement towards the enemy, or at least a concentration of the army previous to taking the field. We were cantoned around Denderwinche, as in the neighbourhood of Oudenarde, the nem in the farmhouses, and abundantly supplied.

On going round their quarters I did not find this to be the case; there are more troops in this neighbourhood, and many of the men are in cottage, but those in the farmhouse are as well supplied as in the last quarter. Headquarters of the army are at Brussels, with a considerable force of troops in the immediate vicinity. Lord Hill, with a party, is at Grammont, and the Earl of Uxbridge, commanding the cavalry, is at Ninove.

The Guards are at Enghien, and there is a brigade (if noot two) of troops of the King of the Netherlands at Nerville. Sir Thomas Picton, with a division of British infantry, is in the neighbourhood of Waterloo; and from the general disposition of the army, I should say it was the Duke's intention to cover Brussels on either road the enemy advance, and at the same time not his intention to attack until the other powers come up. We hear of their advance, though it is said they cannot be so forward in six weeks as to admit of a forward movement on our part.

The Duke de Berri id, I believe, at Hai. He draws rations from the British army, and is said to receive an allowance for ten or twelve horses (per diem), which he profits from by only keeping a couple.

June 16th. My brother Henry, who had come out from England about a week (the 7th he arrived at my quarters), was impatient at the idle life we were leading in our quarters, and was anxious to go and see the country in our front, and visit some of the towns occupied by the Prussians, for the purpose of seeing their troops and the towns they occupied. Soon after daylight my servant came into my room saying there had arrived an order to march directly, and that the whole army was moving. We were ignorant of the cause and heard rumours that it was occasioned by an attack the enemy had made on the Prussian outposts. On our arrival at Enghien, we found that the Guards had left it, and it was said we were to remain in its neighbourhood for the purpose of watching the road from Enghien to Mons. We halted for a considerable time near the town waiting for orders, when we moved on towards Braine-le-Cornte. This we passed, and when we had got about a mile on the other side, and at, I think, about 2p.m, we began to hear some firing beyond Nivelles, on which we were moving.

When within about a mile of Nivelles, an order came for us to proceed on without delay, the enemy having made an attack on our troops beyone Nivelles. We threw away the bundles of forage(hay) we were carrying, passed Ninelles at a trot, proceeding on towards Quatre Bras with the least possible delay. The firing continued, the cannonade was sharp, and on our getting nearer, musketry, and in a heavy fire, was distinctly heard. We met several wounded, who told us the enemy had made a sharp attack and had been replaced. The earl of Uxbridge commands the cavalry. I do not know what his orders were, yet it appeared to me no decided point was given for our brigade to move to. Had the brigade in the first instance received an order to march on Nivelles, and proceeded directly there, we should have been up in time to have acted, and though our numbers would have been much inferior to the enemy's force, yet it was very desirable to have cavalry, and, however few, considerable advantage would have resulted from it. We should have been the only brigade up, and have had to contend with a force very much our superior. We most likely should have suffered greatly. From the obstinate manner the ground was contested in, and being held by such an inferior force on our part, it was evident the object was a great one, and we, of course, should have come in for the same fate which fell to the lot of the infantry, I n being opposed to a superior force, though in cavalry the odds would have been greater against our one brigade than the force of the enemy's infantry was to ours.

From Lord Uxbridge being a Hussar, it was said he would bring them forward on every occasion, and therefore a subject of regret on our part that the brigade should have missed a chance in which we alone would have been employed. On approaching Les Quatre Bras we formed in line, advancing to the point where the two roads intersect each other, when we brought forward our left shoulders, advancing on the enemy. They had discontinued their attack, being repulsed at all points, and we only moved forward under a slight cannonade for the purpose of showing ourselves, and to prevent any small party of our infantry being molested when withdrawing for the night. The enemy did not show any inclination, and all was quiet, excepting a chance shot occasionally from the sentries. It appeared that the 1st Division, under Lieutenant-General Cooke, had occupied a wood to the right and in advance of Quatre Bras, where a brigade of Guards, under General Maitland (2nd and 3rd battalions of the 1st Regiment) had been sharply engaged, repulsing every attack. The 5th Division, under old Picton, had arrived from Waterloo in the nick of the moment, and advanced to take up a position on the left of the wood. Here they were repeatedly attacked, and more than once charged by the cuirassiers of the Guards. On going over the ground, we saw several cuirasses lying scattered about. Some of them had been carried away by the infantry and used for frying their meat, the baggage being in the rear, and nothing to cook with then up with the regiments. They were attacked very suddenly, and had to form in square, without loss of time, in the standing corn. The enemy attacked most gallantly, but were received so coolly, and in such order, that it was impossible to succeed unless they had ridden the square down by main force. (A thing never heard of. The infantry either break before the cavalry come close up, or they drive them back with their fire. It is an awful thing for infantry to see a body of cavalry riding at them full gallop. The men in the square frequently begin to shuffle, and so create some unstaediness. This causes them to neglect their fire. The cavalry seeing them waver, have an inducement for riding close up, and in all probability succeed in getting into the square, when all is over. When once broken, the infantry, of course, have no chance. If steady, it is almost impossible to succeed against infantry, yet I should always be cautious, if in command of infantry attacked by cavalry, having seen the best of troops more afraid of cavalry than any other force). The 28th, 42nd, 79th, and 92nd Regiments (the three last Highland) are named by Lord Wellington as having distinguished themselves. The 79th, I fancy, had more to do than the others, and was said particularly to distinguished itself. Of all the troops to resist cavalry, where great steadiness, coolness, and obedience to orders is required, I should select the Scotch. In outpost duty, or any service where quickness is required, and immediate advantage to be taken of any sudden change, I do not think they are equal to others.

Napoleon is in command of the French army. He has only the Duke to beat that he may say success has attended him with every General in Europe. It is an anxious time.

We remained on the ground we had halted on until after dark, and then retired for the night to the rear of Quatre Bras, having piquets in our front. Through the whole of the evening and after dark we heard a very considerable fire on our left in the direction of Sambref. This was an attack of Napoleon's on Prussian army, in which he employed his whole force with the exception of the 1st and 2nd Corps-those attacked us at Quatre Bras. Ney conducted the attack on us, in which, from the numbers he brought, and the hurried arrival of our troops who were obliged to occupy the first ground which presented itself, he had a fair chance of success. The French troops behaved well. The attack on the Prussians was very decided. The enemy, more than once, attempted carrying the villages of St. Amand and Ligny, which Blucher occupied, in which for some time they failed. French troops and in greater numbers were brought down, when the French succeeded in occupying these posts, but not so as to oblige the Prussians to abandon their position. The, however, after repeated attacks, succeeded in driving the Prussians from the two villages of St. Amand and Ligny, and Blucher, not being joined by his 4th Corps and Liege (under Bulow) retired in the night, and on the 17th on Wavre.

Blucher, at one time, was nearly taken, and his horse was killed. He was said to be saved by a charge of cavalry.

From 6 until dark the different corps of the British continued to arrive at Quatre Bras, and, before midnight, I think, the whole was assembled. We bivouacked as we could find ground. I slept on a door with my brother Henry. It was the first time he had ever been in bivouac, or out all night sleeping in the open air: I rather think I slept better than the amateur. At daylight our men were discharging their muskets, when he bridled his horse, thinking it was an attack on our troops. The point where we passed the night was close to the main road and neat a house with a well near the road. Our brigade close to Quatre Bras, is rear of the infantry.

The night was fine, but considerable inconvenience was felt from the scarcity of water, there being no running stream or other water near where we were, and the wells exhausted before our arrival. I attempted to get water at a well, but found so many Belgians it was impossible. A cellar of wine had been plundered by them, and I came in time to witness the conclusion, a contest betwixt two parties for the last barrel in it.

From the scattered position of the troops, and their manner of moving on Quatre Bars, much has been said of the Duke of Wellington allowing himself to be surprised. From the force the Prussians had in front and around Quatre Bras, I do not conceive he was much called upon to watch, in any force, that point in the line which the two armies had occupied; and as there was a considerable extent of country on the right by which the enemy might move on Brussels, he was obliged to protect the frontier on that side. He heard of the attack on the Prussians at Charleroi on the 15th, and immediately (I believe) sent an order for the Guards from Enghien to move on Nivelles, and an order for the whole army to hold itself in readiness to march.

Major-General Alten, stationed at Mons, sent one or two reports of the advance of the enemy, and conceiving, from all he could collect, it was with a view to attack with their whole force, he sent off his aide-de-camp with another report worded more decidedly. He arrived at Brussels about three on the morning of the 16th, and going to the Duke's house requested to see him. He was shown into his room, where the Duke was lying down in his clothes. He told him all he had heard and delivered his letter. The Duke said, "Then it is your opinion it is in their intention to attack us?"

He replied it was his opinion they would. The Duke then said, "Ride up immediately to Waterloo, where you will find Sir Thomas Picton with his Division, and order him to turn the troops out immediately." He did so, and five minutes after he arrived the Duke himself rode up and directed the troops to move on Quatre Bras.

I had this from the A.D.C. From this I think it appears that the Duke did not think they would attack, and, therefore, he possibly might not pay that attention to the reports on the 15th which they required; yet, again, it would not be prudent to move his whole force to one point on every demonstration of the enemy.

Something has been said of the headquarters at Brussels thinking so little of the enemy's advance that they were at a ball, and considerable delay occasioned in consequence. If an army receives information at night which require an immediate move of troops, it is of great consequence to have the Quartermaster General and other staff officers collected, in the place of having to seek and assemble them over a large town, There was considerable time saved by this, and no objection to attending a ball twenty miles from an enemy.

June 17th. We heard early this morning from Colonel Ponsonby that the Prussians had retired, and that we were to do the same. I always applied to him for any news from headquarters, and he told me himself. He regretted that we were obliged to retire.

The Duke rode up at daylight to Quatre Bras. We soon heard that in consequence of the attack made on the Prussians last night they had retired on Wavre, and that we were likewise to retire to a position in our rear for the purpose of covering Brussels. The infantry withdrew quietly, leaving the cavalry to cover their retreat. We remained on the ground we passed the night on until about 2p.m, when, in consequence of the enemy showing some cavalry, we turned out, forming in three lines, to the left and rear of Quatre Bras. The two brigades of Hussars were formed by Lord

Uxbridge in the first line. The Light Dragoons (Sir J. Vandeleur's brigade) in the second, and the Heavy Cavalry in support, some distance in the rear. The intention of Lord Uxbridge was to keep the Hussars in front, to take advantage of any favourable chance, and on the enemy advancing in such force as to oblige us to retire, they were to pass through the second line, and for it to cover the retreat. Nothing can show more clearly the result of the affairs of yesterday than the late hour at which the enemy attempted a forward movement. They did not move a man in pursuit of either the Prussians or English until late in the day, and not until all (excepting the rear guard) had withdrew. Had either of the affairs proved successful they would have attempted a forward movement against the beaten opponent at daylight. (They were successful against the Prussians because they obliged them to abandon their position. Two more such successes though will ruin their army; they suffered greatly).

Both affairs ought to reach them that good judgment and good conduct in their troops will be requisite to ensure success, and in case of a reverse on their part they have not their usual resource of averting the evil by a suspension of hostilities or profiting in any way by intrigue.

Blucher is exasperated, and the Duke determined; they act together with cordiality.

I saw the French cavalry when moving out of their bivouac, and thought from their numbers we must either bring all our force to oppose them and keep our ground, or that, if a retreat was determined on, the sooner we moved the more prudent. They advanced in very large bodies, and Lord Uxbridge soon saw that so far from having any chance afforded of charging he had nothing left but to get his troops away without the least delay. They came out column after column, and in greater force than I ever recollect seeing together at one point. We, in the second line, were ordered away immediately, and retired leaving Genappe to our left (in retiring). The first line got away without much loss, retiring with the Heavy Cavalry on Genappe, but had not time allowed it to retire through the second line, as first intended. There was not time for the

Hussars to pass through our brigade, the enemy were so close upon them, and had we not got off with the least possible delay the Hussars and our brigade would have been in one confused heap. We had learnt the necessity of making way for those in front, when we and they were retiring, from acting in the narrow roads of Portugal, and the retreat being ordered, we fortunately made way for the front line as we were ordered to do. The infantry being all clear, and the enemy showing so large a force of cavalry, we ought not to have waited so long. Retreat being our object, the more easily it was effected the more prudent it would have been.

At Grenappe the enemy came up with the rear, pushing on into the village. Lord Uxbridge ordered the 7th Hussars to attack a regiment of French Lancers. The enemy were formed across the street, and in this position were charged by the 7th. The men rode up most gallantly and attempted to drive them back, cutting them with their sabres, the enemy holding their lances before their horses. The men of the 7th, from all I could hear, behaved well, but were obliged to retire unsuccessful. The French then advanced out of the village, when the 1st Life Gguards were brought down and charged. They advanced most gallantly, and the enemy ran away before the Life Guards got up to them, They were from what I could learn, within about 100 yards when the enemy about, and though the French were awed by their appearance, and ran away before they came near them, yet the charge was entirely attributed to the superior strength of the Life Guards and weight in riding down the enemy. Nothing could be better done than the charge, yet, I much question, had the Life Guards attacked in the situation the 7th attempted, if they would have succeeded. The 7th was Lord Uxbridge's own regiment, and an opportunity desired by him for distinguishing them. He selected the first that offered, fancying he had only to allow them to come in contact with the enemy, and that the result must be to their credit. I have seen the same thing frequently occur, that those regiments which a General wishes to bring forward are either placed where they do nothing, or get into action under unfortunate circumstances, losing many men without gaining much credit. Lord Uxbridge, having all the cavalry under him and detached from the infantry, was aware of the opportunity of distinguishing himself, could he bring about a successful affair. It is a chance few can resist, and in their anxiety not to lose the opportunity, they are frequently led into errors which cause a head of an army to distrust them on any future occasion. They are opportunities desired by all officers, and those serving in the particular corps and regiments engaged are more spoken of in an army that in general actions in which all bear a part, from a desire in those employed to make the most of their own exertions, and from an inclination in those not engaged to be acquainted with what they had not an opportunity of serving, and lost too often with an intention of finding some error to detract from the credit of the affair.

I think the result to the Duke must be, that Lord Uxbridge is too young a soldier to be much relied on with a separate command form feeling that he will risk too much in a desire to do something.

This was the error Crawford fell into with the Light Division in 1810 on passing the Coa, and I think Lord W. was not much inclined to trust him again with a distinct command.

The conduct of Lord Hill (when Sir Rowland) was quite the reverse, through the whole of his operations, distinct from the Duke, when employed south of the tagus. His orders were to watch the enemy's force opposed to him; he never engaged but when obliged, and lost so many chances of bringing on the petty affairs, that the men called his division the Observing Division.

We retired to the rear of the position the army was about to occupy, and bivouacked for the night about a mile and half in rear of Ter la Haye, and half a mile in the rear of the left of our position. During our retreat from Quatre Bras we had been exposed to the heaviest rain I was ever out in, and, in consequence, not a dry thread remained throughout the army. It ceased a little at nightfall, but as it became dark again commenced, and rained incessantly through the night. The country was entirely of arable land, and fancying a clover root (nearly fit to eat) would be drier to lie down upon than either standing wheat or fallow, we selected it as the best spot we could find.

From the appearance of the weather every one was desirous of obtaining wood to keep up a fire. One of our dragoons came out of the village of Waterloo with a clock on his back. An officer from a distance and behind him (Lieut. Luard) called to know what his object was in bringing it. The dragoon replied (not knowing who spoke to him), "If you will come to our troop you shall soon see what I will do with it. I'll make the beggar tick." So far from making it tick he prevented its ever striking another tick by setting the clock on the fire and making a chimney of it.*

With the horses moving about to get their backs to the rain and the men walking to feed them and light fires, the clover soon disappeared, and the whole space occupied by the 16th became one complete puddle. (It was knee –deep at daylight.) I lay down in my cloak, and having been up at 2a.m on the morning of the 17th, and occupied through the whole of the day, I slept for two or three hours.

Battle of Waterloo

June 18th 1815. The rain had fallen through the night without ceasing; the army had no tent; consequently there could not be a dry thread left to us. The fires were attempted to be kept up at the commencement of the might, but from the rain and want of fuel not many were continued through the night. All was quiet at daylight when the rain ceased. The fires in the 16th were lighted, and attempts made to dry our clothes. Occasional showers, however, fell during the morning, though light in comparison with the rain of the night and preceding day. The

---

*On re-visiting the field of battle more than forty years later, my father, on telling his story to his party, was importuned by a Belgian peasant for compensation, on the ground that the clock had belonged to his family!

enemy had brought a considerable force to the hills opposite our position; their fires were seen extending for some distance along our front, and it was evident they had moved to the front of our position nearly the whole of their force.

From the march the army had made yesterday, and the hurried manner in which the position was taken up considerable arrangement of the line was necessary. This commenced soon after daylight, under the immediate inspection of the Duke of Wellington, and was some completed. (Lord Hill was out the instant it was light, and had arranged his own corps before the Duke arrived.) The position selected was across the Nivelles and Charleroi roads from Brussels, leading to both those points. The right was thrown back en potence to a ravine near Merbe Braine, which place was also occupied, and the left extended to the hamlet to Ter la Haye.

A curious scene took place betwixt Price in my troop, and myself when moving from the bivouac we occupied for the night to the ground appointed us in the line. He got off his horse and ran away to the rear before we were engaged, being deranged. He was an old soldier, yet not the wisest, and had been shoemaker to the troop for many years. The men after the day was over did not resent his leaving them, knowing the kind of man and his weakness.

At night I had only one man absent, excepting killed and wounded, and less that one man away assisting each wounded. The one absent had gone away during the advance to plunder, was reported to me by the men, and booted by them on the morning following the action.

There were two farmhouses immediately below the position, the occupation of which was of the greatest consequence to the holding of the position-Hougoumont in front of that part of the line called the right centre and close to the Nivelle road, and La Haye Sainte in front of the left centre. The latter was a single house with a garden, and not affording cover to any great body of troops. Hougoumont was more important. The house, garden and wood in possession of the enemy would enable them to form any number of men unmolested immediately below the position, and admit of their making an instantaneous attack. The wood in front of the house was occupied by a light battalion of Nassau troops and one battalion of the Brunswick Contingent. The chateau and garden were in the first instance only occupied by three companies of the Coldstreams. These were afterwards reinforced by four more companies of the same regiment. The 1st detachment: of three companies was under the command of Lieutenant-Colonel Macdonnell, and the latter, of four companies, under Colonel Woodford. The light troops placed in the wall would, of course, retire on the advance of the enemy's columns, and there being but three companies for the defence of so important a place, I cannot but conclude the Duke either did not think the enemy would consider it an object, or he himself did not think it of consequence. The first effort made by the enemy was repulsed by the three companies, when, finding the point the enemy considered it, the other four were sent to reinforce them. It was entrusted to too weak a force, and would have been carried but for the determined courage of the troops.

The four light companies from the four battalions of the Guards were posted, in the first instance, in the wood in front of the chateau. Some of these retired, when attacked, with the other light troops, which, with them, occupied the wood, and some took shelter in the house and garden, continuing through the day to assist in its defence. In what proportion I could never learn.

Position and number of troops engaged at Waterloo

The second corps, commanded by Lord Hill, on the right.

2nd Division, Lieutenant-General Sir Henry Clinton, placed on the right en potence.

3rd Brigade, Major-General Adam: 1st Battalion 52nd, 1st Battalion 71st, 9 Companies 95th Rifle.

1st Brigade, Colonel Duplat: 1st, 2nd, 3rd, 4th Battalions King German Legion.

3rd Hanoverian brigade, Colonel Halkett: 2nd and 3rd Battalions Duke of York's Corps and one battalion Hanoverian Militia.

Captain Bolton's Brigade of Guns-British; Captain Sympher's K.G. Legion, 12 Guns.

4th Brigade, belonging to the 4th Division, the remainder of which was detached on the road from Brussels to Mons, Colonel Mitchel: 3rd Battalion 14th Regiment, 1st Battalion 23rd Regiment, 1st Battalion 51st Regiment.

FOREIGN 3RD DIVISION, under L.G.B. Chasse, posted at Braine l'Alleud in the first instance, and moved to support the right of the line during the last attack made by the enemy.

1st Brigade, Colonel Detmers: 35th Battalion Chasseurs Belgiques, 2nd Battalion of the Line, Dutch 4th, 6th, 17th and 19th Battalions, Dutch Militia.

2nd Brigade, G.M.D. Aubreme; 36th Battalion Chasseurs, 3rd Battalion Line Belgique, 12th and 13th Line Dutch, 3rd and 10th Battalion Militia, Dutch.

One brigade Foot Artillery, Captain Lux; one brigade Light Artillery, M. Van der Smissen, 12 Guns.

FIRST CORPS, commanded by the Prince of Orange, Centre.

1st Divison, Lieutenant-General Cooke, on the right. Right Centre, posted betwixt the Nivelle and Charleroi Roads.

1st Brigade, Major-General Maitland: 2nd and 3rd Battalions 1st Regiment of Guards.

2nd Brigade, Major-General Sir John Byng: 2nd Battalion Coldstream, 2nd Battalion 3rd Guards.

One brigade of British Artillery, Captain Sandham; one K.G.L., Captain Kullhan.

3rd Division, Lieutenant-General Sir Charles Alten, Left Centre.

2nd Brigade, Lieutenant-Colonel Ompteda: 1st 2nd Light Battalion King German Legion, K.G.L. 5th, and 8th Battalion Line, K.G.L. The 2nd Light Battalion, under Lieutenant-Colonel Baring, occupied La Haye Sainte.

1st Brigade (Hanoverian), Major-General Comte Kilmansegge: 1st Battalion Duke of York, The Field Battalions Lunenburgh Grubenhagen, Verdon, Bremen et las Chausseurs de Sporcken.

5th Brigade (British), Major-General Sir Colin Halkett: 2nd Battalion 30th, 69th, 73rd, and 33rd Regiments.

One brigade British Artillery, Major Lloyd; one brigade K.G.L., Captain Cleeve, 12 Guns.

CORPS OF THE DUKE OF BRUNSWICK-after the Duke was killed under General Olfermans.

Lieutenant-Colonel Butler, one brigade Light Infantry
Major-General Munchausen, one brigade of the Line.
One Regiment of Hussars a la Mort, one squadron of Lancers.
2nd Brigade of Guns, under Mons. De Lubeck, 12 Guns.
Contingent of Nassau Usengen, Geneeral Kruse: 3 Battalions 1st Regiment.

CAVALRY, UNDER LIEUTENANT-GENERAL LORD

Number of squadrons in each Brigade.	
13	1st Brigade, Major-General Lord Edward Somerwet: 1st and 2nd Regiments Life Guards, The Oxford Blues, 1st Regiment Dragoon Guards. The 1st Dragoons Guards had four squadrons.
9	2nd Brigade, Major-General Sir W. Ponsonby: 1st Regiment of Dragoons (Royals), 2nd Regiment Dragoons (Scotch Greys), 6th Regiment Dragoons (Enniskillen).
9	3rd Brigade, Major-General Count Dornberg: 1st and 2nd Regiments Dragoons, K.G.L., 23rd Light Dragoons.
	4th Brigade, Major-General Sir Jo. Vandeleur: 11th, 12th, and 16th Light Dragoons.
6	5th Brigade, Major-General Sir C. Grant: 7th and 15th Hussars.
6	6th Brigade, Major-General Sir Hussey Vivian: 10th and 18th Hussars.
6	7th Brigade, Lieutenant-Colonel Arenschildt: 3rd Hussars, K.G.L., 13th Light Dragoons.

The 1st and 2nd Hussars, K.G.L., had been stationed near Mons. Part of the 1st joined before the action, but the 22nd were not, I believe, present. Part of both Regiments were engaged.

Return of the number of Regiments Employed at Waterloo (Infantry)

No.of each Div	British		Hanoverian K.G.L		Hanoverian Line		Hanoverian Militia		Nassau		Pays Bas Militia	Pays Bas Line		Dutch line		Dutch Militia		Duke of Brunswick's corps	Grand total		
	No.of each Regt.	Total Batt.	No.of each Regt	Total Batt.	No.of each Regt	Total	No.of each Regt	Total	No.of each Regt	Total		No.of each Regt	Total	No.of each Regt	Total	No.of each Regt	Total		No. of Regts	No. in each	Total
2nd	52nd, 71st, 95th, Adams Brgd	3																	25 British	700	17,500
5th Fred			1st, 2nd, 3rd, 4th	4	2nd, 3rd	2	1	1											8 German in British pay K.G.L	700	5,600
																					23,100
4th Brigade only	14th, 23rd, 51st	3																	3 Nassau	800	2,400
																			8 Duke of Brunsick	800	6,400
																					31,900
3rd Foreign Troops												35th, 36th, 3rd	3	2nd, 12th, 13th	3	4th, 6th, 17th, 19th, 3rd, 10th	6		3 Hanoverian Line	800	2,400
																			6 Hanoverian Militia	800	4,800
1st Div	1Gds, 2nd B; 1Gds, 3rd B; 2Gds, 2nd B; 3Gds, 2nd B	4																	5 Pay Bas Line	800	4,000

No. of each Div	British No. of each Regt.	British Total Batt.	Hanoverian K.G.L No.of each Regt	Hanoverian K.G.L Total Batt.	Hanoverian Line No.of each Regt	Hanoverian Line Total	Hanoverian Militia No.of each Regt	Hanoverian Militia Total	Nassau No.of each Regt	Nassau Total	Pays Bas Militia	Pays Bas Line No.of each Regt	Pays Bas Line Total	Dutch line No.of each Regt	Dutch line Total	Dutch Militia No.of each Regt	Dutch Militia Total	Duke of Brunswick's corps	Grand total No. of Regts	Grand total No. in each	Grand total Total
3rd Div	30th 69th 73rd 33rd	4																			
5th Div	1Rgt,3rd B* 42nd 92nd 44th 28th	4																			
	32nd 79th 95th 4th	4																			
	272th 40th	3																			
2nd Div Pays Bas									1&2 Batt. 3rd 1	3		78&27	2					Regts.8	8		
Total		25		8		3		6		3			5		3		6	8			
																			3Dutch Line	800	2,400
																			6Dutch Militia	800	4,800
																			Total		50,300 Infantry 6,900 Cavalry 57,250
																					I consider 55,000 efficient men in the field to be the outside of our force
																				120	Pieces of Artillery
																				100	Pieces effective

I calculate this division at 7,700 British bayonets, composed of regiments, distinguished in Spain The 1st, 42nd, 92nd, 44th, 28th, 79th, 95th, 4th, 27th, 40th have served through the war, and are distinguished for their service.

Brigades	Regiments	Squadrons	Total	No.of men in each Regt.	No.of men in each Brgde.	Artillery Names of officers commanding Brigades	British No.of guns
1st	1st Life Gds	3		320			
	2nd do.	3		320		Capt. Sanham	6
	the Blues	3	13	320	1380	Major Lloyd	6
	1st Dragoon Gds	4		420		Capt. Bolton	6
						Major Rogers	6
							24
2nd	1st Dragoon	3		320		*Attatched to Divisions of Infantry*	
	2nd do.	3		320	960	Major Bull	6
	6th do.	3	9	320		Col. Smith	6
4th	11thLt.Drgn	3		320		Col. Sir R Gardner	6
	12th do.	3		320	960	Major Ramsay	6
	16th do.	3	9	320		Capt. Mercer	6
							30
5th	7th Hussars	3		320	640	*Attached to Cavalry*	
	15th do.	3	6	320		Sir H. Ross	6
						Major Bean	6
6th	10th Hussars	3		320	640	Capt. Sinclair	6
	18th do.	3	6	320			18
							72
7th	3rd Hussars K.G.L	3		320	640	*Reserve* Capt. Kulman, K.G.l	6
	13thLt. Drag	3	6	320		Capt. Cleave, K.G.L	6
			49		5,220	Capt. Symphers, do.	6
2nd	1st Regt Germans K.G.L	4		440		Capt. Braun, Hanov	6
							24
	2nd do. do	4		440	1,200	Brunswick Corps	12
	23rd Lt. Dragoons British	3	16	320		3 Foreign Divs	12
						Total British	48
	1st Hussars K.G.l	3		320	320★	Total	120
	2nd Hussars K.G.L	2		210	210★	★In British pay, and served in Spain; considered part of the British force.	
			65		6,950	Total British and German Cavalry	

There were only a squadron of Life Guards, 3 of the Blues and 3 of the 1st Dragoon Guards.

The 3rd Hussars German are reckoned with the British, and 23rd British are accounted for in the German regiments

From the preceding return it appears that there were only 17,500 British infantry in the field, and, allowing for men absent for baggage, etc., etc., to place the efficient bayonets in the field at 700 each battalion, it is accounting for the numbers present. To this number we must add 5,600 of the King's German Legion in British pay, and having served through the Peninsular Campaigns, and always behaved well, we considered them equally efficient with British infantry. This makes 23,100 effective men. Three battalions Nassau troop of 800 each, and eight battalions of the Duke of Brunswick also behaved well, and must be considered effective, amounting to 6,400, making a total-

British	17,500
German	5,600
Nassau	2,400
Brunwick	6,400
	31,900

The total number of infantry amounted to 50,300, so that there remains 18,400 of Dutch Line Regiments, Pays Bas Line Regiments, and Dutch Militia. Of these I believe the answer made by the Spanish General Alava to the Prince of Orange is so nearly the truth that I mention it to point out the estimation in which they should be considered for their services on the 18th. Both General Alava and the prince had been for many years together on the Duke's staff in Spain.

Question from the Prince:-

"Well, Alava, what do you think your Spaniards would have done had they been present on this occasion?"

Answer from Alava:-

"Your Highness, I do not think they would have run away, as your Belgians did, before the first shot was fired."

They certainly did not behave well, and though placed in the second line, and in many instances under cover of the hill, it was difficult to keep them even in that position. When a man was wounded two or three went away with him to the rear. They took great care of their comrades in going off the field, and then commenced plundering in the rear.

Of cavalry there were forty-nine squadrons of British,

amounting to 5,220 men. Also sixteen squadrons of German cavalry in British pay, and equally efficient, amounting to 1,730, making a total of 6,950. The number of the German regiments is calculated at their greatest strength, and, I think, over rated. The cavalry were considered 6,000, which is probably nearer their numbers. The horses being just from England, and at a time of year when they look well, I think they justified the Duke of Wellington stating to Blucher that he had 6,000 of the finest cavalry in the world. There were several regiments of cavalry of the Pays Bas and of Hanoverian. These did not long remain on the field; indeed, some never came up to the army. They did nothing but plunder the baggage in the rear, riding alongside of the road, cutting at the batmen in charge of it, obliging them to abandon their horses and baggage, both of which they seized. The batmen of the 16th drew their swords, and preserved their baggage. The 1st Dragoon Guards lost all theirs, and the officers nearly all their horses. One officer only of the 16th lost his, and that through the negligence of his servant. (Lieutenant Luard was the officer.)

The position extended, as before mentioned, from Merbe Braine on the right to Terla Haye on the left. There was some strong ground near Merbe Braine which protected the right, and a considerable detachment of troops occupied, or rather were advanced to the neighbourhood of Braine l'Alleud. The appraoach to Brussels from Mons was likewise protected, Major-General Sir Charles Colville being stationed, with part of the 4th Division and a body of troop of the Pays Bas contingent, near Braine le Chateau. He was not employed, the enemy making no effort on that point; therefore the loss of his detatchment and of so old a soldier as their general is to be regretted.*

With regard to the position we held, on our right, it is evident, for any enemy to attack, they must either possess themselves of Hougoumont, or make the detour round it. In doing this they must show the force they moved to that point, and enable a general holding the position of Waterloo to reinforce his right. They could not make a feint with a small body on that point, as

*At Hal.

their object would be defeated by our seeing the strength they brought, and nothing but a very large body would cause any fears; and if a large one, we could spare men from other parts of our line.

A successful attack on our right would open Brussels to the enemy, but would drive us back on the Prussians at Wavre, and so unite the two armies. An attack on our left had the strong ground on that point to contend with, and also some fear of interruption from the Prussians, whose situation Napoleon, from his patrols and information, ought to be aware of.

From La Haye Sainte to the left was likewise strong, and any force attacking at that point had a very considerable length of plain to cross, exposed to our artillery, and also a height to ascend on coming in contact with our line.

The Duke was apprehensive of the enemy making an attack on the right, and getting betwixt is and the wood of Soignes.

From the left of the Nivelles road to the Charleroi road was the weakest part of the position; here the hill was of a gentle declivity, and Hougoumont and La Haye Sainte in the enemy's possession, an attack on that point would be made to advantage. The whole field was covered with the finest wheat, the soil was strong and luxuriant; consequently, from the rain that had fallen, was deep, heavy for the transport and moving of artillery, and difficult for the quick operation of cavalry. The heavy ground was in favour of our cavalry from the superiority of horse, and likewise, in any charge down the face of the position, we had the advantage of moving downhill, and yet we felt the inconvenience in returning uphill with distressed horses after a charge. The difficulty of returning up the hill with distressed horses occasioned so great a loss in the charges made by the heavy brigades.

The ground was so deep that numberless shells burst where they fell, and did little or no injury from being buried in the ground, and many round shot never rose from the place they first struck the ground, instead of hopping for half a mile and doing considerable injury. Many lives on both sides were saved from this circumstance. The corn was laid quite flat, both on the ground held by our troops and before and in the rear of the position. The piquets being posted for the night, and the men going from place to place, soon altered the appearance of the country. In front of the left there was some grass, as likewise on the rising ground near Ter la Haye, and again beyond that, on the line the Prussians advanced by.

From the late hour the enemy had moved in pursuit of us yesterday, it was clear they could not close up their army for a very early attack, and it was past eleven before they assembled.

Napoleon directed the operations from a small hill near the farm of Rossomme, not far from the *chaissee*.

The French army amounted to 78,000 men, including from 12 to 15,000 cavalry-calculated at 66,000 infantry and 12,000 cavalry. This did not include the 3rd Corps d'Armee under Grouchy, which was detached to observe the Prussians, and moved on Wavre. Their strength was said to be 30,000.

The 1st Corps d'Armee, under Comte d'Erlon (Drouet), was stationed on the right. Its right extended towards Smohain, its left rested on La Belle Alliance.

2nd Corps d'Armee, Lieutenant-General Cornte Lobau, was in reserve at the commencement of the action, behind the right wing. The division of the Young Guard was also stationed in rear of the 2nd corps.

The two divisions of the Old Guard were likewise stationed in rear of the 2nd corps.

Artillery-1st Corps d'Armee, including the reserve,				80	pieces
"	2nd	"	"	60	"
"	6th	"	"	30	"
"	A further reserve of			40	"
				210	

We took 150 pieces (the Prussians 60), and there was probably a considerable reserve not employed. Possibly the last forty might not have got into action. In addition to the generals named at the head of corps, Jerome Buonaparte directed the operations of a large force, of possibly one corps and a division of the Guard; he was employed on their left. Marshall Ney had a similar command, and directed the operations on the right. I believe he led the

Old Guard in the last attack. The cavalry was dispersed through their line, a large force being on the right of La Belle Alliance. Their heavy cavalry and Lancers were fine, and being principally opposed to us, we had not an opportunity of ascertaining the state of the remainder. The infantry of their Guard was good, but those taken in the charge of our 2nd brigade, being infantry of their line, were not good-small young soldiers.

At about half-past eleven they began an attack on Hougoumont with the advance of their corps under Jerome Buonaparte, whilst their light troops attacked and carried Papellotte on our left, which was not intended to be held. The attack on Hougoumont was very sharp. The wood in front of the chateau was carried by the enemy after considerable loss, and more than a common resistance on our part, from light troops holding a wood in front of a position. The enemy proceeded to attack the chateau and garden, in which they failed, and retired unsuccessful. The defence, as well as the attack, was gallant.

We (11th, 12th, and 16th Light Dragoons) moved from our bivouac about eleven, and were stationed on the left of the line, below the hill occupied by the infantry; the 6th brigade of cavalry was stationed further on our left, the 2nd brigade on our right, near the Charleroi road, possibly half-way to that point from the situation we occupied. The 1st brigade was immediately on the other side that road, with is left on it, the 3rd brigade a little further to the right, and the 5th brigade on the right again of the 3rd. We moved on the ground assigned for our brigade, and all being quiet on our front, dismounted.

We had not been long on our ground before the cannonade opened and became general along the whole line. Colonel Ponsonby, myself, and some others (my brother Henry was of this party) rode out in front to see what was going on and standing together near a hedge, attracted a few of the enemy's round shot. The enemy's fire was directed against our whole line, and we lost a few horses in the brigade whilst dismounted. Having for some time remained in this position during the attack on Hougoumont on the right, we were ordered to mount, and moved in front of the position to check the enemy's cavalry in pursuit of the 2nd brigade of cavalry, which had charged in advance of the position, and was on its return to our line. It appeared that the enemy, with the 2nd and 3rd Divisions of their 1st corps, under Count d'Erlon, had moved to the attack of the left centre of our position. They advanced in good order, coming close up to our line; at this moment they were attacked by the 5th Division with the bayonet, under Lieutenant-General Sir Thomas Picton, and driven back on their support in confusion. To repulse this attack, the 2nd brigade of cavalry moved to the charge; they went out of the position, charged, and completely upset everything opposed to them. It consisted of 1st (Royals) Dragoons, 2nd Dragoons (Scotish Greys), 6th Dragoons (Inniskillings). It was one of the finest charges ever seen. On going over the ground the following morning, I saw where two lines of infantry had laid down their arms; their position was accurately marked, from the regularity the muskets were placed in. After their success they continued to advance, and moved forward in scattered parties up to the reserve of the enemy, and to the top nearly of the heights help by them. In this scattered state they were attacked by a heavy brigade of cavalry belonging to the 1st corps of the enemy and one of Lancers. They were obliged to retreat, and on our moving out in front of the left position, were seen riding back to our line in parties of twenty and thirty, followed by the enemy, whose horses were not blown, and suffering greatly from theirs being scarcely able to move.

On moving to support them, we had to cross a deep lane, which broke us, and occasioned some confusion; we, however, got forward as quickly as possible, charged, and repulsed a body of Lancers in pursuit of a party of the Scotish Greys.

Lieutenant-Colonel Hay, commanding 16th Light Dragoons, was shot through the body. The shot entered his back, coming out in front. It was the time, supposed he could not live. He had recovered. I think he was shot by our own infantry firing to check the enemy, and not perceiving our advance to charge. There is little doubt of it.

The 12th on our left attacked and dispersed a considerable

body of the enemy, and not being on our left, and not so much delayed with the lane, got in advance. We supported them, having formed immediately after out charge, and by forming line (with the 11th), presented a front which enabled the 12th to retire with safety, as likewise all the men of the 2nd brigade that had retreated on this point. We had some difficulty in preventing the men of the 16th from attacking in small bodies, after the charge, those parties of the enemy which had pursued the 2nd brigade. Had they done this, we should have got into the same scrape; at least, we could not have covered the retreat of the others, but must have retired to form ourselves. The loss of the 2nd brigade was immense, and the more to be regretted; for had they halted after completely routing the enemy's troops (making the attack) their loss would have been trifling, and the brigade remained efficient for the rest of the day. What with men lost and others gone to the rear in care of the wounded, and many absent from not knowing where to assemble, and other causes, there did not remain efficient above a squadron. In repulsing this attack, we had the misfortune to lose three excellent officers,-Sir Thomas Picton, who was shot at the head of his division, leading it to his favourite and decisive attack with the bayonet. He is a great loss- a person in whom the troops had the greatest confidence, and of such experience and knowledge in his profession as to be of the greatest loss to the army. Through the whole of the Peninsular was he had been at the head of his 3rd Division. No division ever more distinguished itself. Had he survived this day, he must have been raised to the peerage, and on the titles conferred at the peace of 1814 (the conclusion of the Spanish was), he said that had his patent been in a fortress with those of the others then created, he believed he should have obtained his nearly as soon. If services only had been considered, he certainly stood before most of the others. I can only except Lord Hill.

Sir William Ponsonby was killed* at the head of his brigade; he had led them to the charge, and, his horse being shot (or he dismounted), was killed by one of the Lancers. Perhaps in the confusion no report is very much to be relied on; but the one I

*Happily this proved incorrect. Vide inf.

have named was the only mention I ever heard of the manner he fell. He had commanded the 5th Dragoons for three campaigns in the Peninsula, and had been in command of the brigade in which they served for a considerable part of that time. He was very much esteemed by those under him, and regretted both as an officer and a gentleman.

A French Lancer thrust his lance into him when on the ground, saying, "Tu n'es pas encore mort, coquina?" He recovered, and told a very discreditable tale of the conduct of a French Lancer when he lay on the ground. The fellow came up and said, "You are not yet dead, villain?" and ran the lance into his body. An infantry soldier then rested his musket on him, firing from behind him, lying down. After a short time he went away, put a knapsack under his head, saying the day was ours.

The third Lieutenant-Colonel Ponsonby, of the 12th, who fell into the enemy's hands desperately wounded, having his horse killed in the charge our brigade made to cover the retreat of the 2nd brigade. He was very much wounded, and remained in the enemy's hands through the day. His loss as a cavalry officer would be great, and in any future war where he has an opportunity of commanding a body of cavalry it will appear he is one of the best officers in the service.

We were told very early in the day that a corps of Prussians were on their march to join us. Being on the left, we were constantly looking out for them. Not knowing by what line they would come, I rode forward to see if there was any road along the valley in our front and leading up to the left. This was near Ter la Haye.

The cannonade continued along the line through the day. Whenever the enemy made an attack, they covered it with all the artillery they could thunder at us, and we again worked their columns in advancing with every gun we could bring against them. One brigade of guns was firing at a brigade of the enemy's which had got their range and annoyed them. They were ordered by the Duke not to fire at the enemy's guns, but direct all shot against their columns. We might run a chance of losing the position from a severe attack of one of their columns, but could not by their cannonade. The manner their columns were cut up in making the attack was extraordinary, and the excellence of practice in artillery was never exceeded. The enemy fired a great deal, yet at times, I thought, rather wildly. During this attack the enemy had attempted the forcing La Haye Sainte in which one brigade of their infantry was nearly annihilated. This attack was at length supported by a reinforcement from their first division and a considerable body of cuirassiers, under General Kellerman. They moved forward to the attack of La Haye Sainte, and from the body of troops moved against it there appeared an intention of carrying our position on that point. They came so forward that the 1st brigade of cavalry, Lord Edward Somerset's (Household), were moved to the charge. They attacked and succeeses against the cuirassiers, following up their success in the same imprudent manner as the other heavy Brigade had done after their charge. They suffered very much, but not, I think, to the same extent as the others.

Towards the close of the evening the whole brigade did not form above one squadron. It could not be supposed so few remained over the killed and wounded. The fact was that the men did not know where to assemble after the charge, and this being the first action they had ever been in, they, I suppose, fancied that nothing remained for them to attend to after this one attack, and many went in consequence to the rear. There was one squadron of the 1st Dragoon Guards in which not above one or two returned. They rode completely into the enemy's reserve, and were killed. The enemy, I suspect, did not spare a single prisoner who fell into their hands. It is impossible to suppose a whole squadron killed without one man surrendering.

The building of La Haye Sainte was occupied by the 2nd Light Battalion K.G.L., under Lieutenant-Colnel Baring. The enemy had attempted to dislodge them from it for some time, and on bringing down their reinforcements, they so surrounded the place and approached so close to our line that the communication with La Haye Sainte was intercepted, and consequently the battalion occupying it soon became short of ammunition. The fire they were obliged to keep up to enable them to hold it was so great that they were soon under the necessity of sending for more; in attempting which, they found the communication occupied, and it could not be procured.

It so happened that the communication with La Haye Sainte was on one side of the building, and not directly in its rear, so that the enemy, by occupying the ground on that side, rendered the approach impossible. There ought to have been a hole broken through the wall directly in the rear, which would have preserved the communication. The Duke said he ought to have ordered this, but, to use his own expression, "it was impossible for me to think of everything." The officers stationed in it ought to have seen its necessity and made the communication through the rear.

They could not retain the post without ammunition, and were obliged to abandon it to the enemy, making the best retreat they could to our line, in doing which they suffered greatly. Their defence had been a gallant, severe affair, and their numbers by it very greatly diminished. The occupation of La Haye Sainte enabled the enemy to form a considerable body of troops close in its rear, and from that point to commence attacks on the troops in position immediately above the house. These attacks were made at intervals for nearly two hours; they were the most singularly daring attempts ever heard of, and in many instances appeared like an inclination to sacrifice themselves sooner than survive the loss of the day. Parties of cuirassiers, from two to three squadrons and frequently less, occasionally supported by a few infantry, and in many instances without infantry, rode up to the hill occupied by our troops.

An officer of cuirassiers rode close up to one of our squares with a detachment of men. He saw he had no chance of success, and by himself alone rode full gallop against the square, was shot and killed. Our men and officers regretted his fate.

The artillerymen at our guns remained at them to the last moment, firing grape on the enemy, by which the cuirassiers suffered. Our infantry got into squares of regiments, and the French Dragoons came riding amongst them, waving their swords and in many instances approaching close to them.

They never attempted in any body to attack the infantry, and after remaining on the position for ten minutes, or possibly longer, retired again. The instant they turned their backs, the artillery in the squares of infantry ran to their guns and commenced their fire against them.

Lord Wellington, in his dispatch, speaking of the artillery thus mentions them: "The artillery and engineer departments were conducted much to my satisfaction by Colonel Sir. G. Wood and Colonel Smyth. It was an action in which the artillery suffered greatly and particularly distinguished themselves." Repeatedly they had to leave their guns and take refuge in the squares of the infantry, and the instant the French cavalry turned to the rear, they ran to their guns, firing at them in their retreat. They were, too, exposed to the whole fire of the enemy's gins without being suffered to return their fire. They were directed to fire only at the enemy's columns. Without meaning any slight to the engineer department, yet in an action such as this there is nothing for them to be employed in, and therefore to couple the artillery with them is rather passing over their exertions unnoticed, and I conceive that if any part deserved to be especially named, it was that part of the artillery placed above La Haye Saints.

Captain Ramsay, of the artillery, was killed near this point; his head was carried away by a round shot. He had been through the whole of the Peninsula, attached to Major-General Anson's brigade, and was invariably zealous and willing to run every risk to get his guns into action. He rode a couple of six-pounders over a hedge and ditch at Vittoria, to get them up to act against the enemy's retreating troops. We all regret him exceedingly.

During the time the enemy were employed in this attack out guns were in their hands, but without any means on their part of either injuring them or carrying them away. It was the most singular, hardy conduct every heard of, and had such gallantry been properly directed, it must have been turned to some account. Had it happened immediately after an attack, or been once adopted in the zeal of the moment by any officer foiled in his object, there might be some excuse; but for such a thing to be continued for any length of time and under officers who had been serving all their lives, is a proceeding quite unaccountable. They made two or three separate attempts from the one just mentioned, all of which ended in the same manner.

The cuirassiers and Imperial Guard were excellent, and from the manner they were always pushed forward, and the selection made of them through the army for the two services, it appears that they alone were considered, and that the others were injured by having their best men taken from them, and broken in spirit from being considered inferior. In a small French pamphlet, giving an account of the spirit in the French army on its advance previous to Waterloo, I believe the domineering spirit of the guard is well and justly described, and that the account of their quarrels with the rest of the army is an accurate one.

The action continued through the day, by the enemy making attacks on our position from near La Haye Sainte, and by occasional efforts to posess themselves of Hougoumont. In one of these they forced the doors leading into the court-yard, and were entering the place when the were attacked by the bayonet and driven back. They attempted to scale the wall into the garden, and on inspecting it the following morning, I found that three or four French infantry had so far succeeded that they had got to the top of the wall, and were there killed falling into the garden. The garden wall was about seven feet in height. The enemy opened a fire of shells on the chateau, and set it on fire, and a considerable part of it was consumed; yet, by the exertions of the soldiers, the flames were extinguished in sufficient time to admit of its being retained as a post, and the enemy repulsed in every attempt they made against it.

About 4p.m we saw a column advance out of a wood beyond Frischermont, and anxiously waited to ascertain by the fire whether it was a corps joining the enemy or the expected Prussians. They had artillery with their advance, and ere long we saw them forming to their front, and their guns open against the enemy. Such a reinforcement during an action was an occurrence so different from former days in the Peninsula, where everything centred in the British army, that it appeared decisive of the fate of the day.

In consequence of the arrival of the Prussians to attack the right of the enemy, and further reinforcement of them expected to join us and occupy the left of our position, our brigade was moved from the left to about half the distance from whence we stood (towards our right) to the Charleroi road. This took place about 5p.m. We halted for a short time in this position, marching to it in rear of the infantry, and occasionally receiving a spent musket ball, and judging of the cannonade from the shots that passed over us. They were very frequent for a cannonade which had been continued through so long an attack.

In passing along the line it appeared to have been much cut up, and the troops, which in parts held the position, were but few, and had suffered greatly. From marching under shelter of the hill we could not distinctly see; yet I conceived, from all I could learn, that many points in the position were but feebly guarded. The opinion I formed was a correct one. The enemy's point of attack for some hours had been La Haye Sainte, to which we were moving, and to the point in the position opposite to which the Duke had assembled a considerable force. The foreign division formed *en pontence* on the right of the army, had been brought to near the Charleroi road, forming in rear of our line. The guards were stationed in their front. After halting a short time in the place I have mentioned, we were ordered to the Charleroi road, which we passed, halting immediately and forming line with the left of the brigade resting on the road. In our front the Guards held the position. Foreign battalions were formed in squares in support of them, and our brigade was placed immediately in rear of the squares. We had not long remained in this position before the enemy commenced their last desperate effort to carry our position.

They had pushed some guns close up to La Haye Sainte, and from these our troops suffered considerably by a fire of grape; they also opened a heavy cannonade of round shot. We were placed just under cover of the hill.

Whilst in this situation my coverer (Sergeant Flesh) was hit by a spent ball. It struck him on the chest, and with such violence that he said he was killed. I fancied the ball had gone through. In a few minutes I saw the ball drop from his overalls at his feet on to the ground, and on desiring him to go to the rear he said he should see it out, and fell in again. He had not been five minutes in the ranks before another spent ball struck him, but not with such violence as the first; he continued with us. The shots coming from the front, I was fortunate to escape them both, as he was directly behind me. He suffered afterwards from not being bled, and taking no care of himself.

A regiment of cavalry of the Pays Bas, not liking to remain so close to the infantry, had withdrawn to a greater distance, and received many shots which passed over our heads. From the place where we stood, we could not see what force came up to the attack, but from the showers of musketry which came over our heads and the volleys in our front, or rather constant roll of musketry, we were aware some important attack was attempted by the enemy, and that from the situation of our brigade, we were placed to meet and attempt to stop any column which might carry our line. It was a most anxious moment. The men were perfectly aware of their situation: they gave two or three huzzars, and had any column made its appearance, I never saw soldiers more ready than the whole of our brigade then appeared to be to do their duty. I never saw them evince greater steadiness.

There was a regiment of the Pays Bas in square. They were not engaged, not suffering much from fire, I may say not in the least cup whilst I saw them. They were immediately in our front, and fancying the affair rather serious, and that if the enemy advanced any further (as their fears apprehended) they would have to oppose them, they began firing their muskets in the air, and their rear moved a little, intending, under the confusion of their fire and smoke, to move off. Major Cholders, 11th Light Dragoons, and I rode up to them, encouraged them, stopped those who had moved the farthest (ten yards, perhaps) out of their ranks, and whilst they were hesitating whether to retreat or continue with their column, the Duke rode up and encouraged them. He said to us, "That is right, that is right; keep them up." Childers then brought up his squadron, and by placing it is their rear they continued steady. The Duke rode away again immediately. Had this one battalion run away at that moment, the consequence might have been fatal. The Duke was hurried, and rode away very quickly.

During this attack we remained stationary, and after a short time the fire slackened, and we were ordered to advance. We moved to the front in a column of half squadrons, left in front, and on getting to the crown of the hill saw the whole French army in the greatest confusion, and the infantry which had made the last attack running away down the hill and over the plain below in the greatest haste and confusion.

The enemy, in this last attack, brought up two close columns of infantry, one in advance of the other. They came with the first nearly to the top of the hill, and then opened a fire on our line. They did not attempt to deploy into line, standing still, holding their ground and firing from their outer ranks. In this position the most advanced column suffered greatly from our grape, and the number of wounded, with comrades to assist them going to the rear, appeared so great to the second column that they almost thought those in advance were retiring and giving way, from the many soldiers who came away to the rear. In this hesitation they were charged by the 52nd and a battalion of the 95th (Rifles), when they gave away, and their retreat became general. I believe some part of the Guards charged at this time, though I could never exactly ascertain. (I believe not.) The 52nd and 95th certainly, for I knew an artillery officer who mentioned their passing through his guns in their advance.

This was their last desperate effort, in which the Old Guard of Napoleon was employed. This is the system they have gone upon every other nation, and have succeeded. They move an overcrawing column or two to one point. It comes up with the greatest regularity, and on arriving at close quarters with their opponents, they carry so steady and determined an appearance that those hitherto opposed to them have generally abandoned their positions without being beaten out of them. The nearer this column gets to the enemy the greater will be its loss from grape and a fire of musketry concentred on it; and if the troops holding the position are inclined to use the bayonet, they have the advantage in being able to move quickly against it, whilst the column must receive the charge from not being able to move at such a quick pace as troops acting in line. At Waterloo they came nearly to the top of the hill, and there halted. They never attempted to deploy into line, and seemed to consider their very appearance, and holding the position they occupied, must cause our retreat. On our infantry charging (52nd and 95th) they set off down the hill, and on our brigade getting to the point from which we overlooked them, they were seen running away on everyside in the greatest haste and confusion. Not knowing when we moved to the front which had succeeded, it was a sight I shall never forget.

On our moving to this front we were ignorant of our success, and not knowing whether we were going to charge a successful column of the enemy or pursue a beaten one, the extent of our success was the greater surprise and delight to us. Being in a column oh half squadrons, we were ordered to form line, decend into the plain and pursue the enemy. We did not feel inclined to lose any time, and the ground being more favourable for a formation to the left instead of to the right (as it ought in regularity to have been), we inclined to our left, forming on the left of the left half squadron of the 12th, which clubbed the brigade. It was of no consequence, as we probably had nothing to do but move on in line, attacking the first troops we met. We were led into the plain by our general betwixt the road to Charleroi and the Observatory, and had to open out and pass over many killed and wounded. In retiring from the last attack the enemy had made considerable haste to the rear, and not until we were lineable with the Observatory did we receive any fire or perceive any intention of stopping us. They were in complete deroute and confusion. On the top of a small hill they at length opened a couple of guns and fired a few round shot. We continued to advance in a trot, and on coming closer to these guns, they fired once with grape, which fell about fifty yards short of the brigade, and did not the least damage. The Observatory was situated at the edge of a wood, and as from the line we were moving on we must leave this in our rear, I sent

Sergeant-Major Greaves of my troop to see if the enemy had any force in the wood. He returned and caught us, saying they had none, when I rode on before the brigade to an eminence (which we were ascending) to see what force the enemy had in our front. From this point I saw a body of infantry with a squadron of cuirassiers formed in the valley, close to a by-road which ran at right angles to the point we were moving on. The infantry were about 1,000 in column, with about three companies formed behind a hedge, which ran alongside of the road in question. I rode back and told General Vandeleur that the enemy had the force I have named, and that the left of the 16th and right of the 11th would (as they were the advancing) come in contact with it; that the 12th had nothing in their front, and if ordered to proceed on to the front and bring forward their right, they would get in their rear and make a considerable number of prisoners. He took no notice, except saying, Where are they? And in a minute the brigade was in the top of the rising ground, in a gallop the instant they saw the enemy, and proceeded to the charge. The enemy's infantry behind the hedge gave us a volley, and being close at them, and the hedge nothing more than some scattered bushes without a ditch, we made a rush and went into their column with the companies which were stationed in their front, they running away to the square for shelter. We completely succeeded, many of their infantry immediately throwing down their arms and crowding together for safety. Many, too, ran away up the next rising ground. We were riding in all directions a parties attempting to make their escape, and in many instances had to cut down men who had taken up their arms after having in the first instance laid them down. From the appearance of the enemy lying together for safety, they were some yards in height, calling out, from the injury of one pressing upon another, and from the horses stamping upon them (on their legs). I had ridden after a man who took up his musket and fired at one of our men, and on his running to his comrades, my horse trod on them. (He had only one eye (Cyclops), and trod he heavier from not seeing them.) Lieutenant Beckwith, 16th, stood still and attempted to catch this man on his sword; he missed him, and nearly ran me through the body. I was following the man at a hard gallop. Captain Buchanan, of the 16th, was killed in the midst of their infantry. After some little delay in seeing they all surrendered; we proceeded in pursuit of the enemy's other scattered troops. It was nearly dark at the time we made the charge, and when we moved from the spot it was quite so. (It was a light night.)

We went up the next brow of a hill, following the enemy, who were scattered in all directions, and on coming to the top the first thing that stopped us were some huts, which some of the rear of the enemy had constructed; and in ignorance of the fate of their army had taken shelter in them I rode into the mouth of one of them, when the men in it turned out and commenced to fire over the back of the huts. I rode back and met Sir Hussey Vivian coming up with his brigade, and told him of our being in his front, fearing the same might occur again.

Sir Hussey told me he had turned the fate of the day by charging with his brigade. The place he charged at was two miles out of the position and half an hour after the enemy retired.

The men were ordered to stop, not knowing in that light what force the enemy might have, and the brigade being scattered we halted and formed. The 16th was the only regiment which came up to the huts, the 11th and 12th being to our right and left, and halted rather before. On forming, we were told a regiment of French cavalry was coming up in our rear and that the men had a general inclination to charge them. We were moving for that purpose, but on approaching we found them to be one of our own regiments-the 1st Hussars K.G.L., the old regiment with which the 16th had such a length of time been briagded in Spain. Each happy to discover its error.

Here the pursuit ended, it being ten o'clock, and the brigade was ordered to retire. The ground was covered with muskets, thrown-away guns, ammunition wagons, tumbrils, brandy, etc. We came across some of the latter, and got as much as the men required. We retired to the edge of the wood near the Observatory, and not half a mile from the point where we charged the infantry, and there bivouacked for the night.

The wood was full of French soldiers, who had run to it for

safety. Most of them got away during the night. We had gone through a very long day, yet had we proceeded, a great many prisoners who got away in the night would have fallen into our hands. From the time our brigade made first charge, until our moving to the right of the position, we had been quiet and dismounted nearly the whole time. We could have pursued through the night, but must have gone on without orders.

Lieutenant Hay*, of the 16th, was killed in the pursuit. His horse was found, but no search could ever discover him. He probably fell in the corn, and was stripped early the next morning by the peasants.

On hearing the firing on the 18th the peasants for miles round assembled the following morning on the field. They plundered all they could get, and in one instance I saw them pulling off a pair of boots from the legs of a soldier of the Guards before he was dead. I made the fellow desist, and attempted to teach him we did not allow such proceedings. Colonel Currie, A.D.C., to Lord Hill, was killed late in the evening. Colonel Egerton was with him and marked the spot, by which means he found him the next morning. He was stripped, and with difficulty distinguished from those around him.

Before we moved, an officer of the Guards came to us, shot in the hip. I put him before one of our dragoons to be taken to the rear. He could not bear the motion of the horse, and was obliged to remain on the field. On our moving to the front, Colonel Canning, of the Duke's staff, lay on the ground. My troop moved to the spot he was lying on, when he begged we would not ride over him, saying he was the Duke of Wellington's aide-de-camp. The men opened out and on my asking him if I could assist him, or leave a man with him, he said it was quite useless, that he could not live long, being shot in the body with grape. I encouraged him, telling him of our success, and that a surgeon would soon arrive on being sent for. He was quite determined not to allow anything being done, and on my mentioning my name and his recollecting me, he begged me to dismount to take his sword and watch, to be delivered to his relations. He did not live above a couple of hours.

*Alexander Hay, of Nunraw (born), 1794.

The Duke himself gave the orders to the 52nd and 95th to charge, and the 71st being in the same brigade and not hearing the order, were retiring. Colonel Egerton* rode up to Colonel Reynell, telling him the 52nd and 95th were charging, and begged him to put his men about and join them. The 71st were halted, fronted, and joined in the charge; and this was done in a very important moment-it was a service of consequence. Colonel Egerton was A.D.C. to Lord Hill, and was desired by him to get up some troops to the crest of the hill. He went to a distinguished corps, commanded by a distinguished knight, but could not induce them to move to the point he requested them to occupy.

To know the point we charged on-it is across a road leading from the Nivelles road to the village of Genappe (I think). On going from the Charleroi road, leaving it at Genappe, to the Nivelles road, you leave the wood we bivouacked in on the right, and the point we charged is about a mile, or perhaps not so far, from the wood.

The Prussians came on the line of the enemy's retreat on Charleroi from our left, and as they came up and proceeded along the road in pursuit of them they greeted us with cheers and acknowledgments for the stand we had made, assuring us there was no necessity for us to proceed, as they would march and complete the affair, by following up the enemy through the night. The officers shook hands with us.

Much has been said of Grouchy not appearing on the 18th, Napoleon directed him to move on Wavre in pursuit of the Prussians; and his failure at Waterloo he attributes to a disobedience of orders on the part of Grouchy in not joining him. The Prussians were more than our strength; therefore to dispose of them and keep their army in check, it could not be considered a large detatchment in employing one corps of 30,000 men, and in weakening his force to that amount, he must be considered fortunate if by so doing he disposed of the Prussians. I have little doubt but that Napoleon considered them so beaten on the

---

*Brother of Sir Philip Grey Egerton, Bart, of Oulton Park, Cheshire. He afterwards married Colonel Tomkinson's sister, and died 1854.

16th, that the corps he sent would prove sufficient to keep them in play, whilst he acted with the remainder of his force against us. If ever the real orders to Grouchy are known, I much question if it will not be seen that his directions were to act against the Prussians without any reference to the British; and that had the Prussians retired before him he was to have continued his advance on Brussels, turning our left, or rather obliging us either to fall back and cover Brussels, or abandon it, likewise effecting by this movement a more important object, viz., the *entrecoupe* of us and the Prussians. When the latter made their appearance on the right of the French, officers from Napoleon's staff were sent to tell their troops that Grouchy was in sight, and up to the last moment Napoleon persisted they were not the Prussians. He was well aware that his only chance was carrying cur position; he determined to persevere to the last; and in this resolution he knew that a report of fresh troops acting on his flank at the close of such a day, would so damp the spirits of his men, that any attack would prove nearly hopeless.

He did right to conceal this truth, and has nothing left him but suppressing his real instructions to Grouchy. It appears since Waterloo (a fact we were not aware of about the time of the action) that Grouchy attacked the Prussians at Wavre.

June 19th. I rode this morning over the field. The loss on both sides has been immense, and the face of the hill near La Haye Sainte, and from thence to Hougoumont, has more the appearance of a breach carried by assult, than an extended field of battle. The wounded have remained all night on the spot where they were hit, and from their numbers and want of means of immediately carrying them away, I fear some will have to remain out a second night. The weather is now fine, and if they are dressed and supplied with a little water and bread, they will not take any injury. Many of the enemy must remain out a second night, and some a third.

There were three men of the 32nd lying wounded together from grape. They begged a little water from me with such earnestness that I got off and gave them a taste of some brandy I had in a flask. The two first I gave it to were wounded in the leg, and on putting it to the mouth of the third, who was wounded in the body, one of the others requested me to give him his share, for his comrade was wounded in the belly, and the brandy would only do him harm. I was aware it was not good for any, yet having been out all night, and probably having had nothing on the 18th, I thought a taste could not injure them. They begged me to send their doctor, and were afraid they would remain out a second night. A man of one on the Highland regiments was employing himself in carrying water to the wounded on both sides, and had been doing so from daylight. Many were looking after plunder, and excellent French watches were sold at a low rate.

A French colonel, wounded near La Belle Alliance, was on the shoulders of four peasants in a blanket, going to the rear. On seeing I was an officer, he spoke much of his unfortunate situation, in being wounded and not better attended to. He requested me to go to the Duke of Wellington and tell him how little attention a French colonel had received, when he assured himself the Duke would provide for him in future. Compared to many of our own officers he was well off, and more of his army had met with his good fortune in finding hands to carry him off the field.

In Hougoumont our troops had suffered greatly, and from the chateau being on fire I almost fear some wounded were burnt to death. The trees in advance of the building were cut to pieces by musketry, and will, I hope, be allowed to stand in confirmation of the heavy fore our troops were exposed to, and the resistance they must have made to hold it through the day against such an attack. The road from Waterloo to Brussels was completely blocked up with commissariat wagons, wither broken down or deserted, and by other carriages belonging to the army. From the many carriages and horses which had passed along it the road was one puddle, and independent of the obstructions on it, had a retreat been attempted to Brussels, it would have been found nearly impracticable. There was some very disgraceful conduct in Brussels from soldiers,-and in some few instances, I fear, officers,-riding into the town and saying all was lost and that the enemy would enter immediately.

An officer of cavalry galloped to Malines, and on his arrival there he stated, that as he left the upper town in Brussels, he saw the enemy's troops in the lower part of the town. Some person with the baggage advised him to inform the commandant of Antwerp, and possibly through his report the gates of Antwerp were shut. They were closed for a short time. A corporal of the Guards stationed in Hougoumont having left his regiment, passed through the 95th on his way to the rear. He was not wounded, and assigned no reason for leaving his corps. He told the 95th that the enemy had possession of the chateau, and that all there was lost. From the point the 95th occupied in the line, they saw our fire proceeding out of Hougoumont against the enemy, and therefore knowing his report to be false, they caught him, and gave the corporal a good booting, telling him in future to beware how he spread such incorrect, dispiriting reports.

The loss and confusion from these reports spreading through those in charge of the baggage occasioned such an alarm, that in one instance a batman was seen throwing his master's baggage into the canal going to Antwerp. Many English families had remained in Brussels, and had no conveyance to take them away. They ran a great risk. The Duchess of Richmond and her family were there, and had they been obliged to move, must have gone with the line of baggage or troops, without the power of getting out of it. The wounded, from being so numerous, were some time before they met with proper attention. They were in the first instance placed under what little cover there was in farmhouses and cottages near the field, and then removed to Brussels when transport could be provided for them. The people in Brussels behaved well to them, taking into their houses the officers as they arrived, and assisting in providing convents or large buildings as hospitals for the men. The day after the action they gave beer away to the soldiers going and returning to Waterloo. In many instances, I believe ladies employed themselves in procuring old linen for the hospitals. To judge of this assistance we should attend a large hospital after a general action, where, from want of linen, the same is used week after week, and the very bandages put round wounds to cure them, are doing more injury than good. Many surgeons came from England for the practice, and on things being arranged, no wounded could be better attended to.

The wounded of a British army generally receive more attention than those of other nations. The French system is to run great risks with a man's life in hopes of saving a limb, from knowing that a soldier without a leg or arm is incapable of service, and probably a burthen to the State. With us, the practice is possibly too much in favour of hasty amputation. There have been instances of officers saving their limbs, from not allowing the surgeon to operate, choosing rather to run the risk of losing their life than being cut out of their profession.

There is one circumstance greatly in favour of all men wounded. An army is commonly on short allowance, and particularly when before an enemy, neither men nor officers are in the habit or have the power of eating more than is requisite to support them. Very early rising, little rest, and frequently none at all, tend to keep down the system and prevent inflammation. The surgeons attribute the rapid cures and extraordinary recoveries to this cause. The inflammation to be contended with in a un-shot wound, on such a habit of body as a London alderman's, or indeed of any Englishman in his own country, would endanger his life, or, at all events, retard his recovery. The scanty fare of an army is possibly more applicable to troops in the Peninsula than in the Netherlands, and to officers doing regimental duty than to those in staff employ. Some of the generals think considerably of their table.

The army marched this day to the neighbourhood of Nivelles. General Vandeleur's brigade bivouacked at Aquesnes, about two miles from Nivelles. Headquarters this night at Nivelles.

June 20th. Boissoit sur Haine-a march of eighteen miles, to near Boeulse. The Prussians are gone in pursuit of the flying troops of the enemy, and it is possible we shall not meet with any resistance for some distance.

21st, Wednesday. Marched to Bellegely, near Malplaquet. Whilst waiting for orders to know where we must halt for the night, the Duke of Wellington passed us. It was our first time of seeing him since the action, and being two or three brigades of cavalry together, we all cheered him. He held his hat off for a short time and appeared gratified with the reception. I got this night into a cottage, and a short time after dark a dragoon of the Belgian cavalry rode into my quarter. He came into the house on horseback, intending to frighten the occupiers in order to extort money, or some other bribe, to induce him to leave their house: he was not aware it was occupied by any of the army. We got hold of him, pulled him off his horse, and gave him in charge to the guard of the 16th for the night.

He was reported the following morning by Major Murray, who commanded the 16th, to the Duke, and a reference took place respecting it. Severe orders had been issued to prevent the troops plundering on entering France, and this being a flagrant attempt, and committed almost immediately on the first villiage we have occupied in France, the Duke was desirous of making an early example. I was asked if I could swear to the man, and on saying I could not, he was given over to be punished by his regiment. Had I been quite clear about it, or indeed, had I stated that which was really the fact, I believe he would have been tied up on the first tree. The man came into my quarter with his pistol loaded in his hand, was pulled off his horse and taken by us to the guard of the 16th. They kept him secure all night, and had no other foreigner under their charge.

June 22nd. Marched to Cateau Cambresis. We are ordered to Pomereuil, about three miles from Cateau. Blucher is advancing in all haste in pursuit of the enemy. He wished the Duke to proceed without a halt, pushing on to Paris with the least possible delay, or rather without a single halt. From the extent of our loss on the 18th, our army is much more disorganized than the Prussians, and a day or two to collect those left to carry away the wounded and allow the cavalry to shoe their horses is requisite, in order that our advance may be made with a little order. The men are all in great spirits, and have not much idea of stopping before we obtain possession of Paris. Looking at our present march up to Paris with a view to dethrone the great Napoleon, and our commencement on a strip of land in the lines of Torres Vedras, then the only army he had not subdued, and that army but a handful in comparison with his hordes in every part of Europe, it appears is great a conclusion to such a poor commencement that we can scarcely revert to the up-hill campaigns we have fought through and believe ourselves the same army not on our advance to the gates of Paris. Napoleon has left his army and gone to Paris. After the defeat he has encounted, his cause may be so weakened as to render his presence necessary to keep down any political party which may be hostile to his government, and under cover of his defeat now presume to show itself.

Lisle is said to have a garrison of 1,500 men with a small force in Valenciennes. It is probable the garrisons in any of the towns around this are not large, as every man would be collected for the advance against is, previous to the battle.

25th. Marched to Fontaine Entat.

26th. Marched to Fanquier, a small village on the high road between St. Quinten and Ham.

27th. To near Royes.

28th. Riequebourh.

The enemy on the 28th attacked the advance guard of the Prussians at Villars Coteret. The main body of the Prussians coming up, they retired across the Marne; being driven by General Bulow on the road near Meaux.

He took from them 500 prisoners. On the 28th, in the attack at Villars Coteret, they lost six pieces of cannon and 1,000 prisoners.

29th. Bivouacked on the other side of the Oise, which we passed at the Pont St. Maxence. The bridge was destroyed on the advance of the Prussians in 1814, by blowing up the centre arch. It is repaired in a temporary manner. Deputies are daily coming out of Paris to treat with the Duke and attempt to prevent the further advance of the army. No terms whilst Napoleon remains at the head of affairs will be listened to. Blucher, with the Prussians, is in our advance, and attempts have been made by them to treat with him. I believe he will not see them, saying, in Paris alone will he listen to any terms. The Duke will not, of course, make a separate treaty, therefore they must wait for an interview in Paris.

Marshal Grouchy, with his corps from Wavre, has arrived at Paris; he has made a rapid march and brought all his material complete.

The enemy have near 50,000 troops of the line, besides the National Guard and a new levy called the Tirailleurs de la Garde-in all early 70,000. Grouchy's retreat was very rapid and well conducted.

Marched to Gousanville, near Louves, within four leagues of Paris. It is on the high road from Senlis to St.Denis. We made a detour from the high road to avoid interfering with the other columns. This took us through the wood of Chantilly. Previous to passing the Pont St.Maxence nothing could be more uninteresting that the country. It is flat and extensive, chiefly covered with corn, without timber, and not affording the least variety. For the last three days we have followed the route of the Prussians; they plunder every village. There are not many inhabitants remaining at their houses.

There were long avenues of cherries in the neighbourhood of Gousanville. More cherries around this village than I ever saw collected in one spot.

July 1st. Marched to Argenteuil and bivouacked in the garden of the Minister of Marine. The Prussians have passed before us, and done all the damage in their power to the house. The looking glasses are all broken; many of them were large and handsome. A bust of Napoleon is split from top to bottom, and the iron railings round the house have been pulled up. I am sorry the Prussians act in such spite, though it is exactly the conduct of the French when in their country. The French deserve it, yet it would have been nobler conduct not to avail themselves of such petty advantages, although the enemy acted to them in the same, or possibly in a more oppressive manner. It is difficult to say what is right. The French should not allow their army to act as they have, and come off themselves with impunity.

Blucher, on the 2nd, was strongly opposed in taking possession of the heights of St.Cloud; he, however, affected his object, and pushed his advance close to the gates of Paris. They occupied the village of Issy. They were attacked at this point on the morning of the 3rd at daylight. The enemy advanced on the Prussians in considerable force, and the affair became severe. They were driven back into Paris, and knowing Blucher would bombard the town, they sent to desire the firing might cease, and that terms being arranged for the withdrawing of the army, they would evacuate Paris. Blucher had applied for our Rocket Brigade, and would probably have employed them the instant they could have got up against the town.

The Duke having thrown a bridge over the Seine at Argenteuil, by an advance on Neuilly the Bois de Boulogne would have been occupied and the two armies in possession of the ground up to the gates of the town. It is fortunate the affair ended here, for had we advanced up to the town, had a successful affair, and in the hurry of the troops, followed the enemy into the town, it is impossible to say what would have been the result. Had the men left their ranks and attempted plundering a town of such an extent as Paris, with a population half soldiers, I fear we should have lost half the army. It is fortunate the business has closed and the troops in bivouac a short distance from the town.

July 3rd. A pontoon bridge was thrown over the Seine yesterday at Argenteuil. We crossed this morning and with the 2nd Division moved on Courbevoye, situated on the Seine close to the Pont Neuilly. The 2nd Division of infantry crossed at the same time, and moved on Courbevoye. A Convention has been agreed upon, and signed this day at St. Cloud.

On the 4th July St. Denis, St. Ouen, Clichy and Neuilly are to be given up.

On the 5th Montmarte is to be surrendered.

6th. All the barriers around Paris are to be given up. The French army to retire over the Loire within eight days.

The enemy are to retire over the Seine and give up Courbevoye, retiring over the Pont Neuilly.

On arriving at Courbevoye they pretend ingnorance of the terms agreed on, and fired on our advance. We had a skirmish with them in driving in their piquet (they knew of the Convention being signed), in which we lost a man and horse with three or four wounded. After they had retired into Courbevoye we had the greatest difficulty in persuading them t suffer our piquet to be stationed (as specified) close to the bridge.

Lieutenant-General Clinton talked with them for some time, and then allowed them then minutes to determine. He moved the 2nd Division to attack if they did not retire, when they evacuated the post, allowing our piquet to be stationed on the bridge. When they saw us determined, they became very civil, and came forward to converse with us. They were dreadfully enraged at the Bourbons, saying, they supposed now that they must receive a king from the English, but that they preferred the Duke of York or the Duke of Wellington to a Bourbon. An officer of Hussar put himself in a dreadful passion, pulled the cloak he had before him in a manner to pull it off his saddle, saying he had seen the Duc de Berri strip an officer's epaulette from his shoulder on parade. We bivouacked in the garden.

July 4th. The Convention being signed, we moved a short distance down the Seine, occupying the village of Aniers. We were well put up, and within two miles of Paris.

July 7th. Rode this day into Paris. The barriers having been only surrendered yesterday, not many officers have entered. They rather looked at us as we rode along the streets. The greater part of the infantry are in bivouac in the Bois do Boulogne. We find a regiment of cavalry daily for duty, which occupies the Champs-Elysees, close to the Place Louis Quinze. On the 16th, marching from Aniers, the first day they took this duty, we did not go the direct way, but marched through a part of Paris, across the Place Louis Quinze, to our station. It was singular to find a British regiment of cavalry marching peaceably through the streets of Paris.

Louis XVIII entered Paris on the 8th; he was tolerably well received. Many, I think, went to see his entrance from the mere pleasure of witnessing such sights, and not from and respect or liking to him. This was, I think, the motive which induced the people in whose house I was quartered at Aniers. They spoke for a couple of days of going to see him, yet had not any particular dislike to Napoleon. The lady of the house and her sister rather feel the situation their nation has sunk to. They were speaking of their troops before the Russian Campaign, stating that had they been properly managed, "they could have given laws to all the world."

The Emperors of Russia and of Austria, with the King of Prussia, have arrived.

A detatchment from one of our heavy regiments of cavalry was sent to escort the Emperor of Russia into Paris. He paid them the compliment of saying "he was flattered by being escorted by such brave men."

Napoleon left Paris either on the 20th or 21st for Malmasion, where he remained until obliged to leave on account of the advance of the armies. He has embarked at Rochfort and given himself up to a British man-of-war off that station. It has sailed with him for England-Captain Maitland of the Bellerophon.

Paris, three days after signing the Convention, was full of officers from both armies, and the Parisians enjoyed the concourse equally with us-at least to all appearance.

The Prussians carry the thing with a high hand. In every house they occupy the owners keep a table for the officers billeted on them. We generally attended any duty required early in the morning, and then pass the day in Paris.

The Prussians were reviewed by the Emperors of Russia and of Austria and the King of Prussia. They assembled on the Boulevard with their right on the Place Louis Quinze, where the sovereigns stood to see them pass in review order. Each regiment, as it moved, played, "The Downfall of Paris." The men are fine, young-looking fellows, yet I think rather disfigured by the stuffing they use in their jackets to pad them out and swell out their chests.

The Prussians having played "The Downfall of Paris" at their review, an order was issued for the British regiments either to play "God save the King," or the national air of their country, applying the latter distinction to the Scotch. It is right to avoid these petty annoyances, the more so as nothing enrages the French more than the good conduct of our army, thereby removing all plea for abuse from them of us.

The British army was reviewed in about a fortnight. We formed along the road to Neuilly with our right on the Place Louis Quinze-the artillery on the right, then the cavalry in line, and the infantry in close columns of regiments. The troops looked well. The foreigners particularly admired the artillery, and also the cavalry. The infantry not being selected for any particular corps (as in all their services), there was no regiment distinguished above the rest, and did not call for any particular comment. There is, however, a steady, determined look in the clean-shaven face of an English soldier which we do not find in the whiskered, moustached countenance of a foreigner. The Landwehr of Prussia (militia) are very fine troops-nearly equal to their regiments of the line. It is said they kept up a considerable force under the name of Landwehr during Napoleon's power, being restricted by treaties with him from having above a certain number of troops in the pay of government.

July 1st. Forage becoming scarce, the greater part of the cavalry was ordered away from Paris to the neighbourhood of Neuchatel, five days' march. The 16th occupied Aumale. The inhabitants expected the same treatment from the British they had heard of the Prussians exercising in many towns they had occupied, and were rather alarmed at hearing troops were moving to their neighbourhood. I found in the house I was billeted a dinner prepared and every attention. We soon established a mess at our own quarters, and were on the best terms with the inhabitants.

Whilst at Aumale, Lord Harcourt came out from England and reviewed his regiment on his way to Paris. He was much delighted, and could only observe that he never expected to have reviewed his regiment in France.

The procuring forage in the town being rather troublesome, my troop moved to the village of Mark, occupying some farm houses around the village. It only consisted of a farmhouse, a poor old chateau, and a few cottages.

October 12th. We, this day, moved to Ville d'Eu, twenty miles nearer the coast them Aumale. The people at Ville d'Eu having heard we were not inclined to give any trouble at Aumale;

presumed on this. And were very impertinent on our arrival; they would scarcely allow us to come into their houses. We were as much at variance with the inhabitants of Ville d'Eu as we had been otherwise with those at Aumale.

It is arranged that a certain proportion of the army is to remain as a corps of occupation for three years, and that Russia, Austria and Prussia are to furnish their contingent. I fear it is our turn for Ireland, and that we must leave France for that country. The whole of the army of occupation is to be under the command of the Duke of Wellington.

We moved from Ville d'Eu on our route for Calais on the 15th December. There were a certain number of our horses transferred to the regiments remaining in France. These we gave up at Abbeville, and then proceeded on our route.

The weather on the march from Ville d'Eu to Calais was the most severe I ever experienced. It was so cold for a couple of days, the men could not ride their horses; they were occasionally obliged to dismount and walk, to prevent their being frozen or rather cut through by the coldest easterly wind I ever experienced. The frost was severe. On arriving at Calais, the weather was very stormy, and it was some time before we could embark. The commandant at Calais threw every obstacle in the way of our embarkation. He would not allow us inside the walls of the town, causing us to make the detour of the walls to the point of embarkation.

We arrived at Rumford, near London, on Christmas Day 1815. We left England for Lisbon April 1809. Returned from France in June 1814. Embarked for Waterloo in April 1815, and returned from France December 1815, making a period of service of nearly six years.

We were the only cavalry regiment in the service that went through the whole of the Peninsula (expecting Sir John Moore's campaign, and no regiment served in both,-those with Sir John Moore were not with Sir Arthur Wellesley), and had the good fortune to be present at Waterloo. The 14th Light Dragoons served the same length of time in Spain, but were not at Waterloo, having left the Spanish army at Bordeaux for America, where they were in 1815.

ALSO FROM LEONAUR
AVAILABLE IN SOFT OR HARD COVER WITH DUST JACKET

EW15 EYEWITNESS TO WAR SERIES
THE COMPLEAT RIFLEMAN HARRIS
by Benjamin Harris

The Adventures of a Soldier of the 95th (Rifles) During the Peninsular Campaign of the Napoleonic Wars.

SOFTCOVER : ISBN 1-84677-047-5
HARDCOVER : ISBN 1-84677-053-X

EW14 EYEWITNESS TO WAR SERIES
ZULU 1879
Selected by D.C.F Moodic & the Leonaur Editors.

The Anglo-Zulu War of 1879 from Contemporary Sources; First Hand Accounts, Interviews, Dispatches, Official Documents & Newspaper Reports.

SOFTCOVER : ISBN 1-84677-044-0
HARDCOVER : ISBN 1-84677-051-3

RC1 REGIMENTS & CAMPAIGNS SERIES
THE EAST AFRICAN MOUNTED RIFLES
by C.J. Wilson

Experiences of the Campaign in the East African Bush During the First World War (Illustrated).

SOFTCOVER : ISBN 1-84677-042-4
HARDCOVER : ISBN 1-84677-059-9

EW12 EYEWITNESS TO WAR SERIES
THE ADVENTURES OF A LIGHT DRAGOON IN THE NAPOLEONIC WARS
by George Farmer & G.R. Gleig

A Cavalryman During the Peninsular & Waterloo Campaigns, in Captivity & at the Siege of Bhurtpore, India.

SOFTCOVER : ISBN 1-84677-040-8
HARDCOVER : ISBN 1-84677-056-4

AVAILABLE ONLINE AT
www.leonaur.com
AND OTHER GOOD BOOK STORES

ALSO FROM LEONAUR
AVAILABLE IN SOFT OR HARD COVER WITH DUST JACKET

EW2 EYEWITNESS TO WAR SERIES
TOMMY ATKINS

Fourteen First Hand Accounts from the Ranks of the British Army During Queen Victoria's Empire.

SOFT COVER : **ISBN 1-84677-022-X**
HARD COVER : **ISBN 1-84677-037-8**

SF4 CLASSIC SCIENCE FICTION SERIES
DARKNESS & DAWN 1
by George Allen England

The Vacant World. A Novel of a Future New York.

SOFT COVER : **ISBN 1-84677-027-0**
HARD COVER : **ISBN 1-84677-034-3**

SF4 CLASSIC SCIENCE FICTION SERIES
DARKNESS & DAWN 2
by George Allen England

Beyond the Great Oblivion. A Novel of a Future America.

SOFT COVER : **ISBN 1-84677-028-9**
HARD COVER : **ISBN 1-84677-036-x**

SF4 CLASSIC SCIENCE FICTION SERIES
DARKNESS & DAWN 3
by George Allen England

The After Glow. A Novel of a Future America.

SOFT COVER : **ISBN 1-84677-029-7**
HARD COVER : **ISBN 1-84677-038-6**

AVAILABLE ONLINE AT
www.leonaur.com
AND OTHER GOOD BOOK STORES

ALSO FROM LEONAUR
AVAILABLE IN SOFT OR HARD COVER WITH DUST JACKET

EW9 EYEWITNESS TO WAR SERIES
THE LIFE OF THE REAL 'BRIGADIER GERARD'
Volume 1 **THE YOUNG HUSSAR**
by Jean Baptiste de Marbot

A French Cavalryman of the Napoleonic Wars at Marengo, Austerlitz, Jena, Eylau & Friedland.

SOFTCOVER : ISBN 1-84677-045-9
HARDCOVER : ISBN 1-84677-058-0

EW10 EYEWITNESS TO WAR SERIES
THE LIFE OF THE REAL 'BRIGADIER GERARD'
Volume 2 **IMPERIAL AIDE-DE-CAMP**
by Jean Baptiste de Marbot

A French Cavalryman of the Napoleonic Wars at Saragossa, Landshut, Eckmuhl, Ratisbon, Aspern-Essling, Wagram, Busaco & Torres Vedras.

SOFTCOVER : ISBN 1-84677-041-6
HARDCOVER : ISBN 1-84677-052-1

EW11 EYEWITNESS TO WAR SERIES
THE LIFE OF THE REAL 'BRIGADIER GERARD'
Volume 3 **COLONEL OF CHASSEURS**
by Jean Baptiste de Marbot

A French Cavalryman in the Retreat from Moscow, Lutzen, Bautzeu, Katzbach, Leipzig, Hanau & Waterloo

SOFTCOVER : ISBN 1-84677-046-7
HARDCOVER : ISBN 1-84677-050-5

EW15 EYEWITNESS TO WAR SERIES
THE COMPLEAT RIFLEMAN HARRIS
by Benjamin Harris

The Adventures of a Soldier of the 95th (Rifles) During the Peninsular Campaign of the Napoleonic Wars.

SOFTCOVER : ISBN 1-84677-047-5
HARDCOVER : ISBN 1-84677-053-X

AVAILABLE ONLINE AT
www.leonaur.com
AND OTHER GOOD BOOK STORES

ALSO FROM LEONAUR
AVAILABLE IN SOFT OR HARD COVER WITH DUST JACKET

EW4 EYEWITNESS TO WAR SERIES
BAYONETS, BUGLES & BONNETS
by James 'Thomas' Todd

Experiences of Hard Soldiering with the 71st Foot - the Highland Light Infantry - Through Many Battles of the Napoleonic Wars Including the Peninsular & Waterloo Campaigns.

SOFT COVER : ISBN 1-84677-021-1
HARD COVER : ISBN 1-84677-030-0

EW6 EYEWITNESS TO WAR SERIES
BUGLER & OFFICER OF THE RIFLES
by William Green & Harry Smith

With the 95th (Rifles) During the Peninsular & Waterloo Campaigns of the Napoleonic Wars.

SOFT COVER : ISBN 1-84677-020-3
HARD COVER : ISBN 1-84677-032-7

EW7 EYEWITNESS TO WAR SERIES
A NORFOLK SOLDIER IN THE FIRST SIKH WAR
by J. W. Baldwin

Experiences of a Private of H. M. 9th Regiment of Foot in the Battles for the Punjab, India 1845-6.

SOFT COVER : ISBN 1-84677-023-8
HARD COVER : ISBN 1-84677-031-9

EW8 EYEWITNESS TO WAR SERIES
A CAVALRY OFFICER IN THE SEPOY REVOLT
by A. R. D. Mackenzie

Experiences with the 3rd Bengal Light Cavalry, the Guides and Sikh Irregular Cavalry from the Outbreak of the Indian Mutiny to Delhi and Lucknow.

SOFT COVER : ISBN 1-84677-024-6
HARD COVER : ISBN 1-84677-039-4

AVAILABLE ONLINE AT
www.leonaur.com
AND OTHER GOOD BOOK STORES

www.ingramcontent.com/pod-product-compliance
Lightning Source LLC
Chambersburg PA
CBHW030229170426
43201CB00006B/154